In Search of Home

Noragh Jones

In Search of Home

Women working, caring, sharing

Floris Books

First published in 1998 by Floris Books

British Library CIP Data available

ISBN 0-86315-276-7

Printed in Great Britain
by Cromwell Press, Trowbridge, Wilts.

Contents

Acknowledgments

This book centres on personal life stories and would never have been written if, over the last four years, I had not had the willing help of the fifty people who sat down and talked to me about what matters to them in their everyday lives. I acknowledge here my gratitude and respect to every one of them. I have changed their names to protect their privacy, but otherwise I have faithfully described their life circumstances when introducing their stories. In a few chapters I have quoted from written sources (see Notes on p.255) which reflect the same concerns, and gratefully acknowledge my debt to these too.

Introduction

What does home mean to women today in all the changes of our life cycle? What kinds of emotional and material support do we need from home to accommodate women's demanding new life styles? — as expressed in this twenty-year-old's ambitions:

> My aim is to achieve what my mum never achieved. So it has to be everything — a good job, a good relationship, and home and children sometime. That's the big challenge for me — wanting the whole of life ... I don't want to be like my mum, who was hardly up to the challenges she had in life. My parents are divorced, and home has never been a very comfortable or comforting place because my mother had such a struggle working and bringing me up and never having enough money. Coming to university has made me more able to meet those challenges. It's made me aware of different kinds of challenge too ... It's probably that I have to prove things all the time, but I know I want *everything!*

The fifty people who tell their personal stories here have been chosen because they embody emotional and moral intelligence in their everyday lives. In our culture when we speak of intelligence we generally mean the cultivation of the mind, but it became clear while interviewing people for this book that emotional and moral intelligence are just as vital for being whole people and bringing up our children to be whole people. So these narratives start with grassroots life experiences and show how women's values are grounded in everyday activities and ways of relating to partners and children, friends and colleagues, neighbourhood or electronic networks. They are re-making home for the way we live now, rather than seeking a nostalgic return to some lost Eden of family values. Their values sometimes derive from Christian or Buddhist or Neo-pagan faiths, but they are never passively accepted religious precepts. They are rooted in personal experiences of relating (or failing to relate), and tested in everyday struggles to reinvent home.

When politicians and churchmen make confident pronouncements about the need to revive traditional values of home and family, they are never very clear about how these are to fit the complicated and messy reality of serial relationships and new kinds of families like gay couples and single parent households. It is as if they have buried their heads in the sand and go on prescribing for a way of life that no longer exists for the majority of people. How do lesbian couples relate with emotional and moral intelligence? How can men and women work out better patterns of sharing domesticity and parenting now that the majority of women work outside as well as in the home? How can we find personal space in relationships to develop individually, as well as caring and sharing with our partners? How can we manage the time famine which the double burden of outside work and home now loads on to women's lives? How can older people re-make home meaningfully when earlier retirement often leaves thirty years of life to be lived without the props of belonging and sociability that we get from going out to work? How can women in their eighties sustain themselves in the final phase of life, when the "homes" they end up in so often deprive them of any sense of control or purpose in their everyday lives?

Many modern people have difficulty with the idea of home. For modern women especially it is weighted down with the aftermath of the Angel in the Home ideology, where man was the breadwinner and the paterfamilias, and a proper woman was a domesticated wife and mother, and nothing more. It gave women little scope for exercising any talents in the world beyond feminine gender roles, and left men emotionally and functionally deprived in areas like parenting and home skills. Why should a woman need a room of her own or a mind of her own, when she could live perfectly well through her husband and children? The Angel in the Home, suggested Virginia Woolf, is the enemy within every woman, the first enemy we must vanquish when we aspire to express our own identity:

> You may not know what I mean by the Angel in the House ...
> She was intensely sympathetic. She was immensely charming.
> She was utterly unselfish ... She sacrificed herself daily, she
> never had a mind or a wish of her own. And when I came to
> write I encountered her with the very first words ... She slipped
> behind me and whispered: "My dear, you are a young woman.
> Be sympathetic, be tender; flatter; deceive; use all the arts and
> wiles of your sex. Never let anybody guess that you have a
> mind of your own."

In Search of Home contains the stories of a few dynamic Angels in
the Home who warn us about disparaging traditional women's skills
in our haste to have careers and be like men. Single mother Gwen
values her home as woman space, and wants to keep alive the
traditional women's skills of mothering, home cooking and making
patchwork quilts as her mother and grandmother did before her:

> I'm a feminist because I'm pro-woman. But I value women for
> the skills they've had handed down over the generations, rather
> than for neglecting the home skills and doing men's jobs better
> than the men. My women friends would bash me over the head
> for saying these things. They want me to get outside the home
> and do other things. But I think things should be made more
> glamorous for the home-centred woman, and she should be
> given more appreciation for bringing up the children well.
> That's really important and never-ending work that you have to
> use all your different skills on. But you don't have the backup
> of community or society to help you now, whatever they may
> *say* about how important mothering is.

But the stories told here on the whole confirm the Demos report on
Tomorrow's Women (1997), in showing that younger women now
want much more than homes and children of their own. Indeed they
even want more than rooms of their own and minds of their own.
They want flexible partners and flexible employers and a supporting
atmosphere (at work and at home) to enable them to combine a good
home life with a good professional life. They want a balanced life

which gives them time for traditional home-centred activities as well as an outside identity coming from a career and a circle of friends. They want to develop both mental and emotional intelligence, and they want their male partners to be better at communicating with them on both these levels. As we approach the millennium the reality of life for younger men and women is that a majority of women as well as men go out to work and have an identity not tied to gender roles. Among the young at least there is a convergence of male and female values, a desire to share parenting, and aspirations to a better balance between work and home. But because the workplace is still geared to the male breadwinner's life cycle, it is not hospitable to the balanced life for women or men. More young men may be in principle willing and emotionally prepared to share parenting, but the number of househusbands is still minute. Two couples (see Chapter 6) suggest why this is so as they tell of their own experiences of role reversal. New Man explains how it feels to be not quite "one of the girls" in traditional mothers' meeting places, at the swings in the park or down at the playgroup; and not quite "one of the boys" when you are a man only working part-time because you are doing parenting work the rest of the time.

Good domesticity and good relating are at the heart of home, Relating is considered to be fine, even among busy modern people, but who wants to be domesticated now? Most women want to avoid the domestic trap they remember settling like a cage around their mothers or their grandmothers — whether the caged bird sang or not. Yet many who pay lip service to sharing domesticity with men find it impossible to let go of domestic control, even when their partners are willing to share. There are still deep dark areas of even the "liberated" female psyche which claim the home and the domestic realm as woman's domain, and continue to repel men when they threaten to breach the boundaries of this age-old womanspace.

However much men and women share in doing the work of home, every individual needs to retain some personal private space to keep a sense of who they are, apart from being somebody's partner or somebody's parent or somebody's child. Home needs to give us this private space, this essential time to ourselves. We all need that personal space, but many of us are not attuned to creative aloneness and use any personal space we have to carry on being busy — busy shoppers, busy chatters, busy bodies.

We are ambivalent when we do have time at home by ourselves in the middle of over-busy lives. The longed for blessing sometimes turns into empty and meaningless time, and all it provides is a sense of absence or loneliness. It is as if the life has drained out of home and is located somewhere else, so being at home conveys a sense of missing things rather than the original sense of home as the centre and focus of life. This is a new problem. For the first time perhaps in social history homes have an uneasy empty feel because they no longer have a continuous indwelling life of their own. They are emptied of adults and children every morning, and have no life during the day until the inhabitants return from work or school. You "get a life" by getting out of home, not by staying at home. Even the tiniest tots commute to nursery schools and childminders. The whole family are commuters now, and the daytime life drains from home and neighbourhood when everyone is out for so long.

To be at home during the day now more often than not means to be off sick, or waiting for someone to fix the central heating, or, worse, out of work and nowhere to go. Home is in danger of becoming a place to get out of, rather than to inhabit with our whole selves — a servicing base, something like a filling station where we wash and refuel ourselves for the next engagement out there where the action is. Is that why people feel a sense of loneliness and apathy when they are at home alone, however much they suffer from overwork and long for personal time and space?

The number of people living on their own has been steadily growing. If being alone at home can be a problem even for those who live with families, what about the problems of these single dwellers? It is easier to be positive about being on your own when you have chosen aloneness, rather than having it thrust upon you as the unwanted or traumatic result of divorce or widowhood or children leaving the nest. *In Search of Home* tries to tease out why it is that living alone can be creative solitude for some, but bring heart-crushing loneliness to many. What does it mean to be emotionally intelligent in loneliness? Single parents often speak of themselves as "alone with the children," for they can feel as lonely as anyone else "on their own," but have the double burden of not giving way for the children's sake. They have a heartfelt need for emotional support rather than the regular blame they attract from public spokesmen who regularly foretell their children's shortcomings in life. Chapter 7 gives the stories of three mothers bringing up children on their own. They explain how they try to teach their children values in the context of everyday relating — to each other, to intermittent dads, and to their neighbours. Each draws on a different value system — Christian, Buddhist and New Age — but all three offer a down to earth guide to values for doing parenting on your own.

Some people find it far harder than others to use emotional and moral intelligence in relating to others and in making a home, because their childhood homes have not taught them any positive meanings of home. They have never had a supporting haven or secure space where they could safely express their personal needs and hopes and fears. In Chapter 13 are the stories of the homeless and the deprived, the "Fourth World" people who have to learn emotional intelligence the hard way in homes which are not homes, or give up on home for themselves while hoping it is not too late for their children to learn enough emotional literacy to make home work for them.

In the process of talking to all the people who tell their stories in this book, I have become very aware of the ambivalence of home for modern people. Most still need and want a home haven, a safe place for self-expression, a private space to recollect themselves and to welcome trusted others. But alongside this basic need for home runs the fear of home as a smothering, a place of confinement that cuts you off from the big wide world out there which you need to explore to find yourself and go on growing as an individual. People told me that home for them is no longer a fixed place or a fixed group of people, as it was for their parents or grandparents. Home is a web of personal networks, globally expansible (thanks to the electronic revolution and the World Wide Web) and able to satisfy one's hunger for new interests and new people indefinitely. Christabel (see Chapter 12) explains why she is more at home in her new style electronic community than in any traditional community:

When you're dialoguing on the Net you run the risk of wimpish nerds sending messages like, "I like to keep abreast of affairs" and "God knows we all need a bit of breast" and other boring little nerd jokes. But we've always had to put up with that kind of chat in the local pub, and it's harder to get away from it in the pub than on the Net. On the Net you're more in control of who you talk to, and about what. You can make your own community instead of being stuck with the one you find yourself in. Old style community gave you no choice at all. You put up with your neighbours, and you were under pressure to conform or get out. Electronic networking is the ultimate choice. You choose your community yourself, and you have the whole world to choose it from.

But shutting yourself off from old style communities of place in order to be at home in your personal selection of contacts from the global village leaves some people uneasy. It diminishes the home ground on which we stand in our everyday lives and which offers us the chance to relate in some way with the people around us, whether they share our interests or not. That kind of relating, with people who are different from us, is perhaps the ultimate test of our emotional and moral maturity, even if it goes against the grain of modern individualism which wants unlimited personal choice. All the people who tell their stories here have learned emotional and moral maturity through responding to their everyday life experiences and shaping their personal values as a result. For some it has been a conscious process, guided by Buddhist or Christian or Neo-pagan beliefs. For others it has been a journey through experience to a way of knowing which can best be described as emotional intelligence. This is the practical art of good connecting with our true selves, with the people we relate to, and with the wider public world. The steps we can take on our personal paths to emotional literacy are summarized in the last chapter (see p.253). Learning and practising emotional literacy are the age-old skilful means we need in our struggles to be at home in the world.

Noragh Jones, Cwmrheidol, 1998

Chapter 1
Our domestic heritage

Women's attitudes to domesticity

When I asked women about good memories of childhood homes, they responded overwhelmingly with domestic scenes of emotional and physical warmth created by mothers or grandmothers. Eliza (37) is a busy modern woman earning her living as a therapist, and has to fit creative domesticity into the thin slivers of time left over from her outside work, but she has aspirations inherited from her grandmother:

> I still have my Cumbrian granny's recipes for gingerbread and strawberry jam. One of these days when I have enough time I'm going to make them, because they are associated with happy visits to my granny's when I was a child. The smells of her baking and cooking I shall never forget, and it would be celebrating her memory to use those recipes again and see if I can get the same results.
>
> When I smell honeysuckle and peppery lupins it always brings back my granny's house too. We went there after she had just died, and the house and the garden looked just the same. There were pansies and those lupins, and potatoes growing out the back, and little kids' tents made out of a clothes horse like we used to do thirty years ago. I wept and wept for what was lost and for what I could never go back to. It was to do with roots, with some symbol of home that my grandmother's house has always been for me from the time I was just a kid. She took me on walks and taught me about the flowers and plants that grew along the Cumbrian lanes. When she was making a new rag rug for the kitchen floor she would give me a little corner of it to do and show me how to do it. So the rug by the fire wasn't just a familiar bit of granny's

house. It was something I'd had a share in making. On washdays too we'd all help her, taking turns at pounding the clothes or rubbing them on the corrugated board or putting them through the mangle. Grandmother brought you into everything she was doing, and she taught you all the things she knew herself.

Sister Teresa, a scholarly nun who now does academic research, has equally nostalgic memories of being brought up on a farm in the west of Ireland:

We learned heaps of skills at home from the time we were very young — embroidery, crocheting, knitting and cookery. So home was a teacher, giving you skills of all kinds. When we were very tiny my mother allowed us to use the sewing machine and to potter in the kitchen making things to eat. I think that having access to a large family kitchen was important. It was the social focus of home. The meals were served at the big table in the kitchen, and the table was full, and everyone sitting around it. That kind of experience is gone these days with the coming of the TV. There were occasions around the farming year when there would be special feasts of food, and we children participated in the hospitality, carrying the big apple tarts and the brack and the rest of the afternoon tea out to the hay-makers in the fields. There was a lot of story-telling and joking. The women's side of the house would be working at making sure everyone was well fed, and nobody got left out. There was great pride in the home baking, and competition to produce the best pastry or the lightest sponge cake. The domestic round followed the cycle of the year with different kinds of food and family feasts marking the passing of the seasons.

But such woman-centred domestic nurturing was not an unmixed blessing for those who gave it or for those on the receiving end. Eliza the therapist loved going to her grandmother's, but could hardly wait to get away from the daily domestic oppression of her mother's house:

You had to stuff yourself to show appreciation of all that heavy domestic ritual. Christmas dinner was specially horrendous because then you had to stuff yourself to the ultimate degree. Once my mum bought a turkey so big it wouldn't fit in the oven and she had to chop off the legs and cook them separately. After the dinner you'd have to eat chocolates on top of everything else. Then there would be tea and The Cake at four or five, and a fry-up of the leftovers in the evening. At Christmas and Easter and birthdays you'd have to eat the feasts because if you didn't eat enough to show appreciation of the cooking skills and efforts that went into the feast, it was really rude and you were rejecting her love ... My mother and I have very different ideas about where and what home is. We (my parents, my sister and I, and the cat) lived in a two-bed council house in the northeast with the sulphurous smell of the coal mines hanging over it. My mother never wanted to leave home — that was *her place* — but my dream was to get away, to have a room of my own with a lock on the door.

So the influence of domesticated mothers on modern women is rarely straightforward, and time-starved professional people are very ambivalent about creating good domesticity, although they are all in favour of "quality time" at home. For many cooking and shopping and cleaning and gardening are nothing but chores to get through as quickly as possible, to leave more time for the "real" things in life. But others are uneasy when they remember that these "chores" are about fundamental caring, and have been for most of history the real things of life for men and women. Perhaps after all domestic skills are bound up with a deep and continuing human need to make home a warm and nurturing place where people eat together and talk together and share their everyday concerns? Either way we have different problems now from previous generations, because the majority of women go out to work, but the majority of men do not yet share the domestic business of making home. And some women would not want them to, for domestic space is traditionally womanspace. Even career women sometimes have emotional difficulty letting go of domestic control to their partner, though they accept the rational arguments for doing so. Women, too, still have a head start over men in domestic skills and home-making nuances. They absorb home-making ways at their mothers' knee, however reluctant or determined they are to avoid the "domestic trap." Mothers, however, seem to be making a poor job of teaching their sons to do even basic cooking and caring. An illustration of this is that many of the women I interviewed, but none of the men, had vivid memories of their mothers teaching them to cook. The men who do regular cooking and enjoy cooking acquired their skills in adult life and are much more dependent on recipes and documentary aids, because as boys they were not part of the "women's mysteries" by which many of the women absorbed their foremothers' domestic skills and the emotional weighting that goes with them. Edie (43) who runs her own information technology business still values (and uses) the domestic skills she inherited from her mother:

> We children started cooking with Viota cake mixes when we were very little. Then we were given scraps of pastry to make into jam rolls and put in the oven alongside mother's proper apple tarts. Sunday was work day in our house, because mother as well as father worked all week. So she cleaned the house from top to bottom on a Sunday, and my job (from the age of nine, when I was old enough to manage the gas stove) was to cook the Sunday dinner. I did the joint and cut the potatoes and veg and cooked them. My father worked shifts and was rarely there at mealtimes. After our Sunday dinner was over your next job was to make cakes for father's tea — madeira cakes, maids of honour, jam tarts. I was a good pastry maker and still am. I've got a skilled job working in computers now, but the kitchen's still the room in the house for me. That's where I'm at home, because there I can still use all those skills my mother taught me.

Men seem to acquire domestic skills when they have to, as a practical addition to their life skills inventory. Women absorb domestic skills from other women, and grow up with a degree of domestic literacy which enables them to read the emotional messages given out by any domestic ménage. Women who have not absorbed a domestic inheritance from their mothers may thus experience an emotional as well as a functional lack, even when they have an outside career, because modern women are above all seeking a balanced life, where work and home, friends and lovers, professional skills and domestic skills are kept in some sort of creative harmony. Making good pastry or doing rainbow cake for a child's birthday party, or laying a beautiful table to welcome friends to dinner, may be rejected by single-minded female careerists, but more and more women are revaluing these skills, though they do not want them to take over their lives as they often did their mothers' or grandmothers' lives. For some it is a way of being grounded in an everyday spirituality which offsets the "convenience cults" that are so tempting. Maggie, a Buddhist and a divorced mother whose children are entering their teens and clamouring for junk food, says:

> Buying pre-cooked food and shoving it in the microwave is very different from our mothers' way of cooking. It's convenient, but you're deprived of the magic of growing things and cooking them with care, by the instant magic of the supermarket. When my mother cooked it was like watching a priest administering a sacrament. She'd start bringing ingredients together in the morning, and laying things out ready for the rituals of good cooking. And there were rhythms to her housekeeping too. She'd do marmalade in January always, and plant hyacinth bulbs indoors in October so they'd be flowering for Christmas. I'm still under her influence, though I don't do it consciously. When October comes I still have the urge to plant bulbs. The importance I give to making bread and pastry comes from her too. My kids rely a lot on bread so I go through regular phases of making bread. They're at an age when they want convenience foods, and if they have good bread it makes up for some of the deficiencies. I see it as a struggle against consumerism and convenience foods, so I think it's important, though sometimes I get so tired I can't find the energy for making bread.

Janey is a green activist, living on a shoe-string budget with her
builder husband and their two teenage children, and she also tries to
ground her domesticity in her spiritual tradition:

> I was brought up a pagan by my mum. Not crystals and gurus
> was my mum about, but living with the seasons, and accepting
> things as they are in their own way, and putting value on our
> ordinary everyday lives. So I don't like the sterile environment
> of consumer homes. I like to see what season it is from what's
> in the house and what we are eating. In autumn now it's mush-
> rooms and dried hops. This is the downtime of the year and
> you want to hibernate. You want lots of good warm food for
> the kids getting in from school. You want a lot of good stuff
> stored away in the cupboards. You want a good hot dinner for
> Dave getting in from his building jobs. I get criticized by other
> women for having his dinner on the table for him, but I do that
> because I'm here in the house then and I *like* providing good
> food for him and the kids. It's a real satisfaction to me. It
> brings up good energy.
>   I learned a lot from my mum who had a lot of good energy.
> She was brought up in southeast London and was quite posh
> compared with my dad who came from a Romany family with
> fourteen kids and always down the pub ... So my mum and dad
> came from very different backgrounds but they had four kids
> together and ran their own business stripping down old Singer
> sewing machines and doing them up. Mum had big muscles
> from handling those sewing machines and loading them on to
> the van. The main thing about her was her endless good
> energy, and that's what I try to be like. When she wasn't
> working for the business she was working in the house —
> piling up the fire to keep it really warm for us kids, or moving
> the furniture around or decorating to make it comfortable. She
> ran up enormous bills with the milkman and baker because she
> was so concerned about feeding us well. I've got some things
> from my mum, because I have the house warm and reasonably
> tidy, with good food, and I like to welcome people around. She
> always used to have people around. She was very neighbourly

and would talk to anybody. Although I'm 36 now and was
very little at the time, I remember that slum area of south
London still. There was a good sense of community, so a
woman from a poor family would always be helped by the
neighbours when she was having a baby. My mum and the
others would clean the place and feed the other kids. It's nice
to have that feeling of community again here in this village
where I am now, because it was lost in London when they
knocked down the slums and moved us to "nicer" areas of
council housing. That "nice" area brought out the worst in our
family. We kids played up and eventually we got evicted and
were moved to Peckham. They told my mum and dad that if
they didn't accept the new place us kids would be taken away
and put into care.

I get more like my mum as I get older. I get a great sense of
achievement out of getting things done, in the house or in
whatever work I have outside. I like ironing, baking the bread,
listening to a play on the radio and thinking about meals I'm
going to make for the family. It's such a struggle trying to get
meals together — the economics of it — never having enough
money — always having to think about the money. But I like
feeding people. Warmth and food are at the heart of making a
home, and they don't come naturally now, economically or any
other way. But we're trying to bring the kids up to know
what's what. They aren't into fast food. They think oven chips
are a great treat. I make the bread and the rock cakes and see
that all the food we have is good and wholesome and made at
home. It is important to me because I'm very conscious of
what I eat and what I give the kids to eat. I'm very conscious
of the health and the good energy that comes from what you
eat. Making bread and in season making jam is part of
everyday to me. It's all the ordinary things you do every day
that make up your life, so my breadmaking and my jam
making are ordinary things that mean something important.

Material things don't matter so much when you lose a real
person and feel it inside. Now I've lost my mum I don't care
so much about the things in the house because I know more

than ever it's the people who are important. Anyway we haven't any disposable income so we can't buy things for the house. You have different worries about material things when you've got hardly any money. You couldn't go in for those sterile three-piece suites even if you wanted to. But I don't, because when you go into those new sterile houses you don't know what to do with yourself. You feel really uncomfortable and not yourself. It's making a home that's important, not the result. So if you go out and buy an instant home it's not really a home. It's the making of it that matters, but people don't make the new sterile homes — they just go out and buy them in the big stores, and think that's it — they've got themselves a lovely home.

Why women find it difficult to share domestic tasks

Even when women and men rationally accept the need to share domestic tasks if both have outside jobs, their very different domestic inheritance often causes emotional unease or deep conflict. Claire and her husband are university lecturers with one teenage son. In theory they approve of men and women sharing domestic tasks, especially when the woman is an equal breadwinner. But emotionally Claire just finds it impossible to let go of the need to be in domestic control which she has inherited from her powerful home-centred mother (a Tory adherent to traditional family values, and an energetic activist in the voluntary sector, which she sees career-minded women deserting in droves, to the detriment of humanity):

> In order for me to feel well-ordered and whole, my house must be well-ordered and whole. My home is like an extension of me, and when I feel chaotic or run down I go in for spring-cleaning sessions (all the year round). Doing up the kitchen or the bathroom or the conservatory in a completely new colour scheme or style is therapeutic. It's like patterning an extension of myself and making me whole again. Of course my partner and teenage son hate my sessions of reordering the house.

They see no need for it because they don't invest their feelings in the house the way I do. Of course we're all supposed to share in the domestic decisions, because we're trying to run a democratic home. But in practice the decisions are always mine, though I may have to pretend they are not. If they choose the "wrong" colour for the sitting room, say, I will disparage their choice until they come round to the colour I want. I'm prepared to do that because I know it doesn't matter to them nearly as much as it matters to me. They don't have nearly as much emotional investment in a room's atmosphere as I do. So although I like the idea of sharing domestic decisions with them, I don't like the reality when it comes to diminishing my control over domestic space.

Another common cause of domestic conflict when men and women try to share domesticity is the different standards they have about cleanliness and comfort:

My males want the house to be comfortable but they are not so concerned about it being clean, as I am concerned. They don't notice so much when it is not clean, so although they help with the housework I am the one who is continuously aware of degrees of cleanliness and squalor, the one who has to take the domestic initiatives. My partner says he's always doing cooking and cleaning, but when he says that I want to make it an issue with him to make him feel guilty — "He doesn't help me enough in the house — poor me!" I know it's to do with my being into domestic power and control, and it goes quite deep and totally against my rational self, but I can't help myself ...

The way men do cooking can also be a source of irritation to women, even though they are supposed to be glad that men are doing their fair share in the house:

He's a very good cook and enjoys cooking, but he always leaves the sink piled high with saucepans and things when he's finished. There's a horrendous amount of washing up to be done, and it's like a reminder of women's domestic oppression through the ages. It stirs up primeval memories of women's domestic burdens and domestic slavery.

Some women simply cannot bear to see men doing "women's things" around the house, because it is experienced as a serious invasion of the female queendom by the male. He dominates in the outside world and now he has the nerve to try and dominate in the one female sanctum that is left — the kitchen! These women often rationalize their fears of male invasion by inventing a "domestic instinct" that women enjoy and men lack, so it is useless trying to "housetrain" men. An elderly woman whose life had been invested in keeping house for others eventually took in an invalid uncle to have someone to look after when her parents died. Her strategy to maintain the female sanctum inviolate was ridicule:

> My uncle wanted to help in the house at first. He hung out the washing once or twice, but he looked so funny — a man hanging out the washing — that I laughed and laughed, and he didn't do it again. While his wife was alive we visited once, and he put an awful old tablecloth on the tea table till his wife told him to put on the nice one kept for visitors. Men just don't notice things like that. They haven't got the domestic instinct.

For this woman a well-developed and sensitive "domestic instinct" is the whole justification for her life. She has always related (in a warmhearted if sometimes suffocating way) to the rest of humanity through her cooking and cleaning and maintenance of everyday life. For her everyday home activities have been not just functional but the main means of emotional and religious self-expression in her life. But now in her seventies she is again on her own (since her uncle died) and says sadly, "You reach a point where you're not able to do so much caring, even though that has been my main purpose in being a woman at home." Her defence of past generations of domesticated women is worth hearing as we witness the phenomenon of some high-powered career women turning back to the creative possibilities of a home-based life:

> I've always believed that women at home have a lot more free-
> dom and ways of expressing themselves than women who go
> out to work. You have the freedom to go out and meet friends
> and help people in your community who need care and support.
> You can develop a lot of skills (lost today) like sewing and
> letter-writing and having time for the people who live around
> you. After my parents died I hadn't enough people to look
> after, and I tried all kinds of things like philosophy classes and
> going on holiday with a friend. But it was only distractions.
> None of those things gave me a purpose in life, and that's
> what you need to make home worthwhile. Otherwise you're
> only filling in time. I needed someone to look after. So I asked
> my uncle to come and live here, and it was worth making the
> apple tarts and the cakes again, and keeping a good fire going
> and the garden nice for him to sit out in when it was fine.

Men get their own satisfactions out of doing domestic work, but none of the men I interviewed got anywhere near to making domesticity the central purpose of their lives, as it has been for many women, and still is for many lonely older women like Doreen above, who now has no one left to care for, no one there at home to justify her accomplished domesticity. The big emotional load which women bring to domestic-ity makes it quite a challenge for men and women to move towards a more equitable sharing of domestic tasks and skills, even when it is the rational thing for partners who are both breadwinners.

Marilyn and Don are a cosmopolitan professional couple currently living in Barcelona. Don accepted the "new man" challenge and took over most household things when Marilyn's workload was exhausting her. She was glad at the time but it left her with heavy feelings of being disempowered:

> I'm no longer the woman at the centre of the home. I'm only
> the breadwinner who goes out and brings home the dosh. Don
> even took to making jams and chutneys, the sort of things I

used to do when I was at home with the two babies twenty years ago. As well as that my younger daughter is vying to show off her culinary skills since her boyfriend has moved into the house with us. She does a lot of the daily cooking (very well, it has to be said) and her boyfriend seems to be taking over from me as chief taxi driver and assistant gardener to the household. I'm uneasy at a deep down level about where all this leaves me in the meaning of home, but I suspect it's very much on the fringes. That would be fine if I could sit here in the wooden annexe (where at last I have a room of my own) and do expressive things like writing novels and poems and playing my guitar. But I continue drearily as the chief breadwinner, teaching English to my Catalan and Spanish students. I feel I'm losing out on the work front and on the home front too. Having a room of my own is just an empty irony when you're emotionally redundant. Are you listening, Virginia Woolf?

Marilyn increasingly involves herself in a wicca commune in the hills behind Barcelona as a way of reclaiming her traditional female powers. She has become a mid life "wise woman," insightful in healing lore and learning to gather healing herbs. For her the wheel has turned full circle and she needs to reclaim her traditional women's inheritance by being part of the wicca revival. A well-paid professional career often proves in middle age to be spiritually impoverishing for women. But so does undiluted domesticity which in these days of diminished community is especially isolating and confined. How then can couples find good ways for both partners to be active in the outside world and in making home? Many younger couples are narrowing the learning gap between male and female domestic skills and insights. The first stage is a fairer division of domestic labour as well as outside work. That involves both partners practising emotional intelligence — being open about their true feelings towards domestic control, putting energy into positive skills rather than defensive postures, and empathizing with the other's emotional domestic inheritance. Creative domesticity requires more than democratic division of tasks and well-informed consumerism. It is about the mutual offering of fundamental human comfort and emotional hospitality. Eliza the therapist and her partner Malcolm (a computer researcher) have been exploring this during their first year of setting up home together after an open relationship of many years:

> ELIZA: The comfort and wellbeing are coming along. We generally have at least one meal a day together. We have evening meals together during the week and brunch at the weekend. That's very important to us, to lay the table properly in the sitting room, have candles burning, and eat and talk together. I like food and we put an effort into our meals together. I light candles even if I'm on my own. As a therapist I know that one way of finding out how families work is to ask how meals happen in a home ...

> MALCOLM: Sometimes we share cooking and sometimes we take it in turns. My mum did all the cooking. Here we both do cooking and that's important for sharing our lives.

> ELIZA: We really share and I like that, because I like cooking so long as I don't have to do it all the time like I did when I was married. I was a real little housewife for seven years (as well as working full-time as manageress of a windscreen wholesalers). I had a Rayburn. I baked bread. I grew vegetables. We didn't share any of that. We didn't share anything much, really, and the marriage broke down. It wouldn't have lasted seven years if we hadn't been too busy in our separate ways to realize how little sharing we did.

> MALCOLM: We're really pleased that the house is shaping up after the first year. We have our own rooms to work in, and the sitting room to eat and relax in, and a meditation room for sitting, and the new kitchen so we have enough rings to cook proper meals on at last. All we need now is a pet. A friend advised us to get a cat when we moved in here, because pets are part of making a home, but we haven't got around to that yet ...

For other couples sharing domesticity is not so straightforward. because of the pressures of their domestic inheritance. A man doing domestic work needs practical and emotional skills to reassure his partner he is not taking over her domestic space. He has to reshape his images of masculinity to be inclusive of the everyday life maintenance that traditionally women have taken care of. He has to face his mother and try to persuade her that it's alright for a man to do what earlier generations of women have claimed as "woman's work," meaning their life purpose. A Californian woman who married a Welshman describes one such struggle with her mother-in-law:

> At first I made meals that his mother had made for him —
> sausages egg and chips, baked beans, etc. It was horrible, so I
> went back to cooking the way I cooked in San Francisco. I
> made fresh salad in vinaigrette with casseroles. I made
> Mexican chili and Hungarian goulash and Italian pasta. In the
> US there are so many cultures that you have food at your
> fingertips from every country in the world. I stepped back into
> my real self instead of trying to be a good little Welsh
> housewife. My husband was thrilled. Then I taught him to iron
> his own shirts. I said to him, "These are your shirts and I hate
> ironing so let's be fair. I'll do the washing and you do the
> ironing." My mother-in-law was not thrilled. When she heard
> what had happened her face went white and her eyes grew big
> and she said to me, "In our family the women do that." She
> wanted to take the shirts back home to iron, but he wouldn't
> let her. I was very proud of him.

Even when a sharing of basic tasks has been achieved, there can be stresses and strains because partners have inherited different domestic philosophies and cannot agree on the core question of degrees of hospitality. Inviting people into your home territory and sharing food with them is a universal expression of mutual goodwill but it involves hard work and reciprocal obligations which don't always sit easily with the modern time famine that women especially suffer in combining career and home. Partners too may make different emotional demands on home, and hospitality (or the lack of it) easily becomes a source of tension. A woman in mid life who is now divorced and recovering from being an alcoholic looks back over her mother's life and her own, and sees how she and her mother suffered in their different ways from a hospitality that was out of balance for them:

> My mother's idea of home was people dropping in or coming to stay. I suspect that she was very lonely and her hospitable instincts were frustrated most of the time, because my father classified as a stranger anybody not immediate to the family. His concept of home was marked out by strong boundaries constructed out of ideas of privacy and the puritan ethic. So she never enjoyed the sociability she was gifted in, and really I think she was happiest in her last years, when there were such a lot of support people coming in and out of the house while she and my father were both in their last illnesses. She enjoyed a final sociability with the nurses and home helps who were in and out every day towards the end. Isn't that poignant, that frustrated sociability?
>
> When I was married we invited people round quite a bit. With four small kids I found that difficult to handle at the time, and I sometimes needed the drink in me to be the sort of generous person that my ideas of hospitality (inherited from my mother) demanded. My husband was a great homemaker with almost feminine sensitivity about how the house should be, and whether the guests had everything they wanted. He loved cooking and decorating the house and entertaining people. He was very good at it. He was so good at it that it infuriated me. He invaded my domestic space. That helped me get started on the drinking as well.

Why cats and other pets create a sense of home

It is significant that the electronic pet is the latest consumer toy. It provides a virtual reality substitute for living emotions, a mechanical way of caring without the trouble of empathy, an evasion of the emotional intelligence that we learn from domestic animals. Caring for pets as well as humans has been for many people a significant part of their domestic inheritance. Indeed for some women suffering the instability and impermanence of modern relationships the beloved cat becomes their focal emotional support. Many people I interviewed spoke spontaneously of the part that animals play in making home. Animals are centred in their home place and cats in particular have a deep instinct for enjoying home that people can learn from. Cats are both affectionate and independent. They can be around you without pestering you. They can communicate a whole range of feelings by touch. They give their grave attention to home events and read the changing atmosphere of home like psychic mediums. Many women who live on their own do not really live on their own, they say. They live with their cat who is a significant other in their lives, a furry living presence who keeps the house while they are out and is there to greet them ecstatically with unconditional affection on their return. They give you connections with neighbouring cat lovers and daily remind you about the ordinary loving care that home traditionally means.

Pets are prescribed as therapy in old people's homes, since they provide the comfort of daily soothing touching for elderly folk who no longer have affectionate physical contact in their everyday lives. Pets need caring too, which the elderly are often deprived of, because it is assumed they are in need of care rather than care givers. But everybody at whatever stage of their lives needs to give as well as receive care, to remain in touch with the flow of life. Dymphna, a Dublin woman in her late seventies who now lives on her own with a pair of cats (one pure black and the other milky white), reminisced about the meaning of cats in her life:

> The number of cats in this house waxes and wanes in inverse proportion to the number of people left at home. After my parents died there were only my brother and me left, but we had six cats and one dog. The company of animals is very satisfying. Why is this so? I think it's because when you're alone in the house the cats watch carefully, whatever you're doing, and they have their own daily routines which is very stabilizing. I think they are models of good domesticity, really. They show you how to be involved but independent, and how

to be self-sufficient when you're left on your own. They are models of good grooming, too, which is a reminder to keep yourself smart even if there's nobody there to see what you look like. And they give you endless affection, not just when it's time for the Kite-Kat, but when you get home to an empty house or when you come downstairs first thing in the morning to try and get the day going, in spite of your arthritic twinges or whatever.

Another elderly woman on her own told me:

For many years I kept cats myself when I was living on my own, but now I rely on the company of visiting cats. When my own cats eventually died of old age I didn't replace them because it seemed too much trouble making sure someone would look after them when I was away. Since then I've moved to a more neighbourly place, and I've noticed one of the things that makes it so neighbourly is the way that people look after each others' pets. But I don't need my own pets here because I have made friends with several of the neighbours' cats and dogs. They visit me every day, and I feed them if their owner's away.

The pets where you live are part of the life of the place, and you are more aware of that when you retire and spend a lot of your days at home. You look out and see the dogs you know by name running and chasing, and the cats curled up in sheltered spots or stalking about in sunny weather with their tails up. They're expressing life in their own animal way, and reminding you to express life in your particular way. But I sometimes think it's quite a selfish thing having animals dependent on you and you getting satisfaction from their dependence. So you have to be committed to them, not just pet them and forget them. If you learn to commit yourself to animals you're on the way to be a better human being. It's a good thing to develop the habit of being a conscientious looker-after of animals as well as people.

It's not only old people who need the company of animals. A first year student living in a university hall of residence saw the loss of her pets as grievous, in spite of all the positive excitements of her new-found freedom. "At home," she said, "I had loads of pets — my dog, the cats, fish. You need to have pets. Pets make you feel at home. You can lift them and they don't run away. You can give them a cuddle and they don't cry. When your friends aren't listening to you your pets are there to put your affection on and talk to. Now I have to make do with stick insects. I talk to my stick insects, but it isn't the same."

A woman hill-farmer in Wales describes the good feeling of coming home on winter evenings, and the significance of her animals in that sense of homecoming:

> It's dark and cold and often raining when I get home from the part-time job I do three days a week to keep my hill farm viable. But I love the feeling of arriving home. The cat comes out of the barn mewing, and the sheepdog comes out of the shed to greet me. They're always thrilled to bits to see me home again. I go inside, take off the tights and skirts of my public clothes, and put on my comfortable old trousers and jersey. I pick up my stick and go out to walk around the fields to check that the sheep are alright. After a minute I get used to the night sky and the shapes of the land show up out of the dark. The animals are usually lying down in a sheltered place. All is usually well. I breathe in the clear air and go back to the house with Jip the sheepdog at my heel. That for me is home.

Chapter 2
The modern time famine

Relating work and home

The time famine is the modern epidemic that attacks everyone who is trying to work out a balance between the conflicting demands of modern life — between work and home, between parenting and individual self-expression, between private and public commitments. It affects women more than men, because the majority of women now go out to work as breadwinners or joint breadwinners, but only a small minority of men have taken on an equal share of the domestic and parenting work. More and more women too are college educated with career ambitions, and their self identity demands more than the satisfactions of being a good wife and mother. But when these women get into their thirties they hear the tick of the biological time clock and have to decide whether they want to be mothers, and if so how they are going to combine career and parenting. What kind of balance do women want in their lives, and how do they struggle to achieve this? What makes career women call a halt when their work threatens other facets of life like relationships, friendships and child-rearing? How do they get time to themselves in the midst of the time famine that all these pressures create?

In recent years there has been much talk about the benefits of working from home. Electronic networking makes this increasingly feasible, but what actually happens when people work from home? Are we really reviving the togetherness of parents and children, the home-based work situation that prevailed across Europe before the industrial revolution swept people out of their cottages and into the workplace? Are we about to recover from the two hundred year old hiccup which has disrupted family life and ancient habits of bio-rhythmic work, imprisoning people in offices and factories for eight to twelve hours a day, and calling it normal? Or are the new home-workers just moving the office into the home and putting up new barriers against domestic distractions like their small children? When I talked to people about homeworking the answers were very ambivalent. One of the problems, they say, is that work invades your private space at home. You begin to long for the psychological relief of keeping work and home separate. It's important for many people to be able to leave the office behind and look forward to the sanctuary of home, even if it involves strap-hanging on bus or tube in the commuter hour of the sardine. There is resentment that homeworking is used by some employers as a way of cutting costs by contracting work out to home workers on a temporary and insecure basis, rather than maintaining permanent staff on a decent wage.

There have always been women who have had to find ways of earning money while looking after small children at home, and one of my interviewees, Annie, tells the story of her successful restaurant project. But on balance homeworking is not an easy option for women trying to combine parenting and paid work. But then neither are most conventional work structures, which are only gradually accepting that women's life patterns are different from men's, and require fundamental changes in the workplace towards more flexible working.

It is not surprising, in the light of the time famine that most women experience during the years of combining career and parenting, that more women(including the highly qualified) are choosing to be full-time mothers, if they can afford it. Gwen is the mother of two small boys (7 and 5) and has chosen to stay at home and do fulltime parenting. She says the career woman is overglamorized, and only successful *"Cosmo* women" get to be heard on the excitement and challenge of going out to work. You do not hear what it's like for the badly paid part-time mothers assembling microchips in an electronics factory or sitting at a word processor bored out of their minds with the endless repeated routines of spreadsheets. Nobody talks about the sheer exhaustion of looking after your baby while you're at home, worrying about the child care when you're at work, and never having any time to yourself. For Gwen full-time domesticity while her children are young has to be better than that, even though she is poorer than most of her friends who are young mothers and out working as well. She believes she is working for the community in putting into parenting the skills and imagination she would otherwise be using in paid work. The problem is, she says, that what she does is not properly acknowledged as important work. and so she is invisible in the prevailing achievement stakes which only rate people by the salaried work they do.

Working out a balance between career and home

Sarah's story

Sarah (44) and her present husband are both university lecturers. Her first marriage to a business executive broke up when their two children were small. With the help of a devoted aunt who minded the children she reconstructed her life, did her Ph.D. and got a lecturing job:

> At the moment I'm absolutely exhausted because I've been finishing off things at work and rushing around getting myself and everybody else ready for going off on holiday.. I suppose that's typical of someone who has a full-time job and also has to run a home and family. Normally I'm a fairly happy sort of person. I don't have time to have "interests," but I'm sociable so I do like to spend any spare time with friends. With the children becoming teenagers now I find that fitting my life into theirs is more important than making theirs fit into mine, as I could do when they were small. I don't know how long that will last. I don't see them sharing my life beyond when they go to university or whatever they do after school. Maybe they'll go on being part of my life, but whereas my mother and aunt were always there for me and helped me get where I am today by looking after my children, I don't know that I would be prepared to do that for my own daughter, because I have a life of my own beyond my children, and my professional career is tremendously important to me. But you never know ...
>
> My career is absolutely central to my sense of identity. When my personal life fell apart (my first husband left me for

his secretary) it became extremely important to regain my confidence and find something I could do well, since I clearly wasn't very good at the traditional role of wife and mother where I'd tried and failed abysmally. Getting back into education and doing my higher degree saved my life. I got a lecturing post out of it, but I also found there were things I could do well, and I got back my confidence. Coming from a working-class background where no one had gone into higher education I had tended to let life carry me on, fatalistic I suppose, without stopping to think where it was carrying me. All that changed thanks to my late entry to higher education. I had a sense of control over where I was going in my life, and enjoyed all the academic things I quite unexpectedly found I was good at.

That explains why my career is so important to me. But having said that I'm not prepared to let it take over my life, as I can see happening to some of my colleagues. I'm working towards the whole life policy where you have to get home and work and personal things into some sort of perspective. You can't get the balance right all the time, but overall the whole life policy has to be seen to be happening. That's what will stop me from going for the Head of Department's job which is coming up soon. It's not because I don't think I could do it, but because it would interfere too much with my personal life. And given that my present husband's attitude to work is so laid back compared with my own, it would be an extremely sore point for me to start exercising naked ambition. I just would not have his support, and I'm not prepared to risk that, because I value our relationship too much to risk ruining it. That relationship too is part of the whole life policy that I'm after.

Having explained why I won't be applying for the Head of Department's job, I have to admit there are resulting frustrations. I have often felt dissatisfied because I know I could do a senior job better than the person who gets it. But I can't or won't apply for it. In the early days of my career it was sheer lack of ambition. I never dreamt that a working-class girl like me could take on the responsibility of a senior post. I couldn't even imagine myself in a senior position. I hadn't the confidence. Now I have the confidence and realize I could do it, but it's too late, because my second husband and my children and I have a life to make outside work, and that is more valuable to me than the life of a workaholic.

Maybe my whole life policy is specially important to me because of the way my first marriage broke up. My first husband suddenly walked out on me, and looking back I can see I was at fault as well as him. I was suffering a simmering dissatisfaction with my role as an executive's wife and mother. but I couldn't even mention it to him, because he would never discuss anything like that. So it festered. Neither of us was facing up to the situation, so he just went off one day with another woman, and I cracked up completely. I had given up my earlier career to be a good little wife and mother, and life turned round and kicked me in the face! My aunt saved me, looking after the children, and eventually I was able to cope again, because I'm stubborn and don't let things ride — with the disastrous exception of my first marriage. I come from a family of strong working-class women who when any crisis came up would let the men have their say — and then the women would get together and decide what was to be done. It was the women who coped with the day to day struggles of life. So I coped.

Now I'm really pretty content with my lot. I've got a well-paid job. I enjoy it, in spite of the current frustrations in higher education. I've got two teenage children who are intelligent and who seem to be growing up to be nice people that I could like even if they weren't my children. I try to get them to respect other people and am pleased that, for example, my son wants to know and seems to care about wider issues, like what's happening in the African conflicts. I'm happily married second time round, and home is now a good place where I can be with the people I care about.

I'm not domestic though. I don't get any pleasure from traditional feminine skills like baking or cooking more than have to. And I need my own personal space. I was brought up in a close extended family with a lot of people about always, and no privacy. The women always seemed to be sitting around chatting, or cooking and being very domesticated. I was the odd one out because I used to go off upstairs by myself to the bedroom to get my homework done. You were funny if you went off into your own space. When my mother visited us here she could never understand why we weren't sitting together, why we were all doing different things separately in our own rooms. For her home was sharing your space with other people. She's dead now, and one of the things I dislike about myself is that I didn't stay as close to her as she wanted me to be. I put up barriers towards her because I wanted a different kind of life for myself than the traditional woman's life she had had. I see now that I didn't need to do that to protect my life style from her disapproval or misunderstanding. Because what you inherit from the women in your family is indirect rather than direct imitation. I've got from my mother and my aunt some of my strength and coping and stubborn qualities, and I can recognize those in myself, even though I use them in a very different context, professionally in the academic world and at home with my own very different family.

The one thing I would like to change in my life is that I'd like to have more time. I never have enough time to maximize my whole life policy. But I have chosen my life, so it's my fault that I have so little time. If I had more time I'd fill it up with something ...

Marge the Workaholic

Marge is the head of a large primary school in an inner city area. Her husband is an estate agent and her two children are independent teenagers. This is how she strives for a balance between all the different facets of her life:

I have a very good life. That for me means I am really doing what I am capable of doing, and I am never bored because there's always something new for me to learn or to see, and new people to meet. I'm a bit of a workaholic. I tend to take on more than seems to be humanly possible, but I just do it. It's a way of life with me. People say to me, "You can't run a big school like that, and run continuing education courses for other primary school heads, and study theology in evening class (because that is my personal interest), and be a wife and mother ..." And I say, "Yes, I can." And I do it all. But one of the things I'm working on is being able to say no, and being more discriminating in taking on what I do. I need more time for myself, more personal space — time to be quiet, time to be alone. I actually value the long drive to my new school because alone in the car I can switch off for a while. Making space for myself is important, and learning to pace myself. Because I'm a doer I tend to do too much myself, instead of delegating more. I'm trying to delegate in my new bigger school, where it's easier because we have enough teachers to spread the load. Being a workaholic I have a lot of energy myself, and I find it difficult to handle people who are — not less competent, but complaining all the time about all the things they have to do. I'm working on tolerance ...

What drives me in my work? I would say it's the power of influence. It's also the influence of power. I have a clear notion of what's good for little children, what kind of educational atmosphere is the best way to stimulate their development — not just intellectual but social and aesthetic too. It connects very much with my home life, because being a mother and watching my own children develop in those ways I wanted to work out ways you could catch that enthusiasm in the school system. I wanted to influence educators along those lines, and becoming a school principal is a way of doing that.

Personal ambition has to be part of it too. From an ego point of view being principal of a big school matters to me. But after that first fine ego frisson it's the challenge of the work that occupies your energies. My school is in a very challenging needy area with multiple problems. I've set up a problem-solving staff group to meet regularly and work on those problems. I like to do a lot of listening and information gathering before making a decision. I like to take people with me when I take decisions, not to be out there on my own imposing things. I've met quite a few women managers who like to do that, so maybe it is a female tendency. But however hard you try to have a sharing model, being in a leadership position is lonely. So I need my Women in Leadership network to fall back on. There's always someone there to help you or back you up when you're down. I couldn't do without that terrific support network.

The satisfactions I get from work ultimately come from seeing the results of decisions we have made since I came to the school. It is everyday things like walking round the school with a visitor or group and seeing children's work up in the hall, showing the influence of staff development courses my teachers have gone on. I like to see the children gainfully employed, and the teacher not yelling at them, when you open the door of any classroom. I like the sound the school choir have achieved as a result of giving the music teacher free rein and making music more valued in the curriculum.

Going for a senior post like this would never have been possible if my husband weren't behind me. He's there for me. He gives me a lot of support at home. He recognizes my need to be superwoman and take on these things because if I didn't I'd be bored and restless, with huge parts of me unfulfilled. How did I fit in mothering with an interesting career? When the children were smaller I rationalized that what mattered was quality not quantity of time I spent with them. I packed more into that three hours of quality time before they went to bed than I ever did when I was at home all day, or than many full-time mothers do. Now they joke me about not being there to give them milk and cookies when they got home from school. The great thing is they can joke about it! I even hear a touch of pride in their voices sometimes when they tell their friends what their mummy does — "My mum's head of a school." So at home satisfaction comes from seeing that the children are growing up to be well-adjusted people in their own right, more confident about their abilities than I was at their age, more free to express themselves at home and bring their friends to the house whenever they want than I was with my full-time mother.

There are sacred moments at home, like Sunday dinner, to keep us all together and catching up on each other at least once a week. I enjoy cooking when I have the time. So I make that Sunday dinner a feast, and we set the table properly, and that's about the only meal we have together as a family any more, because we're all going every which way.

Cleaning the house is just drudgery for me. I resent it because Saturday is the only day I have to do all that silly cleaning, and my woman's conscience makes me feel guilty until I have done at least some of it. The children help sometimes but I'm the one who feels responsible for minimum standards of cleanliness. Fortunately we live in an old house where regular dusting seems to make little difference, so I don't bother. My husband and I use home as a place to be comfortable in, not a showpiece. The kids are shocked because we stay in Saturday nights and play Scrabble. We started playing Scrabble to help my husband learn English. Now we're champions and go on playing. I almost resent it when we're invited out at weekends because they're the only time we can be together on our own at home.

I suffer from the time famine — like all other women I've met who combine careers with marriage and kids. There are bad moments in the life of a workaholic, times when I feel I'm losing control, that too many things are piling up and there isn't enough time to do them all. Usually I'm fairly organized, but if I have a heap of ironing because I've no clothes left, if the house has not been cleaned for a month and there's someone coming to stay, if I've got a report to write that needs several hours of concentrated work and has a deadline tomorrow — if all these things are happening at once, and one of the kids needs me to listen because they going through a rough time — then yes, I get bothered. I have a sense of losing personal control. But then I pull myself together and organize myself a set of deadlines — the last possible time for minimal cleaning the house before the staff party, etc. It's all worth it in the long run, to live the life I'm capable of living, to do all the things I have it in me to do, to keep up all the personal relationships that home means to me.

The pros and cons of working from home

Alice and Hugo's story

Alice and Hugo have been running workshops in personal development in their peaceful country house for a dozen years now. The original idea was to share their home completely with the people who come on the workshops. But it turned out much more difficult than they had imagined to make no distinction between home space and work space. Alice explains:

> It's a very interesting question how you share your space with other people, even when they are people with similar interests to yourself. We enjoyed welcoming into the house those who came on our workshops, and it took us some time to realize how it was affecting us having new people constantly coming into our home space. Eventually it was taking a toll on our health and psychological state. Although we were enjoying it on one level, it was very demanding at another level. If friends come and stay there's a hidden code and they (mostly) respect your space and privacy. But people paying to come on workshops have a different code, naturally enough. They feel a kind of proprietorial right over your home while they're there, and you end up sharing more of your private space than you expected. We realized that to give out to other people (as we were doing intensively on the workshops) we needed to look after ourselves more. If we were to renew our energies we needed to keep back some private space for ourselves in the house. We found that allowing ourselves quality space and

time on our own enables us to give quality in turn to the people who come on the workshops.

As we took back some space for ourselves over the years, the space in the house became ambiguous, and that was another problem. People didn't know how to deal with that ambiguous space. Could they make tea for themselves late at night in "our" kitchen? Should they help or not help lay the table for meals? If anybody and everybody helped with the table how could we keep our aim of a comfortable and welcoming environment with the "beautifully laid table" (candles, flowers, etc.) at the centre of the domestic sacraments? In the end we acknowledged the underlying tensions of sharing home space and workshop space. We separated out personal and workshop activities, and now at the end of the day I have a sense of going home and putting my feet up. We always had a sitting room of our own but never used it as long as we felt we had to be with the people on the workshops every hour of the day. Now we've reorganized things so that they have sleeping accommodation in a separate part of the house, and a room where they are free to make tea and coffee anytime. I hear them chatting late and night, because our room is above that, but we are completely separate and I no longer feel we have to be with them all the time, joining in the chat.

Another thing that's happened is that Hugo and I have developed a different way of sharing and relating, as a result of our experiences of trying to combine work and home. We ran the centre together in the early years, but now I am running it and he has taken work outside again. We used to battle a bit over how to do the workshops. In our own relationship too we came to realize we each needed a bit more personal space. For us it's more healthy to have separate areas of work. Letting go of each other was necessary for Hugo and me. It was hard to do without a lot of recriminations, but now it's done it's much better for me running the centre on my own. I am learning to do the accounts and the admin (which he used to do) as well as the planning and the programmes for the workshops. I'm taking on the whole range of work from initiating ideas to the detailed programmes and the financial side. I wanted to have control and I had to be honest about that. Now we don't battle over work or home, because when Hugo comes home from work after a heavy day he doesn't have to join in and share other people's concerns. Now that work and home are separated out again it's helped us move towards a more equal relationship, which so many couples these days are struggling to reach. He is a hundred per cent behind what I'm doing with the centre, but has his own work outside. We meet at the end of the day and share what we're doing, but we've got our individual space as well as coming together in our shared space.

Homeworking: relating to spouses

Max and Emily are an American couple in their thirties, currently living in Britain. He designs and weaves beautiful wall hangings in an attic studio while she goes out to work for a big corporate institution. Max says:

Emily's plugged into institutions, people, activities through her work, and is leading a very satisfying life professionally. Her work uses her and challenges her, and she likes that. It's a lot different for me. I'm sitting up here in my solitary attic all day, working at my loom on my own. It's a totally inner life. I have no outer life, except through Emily. So we have very different reactions to our new life in Britain. Back in the States we had developed an ability to lead very disparate lives without feeling it any kind of threat. We had been geographically separated by work for various periods. But this is the most disparate we've ever been, even though we are actually living together in the same place. Before, in our house in Madison, we had a wonderful time with our lives centred on the same place, and both of us related in the same way to that centring home space. But now it's different. We have very different relations to the centring space, and I'm not sure it is a centring space for us both, because we use it so differently and have very different needs to satisfy. I'm here much more than Emily, and I notice myself feeling proprietary towards the house. She sometimes brings work home and if she spreads her papers out over this room I would resent that because I need to protect my particular space — or my right to my half of the shared space. She has other spaces outside, but I haven't. This is all the space I have for living and working.

Since I've converted the attic into my studio it's better. I don't feel so proprietorial about other rooms in the house. It's an enormous attic running the length of the house, so we've turned one end of it into a sociable space, with the TV. That means Emily needn't feel that part of the house is off limits because it's my work space.

While Max and Emily are sensitive to each other's problems, Charles and Nan are a couple in crisis because they have not yet managed to work out a way of reconciling the conflicting demands on home as a family place of relating and as Charles' workplace. When they were first living together they both went out to work and enjoyed a lot of leisure time together at home. Then they decided to start a family, and their little girl was born six months ago.

They were very rational in working out how they were going to manage the new situation. Charles decided he could make more money by setting up his own business from home and doing contract work instead of salaried work for an employer who took the profits. This would mean Nan would not have to go back to work but would be able to stay at home and look after the baby. It all seemed very reasonable but six months later the situation is putting unexpected stresses and strains on their relationship. Charles is doing well work-wise, but cuts himself off totally in his work space every day, so although he is at home, he might as well be still going out to his office.

Nan has felt really isolated and unsupported during that nerve-racking changeover from being a professional woman with a career to being a full-time housewife and mother. If the baby is getting too much for her there is no relief, because although Charles is just the other side of a door, that door carries an invisible prohibition: MAN AT WORK — DO NOT DISTURB. She feels that she has ended up with the worst of both worlds. Charles is at home but not there for her and the baby. And she has no excuse for resuming her career at least part-time as a relief from full-time baby minding, because Charles is making enough money for both of them — so long as he concentrates on his work and gives no daily time to his wife and baby daughter. She goes off now every other weekend with the baby to her mother's in Surrey, because that is the only place she can get the emotional and practical support she would like from Charles, but does not get. He resents her going off on weekend visits to her mother but won't go with her because he hasn't changed his way of thinking since the baby arrived. He thinks they should be having the same kind of relationship and leisure weekends like they used to when they were a twosome. It maddens Nan that he does not even see that having a baby turns your life upside down, and you have to learn to be different though you're still the same people — the parenting paradox. He doesn't acknowledge the parenting paradox, so they are drifting apart, although they spend more time than ever before at home. Working at home may not be such a good idea after all, even though the new technology makes it so feasible.

But the new technology has turned out to be a great opportunity for Ellie, who has managed to combine bringing up her babies with keeping the rest of her faculties in use. Her husband is a teacher, and when the two boys were little they needed more money coming in. In any case mothering was not enough for her, however creative and fulfilling she tried to make it. She missed being professionally active:

> I work from home doing typesetting and editing on my own computer. I'm quite good at keeping things separate — my work time and my home time. Working from home is a way of combining things in your life, and that's no bad thing to learn, instead of having everything in separate compartments as usually happens when you go out to work. If I get stuck in my work I can come down and do some housework. When I'm doing creative work, as I am at present, I fit home things into

my work pattern, because it's the creative side of me that's important.

But when the boys were babies (they're both at school now) I tried to be creative about raising them, so I fitted my typesetting contracts around my looking after them. Because it's so important for me to be myself as well as being a "housewife and mother," I've always tried to keep some sort of professional work going, and working from home has turned out to be a life-saver for me. I did take a part-time job for a while from when the eldest was six months old till when he was two. The childminder was very good but she did things I completely disagreed with. After he started to walk she tried to potty train him and I was completely opposed because he was in no way ready for it. Another thing was that she heard him say his first word, not me, and that upset me. Even though he was only with her five hours a day three days a week, he saved his first word for her! So when I had my second child I became a full-time mother — nearly. I still worked from home typing and writing some articles when the babies gave me a chance. As the baby stage eased off I gradually took on more work.

So I would say from my own experience that the new technology is a great opportunity for women who need to work from home. I can do typesetting and desktop publishing right here on my IBM. There are a lot of women now working at home, and it doesn't always mean you have to take your own initiatives like I do, because the big companies spread a lot of employment around for electronic homeworking.

But I know too that it can be a very lonely way of working. When I was building up my business it was satisfying because I was working for myself, but I still missed the camaraderie of going out to work, having chatty coffee breaks, lunching with people from the office. At one point I felt so socially isolated with the babies and my lonely work that I was almost driven to take an outside job just to have regular breaks with people I knew! Then I realized I'd created my own isolation by not taking the first steps to a social life myself. So I took the initiative of setting up my own lunches and coffees with friends. That has to be part of the homeworker's weekly schedule.

"I *do* work at home — bringing up my children."

Gwen's story

Gwen (26), with two children aged seven and five, takes up an opposing position to all the women we have heard so far who believe so strongly in the "whole life policy" of having an identity outside as well as inside the gender role of housewife and mother. She has recently come back to live in the community where she was brought up and is devastated by the changes in one generation:

> There was real women's solidarity in that old community that my mother lived in when she was bringing me up. Now there isn't any of that left here. It's the same place but there isn't any community, because it was women who made that community. The women stuck together and there was plenty of company about the place. It was just casual with people dropping in and out of one another's houses, and helping with the kids when there was a crisis of any kind, or another baby coming. Now you don't get that any more. People are in their little boxes and if you want a baby sitter for an hour or two it has to be fixed up formal and paid for. When I was a child money never changed hands. People round here were poor and nobody had any to spare. But you did favours for other people and they did favour for you in your turn when you needed it. Now women are supposed to express their female solidarity by going out to work and shouting about independence and freedom. But if you haven't the freedom to bring up your children at home, you've lost a basic woman's right, haven't you?
>
> Another thing I can't understand is how the idea of "work" has changed. "Work" only counts if you go outside the home

to do it. I don't see how it can be right to run down traditional
women's skills like cooking and sewing and doing up the
house really comfortable and nice. I've noticed a lot of my
women friends who go out to work laugh at all that. They're
proud of their awful cooking. They think it's great to take
something out of the freezer and put it in the microwave, and
call that dinner — night after night. Well I couldn't be like that
because I have too much respect for my mother and my
grandmother and all those women who handed their
homemaking skills down to their daughters. So it's like I have
to make good home-made dinners and my own cakes, like that
apple and walnut cake we're having — do you like it? (Yes, I
did. It was delicious). According to my friends who go out to
work it's supposed to be a bind making meals or something
special like a cake. But I enjoy it. My mum's dead now but I
still visit my aunties and there's always an exchange of home-
made cakes. I have my mum's recipe book and when I make
something out of that it's special. Because only close family
were meant to have her recipes and when she died they came
flocking to find out her recipes. Women valued that then. Now
they don't usually, because work and home have been
separated out. But I go on valuing it. Because for me work and
home are the same, and you shouldn't separate them out.

Making a living from good cooking

Annie's restaurant

Annie is now in her seventies, and has severe arthritis, but she still
manages to write about cooking good food, which is her life-long
passion. She reminds us that in previous generations too there were
women who had to earn a living while bringing up their children.
They often, like Annie, had no choice but to find a way of turning
traditional home skills into a money-making proposition. Annie
achieved this a generation ago by opening a restaurant that got into
the *Good Food Guide*. This is her story:

The idea of creating a restaurant came when I was stuck with two children (4 and 6) on my own. After the birth of the second little girl my husband became violent towards me. It started quite suddenly and I was very frightened. He couldn't stand being ticked off by a woman and as both the children were girls it got worse. I remember once one of the little girls sat up in bed and said to him, "Stop shouting at Mummy, Daddy. You're upsetting her." I could see what that was going to lead to, so I had to take both myself and the little girls away from him, before he started on them as well as me. I had always wanted to have a restaurant since I was about sixteen, but my father wanted me to have a professional career. Back in the 1950s that was the middle-class conventional thing to do. He said, "I didn't educate my daughter to do cooking ..."

I got my restaurant in the end, but only after I had gone through all the things a nice girl in the 1950s was supposed to do — have a good education, take a professional job for a few years, then get married and settle down.

My restaurant was my life for the ten years it lasted. It was my home, my work and my living. If you were careful you could live out of the business, eating the food and using the heating and the overheads that you had to have for the business anyway. The restaurant employed and developed all my skills for cooking, advertising and promotion, and interior decorating too. But it got a bit frightening as it took off and became a success. It was woman's thinking that was my problem. A woman wants security, so I used the money I had to buy the place and was then short of capital for expansion. A man would be more of a risk taker, more likely to borrow money on the property and use the leftover capital to build the business. But I was lucky. I got the place cheap because tourism hadn't really reached that small coastal port in the sixties. Later it came and the customers were there. I got a licence and opened to nonresidents.

I had this idea of doing different food, good food. I'd have made a bomb out of steak and chips, fish and chips, etc., but my friends and I wanted to be different. We wanted to

introduce people to good food. I had fallen in love with French
cooking, the kind you get in the provincial family restaurant in
little French towns and even rural villages. Elizabeth David's
French Provincial Cooking was my Bible. When two French-
women came in for dinner one evening and were a bit
suspicious at first, I helped them choose and advised them.
When they had finished (with the syllabub for the sweet
course) they said to me, *"Merci bien, Madame. C'est
formidable.* If you were in Paris they would queue at your
door." Tears in my eyes! But they already appreciated good
food. The other sense of achievement came from converting
ordinary people to good food. One night four youngsters came
in for dinner and ordered the salmon steaks, thinking it was a
variation on steak and chips. When it came they looked
suspiciously at the food but risked eating this strange looking
stuff. Then they said to me, "We didn't know there was food
like this. Can we come every night for the rest of our stay in
the caravan?" And they did. More tears in my eyes!

Nobody now has the sense of service that I gave my
customers back in the 1960s. I believe that it's the wonderful
attention to service in every detail that matters, always with the
aim of making the customers feel completely comfortable and
pleased with the whole experience. Over my lifetime (and I'm
now in my seventies) I've seen the idea of perfect service like
that come and then go again. All it is is making people
perfectly comfortable, but that requires such care and attention
to get it right for all your customers.

I lost the restaurant after ten years because of a combination
of reasons. I had exhausted myself. There were financial
constraints. My health was giving way. Eventually I lost
everything I'd worked for. It was very traumatic for my
daughters as well as me. One was becoming a marvellous cook
and if I could have held on she might have come into the
business, but she was only fourteen. It's very satisfying
keeping a restaurant in the family and keeping up the cooking
tradition. But it didn't happen, and that makes me sad.

I'm still doing cookery writing, and I keep up my lifelong

concerns about food. I've got a long-term concern about hospital food. I believe that the way you eat is part of your being well or ill. I did a paper on public eating in institutions like hospitals on the theme that you should be eating to get better. I've talked to hospitals about the value of vegetarian eating, and one or two places have taken it up. We make a lot of mistakes in the way we eat today. We go on eating as if we were farm workers when we are not doing enough physical work to burn up the fat and carbohydrate. We've lost the habit of unselfconscious eating because of worrying about the health aspect and being so weight conscious from a dreadfully early age. One advantage in getting old is that my memory goes back to world war two and the food revolution that occurred after it. The healthiest eating we ever had was under wartime restrictions. Our diet was low in fat and sugar and meat, with plenty of good bread and potatoes and fresh vegetables. With the end of rationing everybody went mad for fat and sugar. And food technology began to have a field day, persuading people that they should stop making home-made soups and cut open a packet of dehydrated chicken noodle with preservatives instead. We lost too the seasonal instinct for different fruits and vegetables to mark the turning of the year.

So you see, although my restaurant is gone, and I am 75, I still care passionately about good food and go on fighting for it. And I worry sometimes that today's young women don't see the point, and don't care enough, because they are afraid of getting caught in the "domestic trap." They want richer more varied lives than previous generations of women. Good luck to them, but I beg them not to throw away the good in traditional women's lives (the cooking of quality, the attention to comfort, the aesthetics of home) when they're tossing out the restrictive and the bad.

Chapter 3
Keeping your own space

Women and men on living together

All the couples I talked to were emphatic about the basic human need for keeping a bit of private space when you share your home with a partner, whether or not you have children as well. One woman explained it like this: "The space for a husband is different from the space for children, and your own personal space is different from both." When your personal space is squeezed out, your self-identity is threatened and that begins to undermine a relationship that was founded in the first place on the attraction of two separate and different personalities. But how do couples maintain their personal space without losing the intimacy between them? In this chapter couples who have faced these quandaries in a positive spirit tell their stories.

At one end of the scale are partners who keep their own places and spend "quality time" with each other. Eliza and Malcolm's relationship was sustained like this (on and off) for about ten years, but a year ago they finally set up house together. They describe how they have tried to work things out so that each has enough personal space in the new arrangement to help them go on feeling independent and individual while living together. They are a fairly affluent dual career couple (without children as yet), so they have freedom of choice in how they pattern their relationship. More often two-household coupledom is the enforced result of the "commuter marriage" that is evolving to enable both partners to follow their own careers in different parts of the country, only spending weekends and holidays together. Gerald and Elaine next tell their story of how a commuter marriage has worked out for them.

Achieving a happy mix of commitment and independence is easier materially if not emotionally for relatively affluent professional people, but you can get your breathing spaces in a relationship if you are sufficiently determined on building them into whatever circumstances you are in. Janey lives in a cramped rural terrace cottage with her husband and two children, on a low income, but she still manages to get a bit of personal space to herself. She says:

> When your husband and kids seem to be taking over the home you have to try and keep a little space to yourself, have a few hours on your own in the house, and a corner (even if it's only a passage behind a curtain) where you can slip away and they know not to disturb you. I like sitting outside too, just letting my body relax and being connected with outside. That brings back my energies. I can sit for quite long periods now outside and feel the energy coming back to me. It's like it's coming up out of the ground and from all around. That's what great about living here in the country. Another thing I do when I'm on my own in the house is dance and bang my drums. That puts me back in touch too, brings up my energies when I'm feeling down or cut off from part of myself. I'm a pagan like my mum and I know from her that you've got to raise good energies and not let yourself go down.

Couples have to work at getting the right balance between shared space and personal space, because partners have very different tolerances and expectations of how much time they will spend together. Everyone is vulnerable to feelings of neglect and jealousy over a partner's excluding behaviour, whether it be a career obsession or a same gender meditation group or cuddling the cat more than the partner. Many people too turn out to be very ambivalent about private solitary space. They have a deep sense of needing it, but when they get it they may not know what to do with it. I have talked with women who lead busy demanding lives and long for a breathing space to themselves, but if they actually find themselves alone with time on their hands all they experience is boring emptiness. The longed for personal space has lost its meaning and they rush into the next bit of busyness to cover up the gaping void. For other women the problem is that taking personal time and space for yourself is in conflict with the traditional female caring roles we have absorbed, consciously or unconsciously, from our foremothers.

Usually these days women have developed external roles as well, but that may only make them feel guilty for not giving enough to their home life. They are torn between the need to be there for partner and children, and the equally pressing need to take a few hours off from the double demands of work and home continually pressing down on them. One woman said to me:

> Sometimes I'm just not able to enjoy the hard-won time off I manage to wring from my loving family. Sure, I can take off for a few hours on a Saturday afternoon and shop till I drop. That gives me a lift. Otherwise if they went out and I was alone at home, I'd just fall into the sleep of exhaustion, and wake up feeling guilty for not spending the time with them. Shopping for clothes at least doesn't make me feel guilty. It's a nice way of looking good and expressing myself and enjoying the money I work so hard to earn. It's a lovely consumer version of personal space. It's much simpler than going to Saturday workshops on meditation for stress relief or personal development or something, like one of my friends does. I've got plenty of personal development in my life already, what with work and home, and buying clothes is my particular form of stress relief — a totally absorbing and delightful bit of self-expression in my own shopping space.

Couples in mid-life may be free of the stresses and strains of frenetic youth, but they have their own dilemmas. If the relationship lasts for twenty years or more, as with Amanda and Robert, who tell their story later in the chapter, how do you ensure that it grows rather than declines, remains rich and varied rather than monotonous and predictable? Amanda and Rob describe their "keeping company" marriage with its ever widening circle of interesting friends. There are Frank and Caroline too, another delightful intelligent couple who on first acquaintance seem very like Amanda and Rob. Both couples are in that well-groomed, well-dressed age group of forties or early fifties which is so hard to read from outward appearances. Both are childless and their energies go into interesting work and elaborate social lives. But Frank and Caroline only met two years ago, on a walking holiday abroad. Frank's marriage was breaking up and Caroline was living on her own. A mid-life romance blossomed, and now they are re-making home together in a charming old farmhouse which they use for their home and work base. They explain how they are working to create good patterns of personal and shared space.

Eliza and Malcolm's story

Eliza and Malcolm are a professional couple in their late thirties. Their working lives are important to them both, not just to bring in money, but as a vital source of self-identity and people contact. She earns her living as a therapist and he has had a succession of academic research contracts in the field of information technology. A year ago they finally set up house together, but they have had a lasting though fairly open and intermittent relationship over ten years at least. Now they have made a commitment to greater intimacy and closeness, and they may decide to have a child. But this new phase in their relationship has involved much agonizing and negotiating with each other over the issue of personal and shared space. Malcolm says:

> We come from different sides on the home question. I'd been bombing around for years, so it has been my shot at stability of every kind. It is turning out very stabilizing for me. Once I got into my thirties I found it so undermining having no stable base or centredness in my life. So this feels very good, as simple as that. Then it's a testing ground for our relationship, because it's the first time we've shared a place together. We both knew we wanted to have our own space. We didn't want to be always in each other's gloves. So I have a room of my own and Eliza has a room of her own, though we share the rest of the space. We have a friend who's never been apart from his partner for more than a week, and just couldn't understand how Eliza and I need our own spaces, and can be apart regularly as well because Eliza's work takes her abroad half a dozen times a year for ten days at a time. So us having

separate rooms shocks some friends. Traditionally it's supposed to be a sign of a relationship that isn't working. For us it's a sign of a relationship that is working. It's a way of living together and having a good relationship which leaves private space for each of us, as well as sharing things together which we enjoy. We can choose to do things together rather than getting into the habit of just assuming we are going to do things together all the time. It's a positive choice, rather than taking things for granted.

And Eliza said:

We go further than most couples in having our own spaces. We started off being a bit overcautious and too distant with each other, because we were trying so hard to respect each other's spaces, We negotiated and are closer now. But I would hate my partner clinging onto me all the time. When I was in my twenties I was married for seven years and never spent one night apart from my husband. And I was brought up in an overcrowded council house, so one of my earliest dreams was to have a room of my own with a lock on the door. It still affects me. I think I'm quite easy to live with, but there's not a lot of people I could live with — partners or women friends — because they invade my space and they have no idea how difficult I find that. Here it is working out fine. Malcolm and I seem to drift in and out of each other's space easily enough. We keep things open between our spaces, offering random sociability and cups of tea. We don't have to process things much or engage in elaborate negotiations, which would be exhausting. We can read each other most of the time ...

The last year has at the same time been a great upheaval for me. When we set up house together it meant leaving so many things behind in London. I left my friends, my home, my support network, and bits of my work. I left my hairdresser, my chiropractice, all my familiar support things. I've not replaced all of those yet, but it hit me hardest when I first got here. I walked through the door and I thought to myself, "What am I doing here in this house with this man?" — even though at last Malcolm and I had the home together that we wanted, and the house that we wanted to turn into home. Home is to do with familiarity — with people and friends rather than the house or place. I still miss my friends popping in for coffee or lunch or supper, as they did in London. Making friends I always took for granted till the last few years when I got into my thirties. Making deep lifelong friends doesn't happen all that often, and I feel now my friends are very scattered and I don't see them often enough. That's more to do with the move up north here than with Malcolm and I setting up house together, I think.

I've spent a huge amount of energy in this first year on the material side of turning the house into home, and I'm sure that's got a heavy emotional load as well. I've discovered there's a fine line for me between making the house home and tipping over into rampant consumerism. I'm discovering I can easily go too far. Malcolm and I tease each other about our magazines. The man has porno mags or computer mags under the bed and the woman has piles of Ideal Homes, Perfect Home and B&Q magazines under the bed. That's my porn. The important thing about how we've done the house is that there's a place to go to when you need personal space, and there's places to be in when you want to be with your partner. You've got the choice. Of course there has to be mutual agreement when you feel like sharing, but a lot gets understood without being explicitly stated. Learning to be intimate includes learning to read your partner and to respond.

A commuter marriage

Gerald and Elaine's story

Gerald and Elaine began their working lives in the southeast of England as hardworking professionals. Elaine was married before and has a grown-up daughter. Gerald and she have not had children. At the end of the seventies they decided to get away from it all and opt for the good life. They bought an old farmhouse in Wales with a few acres of land and rebuilt the house with their own hands, learning the skills as they went along. Now it is an idyllic country home. In the reconstructed inglenook in the sitting room a fuel efficient wood-burning stove stands on slate slabs under the oak beam. An elegant oak staircase rises from one corner of the sitting room, and below it a door leads out into the big farmhouse kitchen, always warm from the Rayburn stove which is used for cooking and central heating. In the early years Gerald and Elaine reared pigs and sheep, but they only had a small bit of land so they had to find other ways of earning their living. First they tried "Grannycare" — bringing an old person to stay with them for a week or two while the permanent carer had a break or went on holiday. However they found themselves vulnerable to (or even victimized by) the vagaries and demands of the succession of old persons on the hearth, as well as finding their constant physical demands exhausting. It was an invasion of home, and they had no space of their own left, so Grannycare lapsed.

Eventually Gerald got a small business going on the basis of the skills he had taught himself doing up their own house. He has now been installing and servicing stoves for ten years and has built up a steady trade. He is known and trusted, and is recommended to new customers by other satisfied customers. Elaine though did not find the same satisfactions in the work available to her in rural Wales. She is a qualified teacher of disturbed children and has trained in counselling. But jobs in her speciality are few and far between, and the only counselling work to be had in rural areas tends to be voluntary and does not bring in any money. She felt very frustrated and unused, for work outside the domestic confines had always been an important part of her life. She and Gerald talked and talked over the problem, and eventually agreed to try out the "commuting partners" pattern that more and more couples seemed to be opting for (out of necessity rather than choice in most cases). She applied for, and got, a job in a residential home for seriously disturbed children, back in the south-east, During the week she lives in a flat provided by her employers and most weekends she commutes back home. It is a very challenging and demanding job, which is what she needs and wants, but where does that leave her in relation to her life with Gerald back in the Welsh farmhouse they rebuilt together? What is it like to be split between two homes? Elaine says:

> I need my work to make demands on me. That gives me more
> energy, not less, at the end of a day. When I'm bored my
> energy decreases, and the feeling of inertia spreads from work
> to home. Before I went away I had a job here — working in
> an old people's home — that was very unstimulating and left
> me stupefyingly dull and inert at the end of the day. A bit of
> that boiled cabbage atmosphere still clings when I come back
> here even now. Sometimes when I come back I still feel dull
> because of the bad work associations here, although I'm now a
> different person in my other home. When I'm working with the
> disturbed kids it keeps my energies high. The more energy you
> put in the more comes up. I'm putting a lot of energy into the
> job but it doesn't drain me. It stimulates me to put more
> energy into my home there and the supporting networks that
> make me feel at home in my life generally. I feel I'm more of
> an individual. I have opinions of my own, and people to listen
> to them. I'm clearer about what I want, and I can do so much
> more in life from my home in the southeast than I could ever
> do here — there's everything set up for you there, from
> women's networking to bonsai courses. Here in the country it's
> difficult to make the same kind of social network. Even if I
> could I'd have to think about how Gerald would get on with
> my women friends, and they with him. I get a lot out of that
> women's networking in the southeast. I need my women
> friends and I'm different with them than at home with Gerald.

It feels a bit schizophrenic really being at home in two different places like I am, and having to relate differently to different people. Gerald can find some of my foibles a serious problem, but my women friends in the southeast can laugh at them. You just have to accept different experiences with different people who matter to you, and see that they're good in different ways. They all help you to grow in one way or another. You learn not to expect the same responses from different people, but just accept the diversity — or even appreciate diversity. I've been to Springs (the health farm) three times in the last year. Once I went with a woman friend and that was fun. Once I went with Gerald and that was serious. Once I went by myself, and that was just relaxing. Different experiences of home are a bit like that. They all add up so you are using all of yourself, but in different places, with different people. Building up friends and leisure things is strange when you have two different home places. There's a Sod's Law factor which means you always find yourself in the wrong place when there's something good on in the other place. Like recently there was a music festival on here in Wales, and Gerald and I would have gone to that together, only I was in the southeast. We both love swimming too, and Gerald really goes for the big wave machines and fun chutes, but it's a long drive to the nearest one in Wales, while I've got one just down the road from where I work, but never have time to go to it.

Friends and family have problems over my two homes. It annoys me when people don't visit me in my work home because they don't see it as my "real" home. I've got space for people to stay, because I've got a staff flat. But nobody comes because of this thing about it not being a proper home. My daughter comes to London from time to time but it doesn't occur to her to come and see me there, because to her my home is with Gerald in Wales. At first I shared the flat with other staff because there's too much room for one, but one changed jobs and the other didn't stay long (he was a gay man and didn't like living on the site because he wanted to keep his private life private). So now I've got my own space to myself again there, and that does feel better than sharing with people you're not close to. It's alright sharing with whoever turns up when you're about twenty, like students do, but later you get more choosy about who you share with.

When you move between two homes you need all kinds of support and so does your partner, the one who's still at home, because you've got two homes but he can feel like he hasn't

got any home left. You have to work things out with your
partner all the time, because when you're so much apart you
stop picking things up unconsciously like you do on a day to
day basis. We both need all the security we can get, because
all sorts of little insecurities to do with home pile up. We have
difficulty with time when we're together because we have to
do a lot of talking and doing things together. The most basic
things get problematic, like cooking. Cooking has got difficult
because Gerald and I put things in different places in the
kitchen, so when I come home I can never find my favourite
herbs and spices. The kitchen feels like Gerald's kitchen, not
our kitchen, since I've been working away. I even eat quite
differently in my two homes. I don't eat meat there, but I do
here because we've reared our own pigs and lambs, had them
slaughtered in the local abattoir, and stuck them in the deep
freeze. I feel maybe I should be vegetarian rather than going
on buying pigs to fatten and kill off and eat. But Gerald and I
aren't really together on that one, and I can understand. When
you're here in the country it feels good and natural to have a
couple of young pigs rooting about out there (they're great for
digging up the ground if you want to grow things later) and
having a free and healthy (if short) life. When you're in the
city and the supermarket meat is all factory farmed, it's very
different, and you get this vegetarian urge.

When you're the commuting partner you have to try and not
arrive home at weekends totally exhausted and inert, however
hard your week at work has been. Because you're meant to be
spending quality time together to make up for the absences in
between. But when I've had a long drive home on Friday night
I'm not always in the mood for instant happiness and glad
welcomes. I'm just tired and need to recover my energy before
I can be my vibrant self!

When you're apart the phone's your lifeline. If my phone
isn't working for some reason I can't stand it ... because the
phone is home for me. We keep in touch on the phone most
evenings. That's important, just talking about ordinary
everyday things to keep in touch with your partner.

Personal space and shared space in midlife relationships

When a couple have been together for many years their individual and joint needs evolve, together and apart, and so they need to rethink the combination of private and shared space that suits them best. Different stages in the life cycle bring new patterns in the way we use our energies. There are shifts in the directions of our emotional priorities — in the twenties to make relationships and find interesting work; in the thirties to do parenting; in the thirties and forties to combine all these things and still have a little time and space to oneself; from fifty onwards to do a midlife assessment and explore new energy flows, emotionally and spiritually. Here are some of the changing midlife needs that women identify:

Louisa (50) says:

> I felt a growing need to acquire my own space and to get in touch with energies in me that I felt I was not drawing on. I took over a kind of annexe to the house that had once been a coach house. It had been used as a store for cast-off furniture and boxes of old books and general junk that nobody would throw away. I was fairly ruthless in sifting through the stuff and clearing it out, because it was my chance to create my own space again and to try and find a way to express myself in that space. I needed that desperately, because at this stage of life, with my daughters grown-up and a job that has over the years become dull and routine, however hard I work at it, I had to find new ways of self expression. I have put a lot of my personality into the annexe, because it was a way of asserting myself and rediscovering my identity after the years of immersion in being a partner, a parent and a breadwinner. I moved in all my favourite books and cassettes and word-processor and felt an unholy joy at being on my own there a few evenings a week, and not have to face the main house with its largely redundant domesticities. Jonathan is a retired man, and the girls are grown-up people with their own lives to

live. It is time for me to explore what else I am besides his
partner and their mother. Of course I've had a "career" as well
as home, and that's supposed to give a woman a balanced life.
It did help my sense of who I was, when I was younger. Now
I'm entering a phase where I'm looking for new meanings and
I'm blundering about in the dark because I'm not sure where to
look. But it's beginning to take shape, and I'm getting a lot of
help from a network on women's spirituality I've recently
joined. I have a strong need for the healing energies you get
from good inner and outer spaces. We have a meditation group
where we learn to sit and (sometimes) shake off that
horrendous busyness we fill our lives with. At fifty you
haven't the time left in your life to be constantly drained by
domestic and work busyness. Once or twice a year now I take
off with some of the women from the network on a sacred site
trip. It's not so much an escape as, yes, a kind of pilgrimage in
search of the bigger truths. We choose a place with mythical or
spiritual associations, and try to relate these to our own lives
— not analytically, just telling our own stories and retelling the
myths for the way we are now. On those trips I sometimes
take my hammock and sleep under the stars, and feel part of
the universe ... When you're fifty years old you need to start
being at home in universal space. You've grown out of family
space and work space. You've got to go somewhere else, and
the bigger, the more mind-blowing, the better.

Amanda (50) perfects her warm hospitality to an ever widening social
network of friends and extended family as her way of finding meaning
in life. She and Rob decided not to have children and have during
their twenty-five years together built up a very close and affectionate
relationship which is supported by a dense social life at home and
abroad, for they travel and have friends on every continent. Amanda
delicately intertwines personal and social, private and public engagement, but at fifty she is aware of certain chasms looming ahead
somewhere in the future. Ageing and retirement from her interesting
information management job might bring elements of isolation and
futility of purpose into their hitherto busy and interesting lives. Her

response is to lay the foundations for an even more elaborate sociability that will keep loneliness at bay and enable her to maintain those caring connections with the outside world that are the heart and soul of everyday life. Amanda explains how she balances the different strata of her busy life:

> Everything radiates from home, and I need to radiate from home as well. I'm keen on the home base, but as a base, not somewhere that ties you down and closes you off. For me home is about relating. That starts with Rob and me relating, but extends to relating to other people, on my own or with him. I have never been at home a lot, and I don't think I would like to, when I think of some of the home-centred neighbours we've had in the past. In our last house they would spend their time looking out of the window, waiting for the evening paper to read, or just watching the crowds of boys who used to gather menacingly on the road in the evenings. For people like that home is a negative thing that closes them off from the world outside. For me the most important thing in life is to keep my mind open, and keep learning how you can get closer to other people. I want to be aware of other people and know how to help them when they need it. I can do that best from having a good home base with Rob, and equally from having my work, which gives me an outside base. If I didn't have my work I would have to find other things to do that were creative or learning things. There has to be something going on to keep the home live and in contact with the outside world, or home is just a dead and lonely place. I like social contacts in every aspect of my life. The main thing about going out to work is the contact with other people, and helping other people (I'm in a service job supplying information). You learn a lot at work about relating to people, and that affects who you are in the rest of your life and how you respond to people in your social life. It's stimulating, and it's a discipline, and both come from the people contacts. I'd say that that's the central thing in my life, in my work base and my home base — the people I come in contact with. It's

not that I go for any kind of sociability, I don't think. It's just that for me life is about being open to the people you meet and responding to them. Those instincts of mine do lead to a lot of socializing, and that's important to Rob and me. Life is more interesting and fuller as a result.

Caroline (50) and Frank (45) have started a new life together coming up to age fifty, and are doing freelance work from their delightful farmhouse in one of the national parks. They are making a fresh start and are free to choose how to plan and share their space, together and separately. Caroline sits in their warm and cosy country kitchen with the Aga purring in the background. There is a ginger and white cat curled up in the winter sun slanting through the window onto the deep window ledge. Outside sheep graze on the unfenced hill pasture, and beyond that wooded hills roll away to the horizon. Caroline says:

It was a mixture of planning and pure fortuitous chance that Frank and I settled here together a year ago. I had been thinking for years that I'd like to leave university teaching. I wasn't unhappy. I was quite good at it. But I didn't like the whole academic thing. It's so narrow and specialized it can cut you off from the rest of life.

So in my forties I was looking for wider visions. I found more interest outside the university than inside it. At one point my plan was to finish teaching and do freelance writing and research. Part of that plan was also to run personal development courses at the house where I used to life. I had been to the Skyros Centre, the Greek island where they run renowned (and rather luxurious) personal development holidays. It was all about liberating the imagination and getting in touch with your natural creativity in a safe and warm community (of other *Guardian* readers!).

Since I was then on my own I found Skyros a good place to go, because the typical Skyrian is an over thirty single professional trying to find him or herself — rather than trying to find someone else, or to escape from themselves. I met a chap there who had the idea of running personal development

courses in Britain. He needed a biggish house to rent
occasionally for the courses, and we agreed on the use of my
house. We did run several courses of four or five days, with
him doing the workshop side and me doing the cooking and
providing the environment. I quite liked the way it went, so I
tried to build on that. I tried to run my own personal
development courses in creative writing, hoping to build up a
series of freelance workshops. But it failed miserably. The
marketing is the problem always. And the house I then had
was too small.

Those tentative moves towards things I could do if I retired
from university teaching at fifty, left me in a quandary. I
wouldn't have any personal development myself if I couldn't
get my personal development workshops off the ground. I was
still keen though to get away from the academic world and
explore the dimensions of life outside the university ghetto. At
that point I quite accidentally met Frank on a group walking
holiday abroad. Purely by chance I heard from an ex-student of
mine that he was running a part-holiday, part-field trip for
people like national park staff and outdoor interests organizers.
That's Frank's field, so there he was, and we met, and he was
in the process of splitting up with his wife, and it all worked
out like a dream romance! Frank decided to move and live
with me, and that made an enormous difference to my life at
that time, personally and professionally. I was ready to make
new kinds of space in my life, but I had felt a bit timorous on
my own, striking out in new directions. Meeting Frank gave
me the confidence to go freelance. And it gave me a new
relationship. I'd only ever had one other longish term
relationship, so I had lived alone for most of my adult life, and
sometimes had the feeling of an excess of my own space. I
was more than ready to share my space. I had found that living
on your own makes it twice as hard to organize a new life
when you feel the urge to move on to a new phase.

With Frank our combined energy was there for the move
into a new phase. So now our personal and our professional
lives are intertwined, but we also have our own spaces within

our relationship, and our own work projects. We are based on this house in the national park. We've made one of the rooms into a shared office, but we're also going to knock a door through into the adjacent barn to give us extra space. I will have a studio there where I can do my own art projects. We decided to set up a company and offer courses and consultancies in the fields we both have interests in. The main thrust is environmental. The sort of thing we've done so far is, for instance, a workshop for third year planning students, where they do an extended role play to take them through all the stages of a planning enquiry. Sometimes we work together like that and sometimes we work on our own. So we have ways of sharing our space and of keeping some of our own space. Sometimes one of us goes off to put on a course, and the other is working at home.

In this first year I've put less work into the company than Frank, because I think I need to stand back a bit after leaving my institutional job. I wanted to move towards a better balance in my life, and have more time to do creative work. But the trouble is it's difficult to get into the creative habit when you have been doing institutionalized things for so many years. It kills the creative spirit, so I need to go deep to recover the imaginative instinct. Frank is at a rather different stage, because he is younger than me. It's the dreaded age of fifty that makes you want to get in touch with neglected areas of yourself. But also meeting Frank like that has meant I have a much fuller personal life, which is very satisfying, so I use my time differently. We do all sorts of things together and it takes up time which I would once have spent working when I was living on my own.

There are wonderful days when we are both at home, and the sun shines, and we just go out and explore the countryside together. Frank's quite a keen mountaineer and rock climber, and whereas I was more timorous on my own, I find myself able to do a lot more when I have Frank with me. So we have both become at home in this stretch of mountain country where we live. Frank likes living in a national park where there is

restricted planning and you don't get bungalows sprouting. In a
way that's a problem for me, so we do have differences
between us about the kind of spaces we want to live in. I have
a problem over escapism, of being part of a protected
landscape where incomers and townees are more protective and
possessive than the locals who make their living here. It's a
problem to do with having privileged space for yourself,
because private space is also part of public space, and I can't
close my eyes to that. I'm more sensitive than Frank to the
issues of us being incomers with different values to the people
who live here. But I agree with him that you can't falsify your
wider concerns about environmental issues, or pretend to see
the same way as the locals when you don't always. The local
farmer here, for example, is against access rights for walkers,
because he is afraid of people breaking their legs on his stiles
and suing him for damages. He's on the community council,
where there's a hearing coming up because some farmer has
closed a right of way. Our local farmer would be very
sympathetic to that, but we wouldn't. So this new home brings
areas of delicate negotiation with it, uneasy spaces between us
and the locals, and occasionally between Frank and me. But
the great thing is to be connected, even if it involves
negotiating ambiguous space, treacherous ground. If you're not
connected you can't even begin to negotiate, and your
everyday life is not grounded. A space of your own is not
enough. You need spaces you can share with significant others,
too.

Chapter 4
Re-making home when you are gay

Lesbians telling their stories

Partners in gay relationships have the same need as straight couples
to negotiate personal and shared space with their partners. But they
have also the problem of negotiating space that is hospitable to their
relationship, with their friends, their families and the communities
where they live. Many (especially if they live outside the major cities)
still agonize over whether or not to come out to their families and
their workmates. Even in places with convivial gay scenes the decision
is not simple. Jennie (35), a senior professional working in computers,
says:

> My partner May and I don't want to be part of the gay scene
> which is flourishing in this big northern city. You have to be
> into a certain kind of style and self-publicity which is not
> really our thing. The gay clubs tend to be more for mad
> extroverts, I think, than for sober "thirty something"
> professionals like us. I can see there's a political point to be
> made for gay lib just as there is for women's lib, so in theory I
> should go on gay pride marches and stand up in public for the
> freedom to live my life with May in a gay relationship. But I
> don't want to do those things. I already feel free to live this
> way regardless of public opinion. It's nobody else's business,
> after all, unless you flaunt your gay relationship in front of the
> neighbours or at work, which I don't. I've noticed that gays
> who "come out" at work tend to be labelled as "gays" first and
> foremost — before all the other bits of their personality that
> might be far more important. Colleagues' responses I would
> find very difficult if I were to be open about my gayness. I
> would hate seeing them struggling between hearty tolerance

and a slightly embarrassed pretending not to notice. But even when you decide to keep your gayness quiet, a few people you are close to need to know, or you begin to feel hunted by secret police (your family) on the most ordinary occasions like Christmas. It can be quite tricky working out how much to tell different people. My mother comes to us for Christmas now, because she's a widow on her own and my brother is abroad. I know she knows how May and I are, but she would hate it to be brought out into the open. She couldn't cope with that because she's got oldie worldie ideas about *the family* and what it should consist of — although her own experience of traditional family with my dad was a disaster. So we don't discuss the fact that May and I are a *gay family*. And that's fine with my mother, because she can see we're happy together, and that pleases her deep down, God bless her!

My previous lover Merida and I used to row over how upfront we should be about our relationship. She is American and very militant for gay rights, and she wanted me to be too. But I couldn't. I tried to tell her about the virtues of European reticence ... She couldn't see it. Fortunately she only came over for holidays and conferences, and the rest of the time we kept in touch with e-mail, etc. I — just — managed to keep my incognito the three years I was with her. It's a relief that May and I see eye to eye over this. It's a lot easier too because she does not seem to have any close family being curious and wanting to suss things out. So we live a very private life, but it's very fulfilling. We don't feel the need to go out Saturday nights looking for "the gay scene." We'd much rather stay in, have dinner and wine by candlelight, and enjoy each other's company. Because we both have full-time outside jobs home is the place we come back to, the place we can be together in. We don't have any problems I can think of about sharing our home space with each other. May does more DIY than I do, and more of the cooking. I do more of the gardening, and of the drinking. But we don't have a Ten Commandments of Domesticity that we slavishly follow. We have a long through living-room where I might be surfing the Internet on my PC at

one end, while May is stitching new curtains at the other end.
But we've chosen the curtain material shopping downtown
together, and she'll often come over to see, when I come
across something amusing on the World Wide Web. We sip
our glasses of wine of an evening, and really quite enjoy
ourselves doing perfectly ordinary domestic things, like your
average happy couple, I presume, whether they're gay or not.

A spirituality for home space in a gay relationship

Kathryn and Alison's story

Kathryn (47) and Alison (42) have been together for six years now.
They are both practising Christians and church members. When they
met each was well established in her own career in the caring
professions, and that was, and continues to be, an important source of
self identity for each of them. Kathryn had never married, being sure
from an early age of her sexual orientation to women rather than men.
Alison had married but her marriage broke up some years before they
met. Kathryn explains how they have arranged their lives to give them
elements of independence while creating the strong and lasting
relationship each wants to have with the other:

> Because Alison and I are a lesbian couple, we said from the
> start that we wanted to create our own patterns for how we
> would live. Not having models is a real problem but it is also
> liberating because there aren't the stereotypes you get in
> heterosexual couples, putting pressure on them to conform to
> masculine and feminine models. We don't have those
> pressures, we have other pressures. There's the ever present
> risk of social rejection for being a lesbian couple. But at least
> we have the freedom to make our own patterns of living, and
> we have done that.
>
> We have two separate homes, just round the corner from
> each other. Our jobs mean we both do a lot of our work from
> home, but my work needs quiet and lack of interruption, while

Alison's is very social and noisy. There would be great
practical difficulties sharing a house, so for the good of our
relationship we keep our separate spaces. Some people find it
difficult to understand that we keep our separate spaces
because of caring for each other in a practical way, not
because we do not care for each other enough. In any
relationship you need to respect your partner's space. That's
part of a positive togetherness. We realize we are very
privileged to be able to keep two separate homes, but even if
we couldn't afford that, we would still try to arrange our house
to respect each other's need for private space.

We make sure we have quality time together. We have a
commitment to each other to say our truth and to hear the
other person's truth. That can take a few tosses, but we keep at
it. We don't try to be with each other every moment God
sends. We try to give each other space, but we also make
space to hear about each other's things. We do attend some of
each other's public functions, to show support and to make
public our commitment to each other. But neither of us is the
other's wife, on those formal occasions or on any other
occasion. We try very hard to take it in turns as to who is
supporting who, both in the domestic domain — cooking meals
and so on — and outside in the public world of functions. It's
important that neither of us becomes exclusively the public
figure and the other only a support person. So we try to keep a
balance between being the upfront person and taking a
supporting role. We have to pay attention to that because both
of us have upfront roles in life.

The thing that's most difficult is for us to arrange enough
quality time together — leisure time on our own. We have to
see to it that we have time together other than when we're
tired out, that we have good emotional space shared with each
other. We get that on our country walking, travelling together,
or just being at home together chatting and relaxing. We have
a lot of fun together, but there too we try to have a mutuality,
so neither of us is always upfront or always supporting or
following.

Our friendship networks are very strong and supporting, and that's important. Alison and I have a lot of friends together, and also each of us has her own friends. Our joint friends are a mix of male and female, but there are more women than men, and quite a lot who are lesbians or lesbian couples. Because one important thing is the support and understanding you get from people who have experienced what it is like to get hate mail or have your job put at risk because you're a lesbian. But there are positive things as well as the defensive things about friendship networks. We go walking with one set of women friends. We are part of a women's liturgy group (by no means all lesbian) which meets once a month. We have a shared meal and it is an amazing feast. We take it in turns to prepare some sort of meditation or celebration. We have very significant, very moving liturgies we do together. Our group is very justice-oriented. Our spirituality, we find, has to be about social justice. We light candles for a friend going through a bad time. We light candles for the people in Bosnia or wherever. The shared meal is as much part of the whole thing as the liturgy. We nourish each other in a practical way as well as by having each other's concerns at heart. Our women's spirituality is about giving and receiving nurturing. It is about preparing and offering food to each other as a grace. And as we give and receive food, we also offer and receive support and strength in our daily lives.

Sharing space in a gay relationship

Chrissie and Flo

Chrissie (37) is a teacher and a practising Catholic who is highly critical of her church's "shifty and uncompassionate views on gay relationships." Until she set up house with Flo three years ago she was a single living in a London studio flat ("basically a large cupboard with a shower and loo extension"). She has over the years built up a support network of feminist women friends, lesbian and straight. Then she met Flo who was working for a distribution business in the Midlands. Flo had been through a traditional marriage (without children) which had recently broken up, and she was trying to put the pieces of her life together again. Although she had never thought of herself as a lesbian she was receptive to the tenderness and everyday company of a woman's love, which Chrissie offered her. They set up house together and their relationship gradually deepened into a lasting commitment, which both, as Catholics, regard as a blessing and a sacrament, whatever their church has to say about it. Chrissie comes from a very secure middle-class background, and sees home as a life centre which energizes you for reaching out to other people and acting upon the outside world. Flo is still conscious of the material insecurity of her working-class background, and sees home much more as an emotional and material sanctuary from worldly harshnesses. So for them sharing a home raises fundamental questions about how the two of them, singly and together, relate to the outside world, as well as how they share their private space with each other. For Chrissie especially it is very connected with her Christian beliefs about living out divine love in ordinary everyday life:

Home and relationship is not about possession. Possession isn't the thing. It's sacred space that is the thing. But I suppose possessing things has never been a big thing for me because in my upbringing I never had to worry about a shortage of possessions, and there were people employed to keep things ticking over smoothly in the house. It's people not possessions that signify home for me. It's my people networks who are home for me. They are what support me and hear my troubles and help me find my way. The way I see home is as sacred space. Sacred space is like a trust you are given. It means giving a lot of yourself to your partner and your network and the outside world. You make your home a sacred space by nurturing everything around you in your life — your partner, your networks, your garden, your dogs ... But you need discernment when you're creating this sacred space, so that you make it open to everyone who also treats it as sacred space, and closed to those who only condemn, and do not try

to understand, the way you live and the way you love. Home is
sacred space, and sacred space is nurturing space. In our
relationship we have different ways of nurturing each other.
But for both of us in our own ways nurturing space means
space where you can give yourself, but also respect other
people's need for personal space.

Flo practises her Christianity in a down to earth way. She is a well-
grounded woman whose working-class roots still shape her work of
homemaking and relating to other people. Chrissie admits she leaves
the kitchen to Flo's ministrations, because she hates cooking and
never learned to do it well, "because of the servants." The kitchen
therefore is Flo's domain and her delight. It is where she does her
domestic nurturing and finds glorious self-expression through serving
good home-made food and wine. It is her sanctuary and sacred space,
the abode of her loving kindness. Flo is reticent with words, but the
little she says is given enriched meaning by the accompanying dinner
she serves:

If you invest yourself in your home, do things together in it, it
becomes more precious because you are putting yourself into
it. You're making the space into something precious with your
partner. Even if the objects around you are nothing special they
all have a meaning for you. They have associations. We did up
an old pub table together — took the rust off, dipped it and
painted it — and it's wonderful. Chrissie's always had a solid
basis of home, so she doesn't see it as a sanctuary as much as
I do. She can go on about home being your networks and that.
But in my background home was a big achievement you could
never take for granted. We didn't own the terrace house (two
up, two down) we lived in, and were always worrying about
where we'd be if my father lost his job. We ate sausages and
cheap mince so we could be sure of paying the rent. But I
learned to cook, because I did the cooking from when I was
nine or ten, to help my mum who went out charring — again
to make sure of the rent. She taught me about cooking, my
mum, and I love it. Though a lot depends on who you're doing

it for. I lost interest in cooking for my husband when the marriage went wrong. You can't put your heart into cooking when your home's falling apart. Anyway we split up in the end. All I wanted to do then was to get away from that marriage and find somewhere I could be safe and secure — yeah, somewhere I could start cooking again for someone who cared, and that I cared for back ...

This home that Chrissie and I have together, this is about sharing. The other one with my husband wasn't. It's important for partners to do things together, because that's sharing. It's not just the big things. It's about agreeing what colours you're going to have when you do up a room, or how you're going to do the garden. Sharing like that doesn't mean you're always together and giving each other no peace to be on your own. We do have our own spaces in the house, and that's important too. I hate Chrissie in my kitchen because she's no good at it and doesn't have a clue, so I'm tempted to say, "Don't do it that way," or, "You're doing it wrong." And we bicker because she's not respecting my holy ground in the kitchen. And sometimes I don't respect her holy ground — her books and papers overflow the house in all directions and I say, "Sell your books." But she says, "That's like being asked to have an abortion."

Gay couples and the outside world

Gay couples suffer from homophobia to a greater or lesser degree, depending on where they live, their networks of family and friends, and whether they are church members or not. It is worse when one or both partners have high public visibility in their work, because they can never be sure how they are going to be received as a couple on public occasions. Kathryn explains what it feels like:

In a lesbian relationship the best way for people to treat you is to treat you as normal people. But people find that very hard to do. Recently we had a very good experience of being treated

normally, and that stays with me because it is so rare. I had
been invited up north to give a talk, and a C of E bishop and
his wife put us up. In the morning he brought us a cup of tea
in bed. Being taken for granted like that is the best possible
way. When people get to know us they seem to manage to
treat us as normal — and then they spoil it by suddenly
making a joke about us being a lesbian couple. They suddenly
bring in something about us being lesbian which has nothing to
do with the context of what we're discussing, and you realize
they can't forget you are "different."

Many people find us threatening for a variety of reasons.
Men can feel not valued, not wanted, if they are insecure in
their own sexuality, and that makes us appear threatening to
them. Women too can feel insecure around us, because being
around lesbian couples calls up any ambivalence in their own
sexuality. But we find that men and women who are secure in
their own sexuality have no problems with us. When people
are sexually mature and in touch with themselves they do not
feel threatened by us. So they can treat us as the multi-
dimensional people we are, not as just sexual beings doing
lesbian things in bed. It can be very hurtful if people are
hostile because you are in a lesbian relationship. Acts of
hostility from family and friends make it feel very bad.
Sometimes you can talk it through, but sometimes there's a
blank wall of unspoken hostility that you can't climb or get
through in any way. There's one person in my family who tells
me that capital punishment is what lesbians deserve for their
unnatural practices. Others who are very upset at first come
round because they can get past the stereotypes and meet us as
individual people. But then when we're not with them their old
ideas about lesbians tend to come back. They're on a seesaw
— accepting us as people, then falling back on the old
stereotypes. My sister and I had an absolutely frank row about
her not accepting Alison as my partner. I said, "How would
you like it if you came and stayed with me for a week, and I
never once asked about your husband or your kids?" I'd been
staying with her for a week and she had never asked about

Alison and her children. "That's different," she said, "they're my husband and kids."

Often it's no use explaining to people, because it's an emotional not a rational reaction. You have to be there on family sessions and somehow become accepted. We worked really hard to get on friendship terms with my family, by being there with them together as a couple. The breakthrough came one morning when my mother said to Alison, "Will you have pears this morning?" It was the first food offered with goodwill, which equals friendship. That felt very good. Because we've been there together in family times of celebration, Alison has gradually been accepted as one of the aunties. The same thing happens with me going to Alison's parents. You are gradually winning acceptance, but then there's a setback — like when they asked me to take the family photo, not be in it! You notice things like that and you never know whether it's accidental or intentional. But it's no use having a temper tantrum and refusing ever to see them again. You have to keep working out ways of helping them not to be thoughtless. It's a cumulative process and there are always new links to be made with the younger generation, who may be more accepting and tolerant.

Relating to a gay partner's children

Laura and Sarah

Laura and Sarah were entering their forties when they began their relationship. Sarah was a single parent with two teenage children, and Laura had to work out what her relationship with the teenagers would be. She wanted to feel part of their family life, but she worried about finding the right balance between becoming a complete co-parent and trying to work out a different way of relating. It was quite a problem because she had no personal experience of raising children herself, and her hard-working professional life had been led totally in an adult world. This is what happened:

I became part of an extended family six years ago when Sarah and I began our relationship. Sarah's two children are Beth, who was then seventeen, and Derek, who was fourteen. Because Sarah had been a single parent she wanted me to co-parent with her, sharing that as well as everything else that was important in our lives. She suggested that we both share the parenting, and was happy for me to take a full part in the everyday parenting — the decisions about ground rules, talking through things with the children when they needed that, being there for them in the same way as she had been while doing single parenting. But I felt from the beginning that the kids wouldn't take it. They were in their teens and had their own ideas about how they related to the people around them. And anyway I wasn't sure what kind of co-parent I would be, with my complete lack of experience in parenting up till then. Could I do it? Would they accept me doing it? Would Sarah be sorry she'd asked me to do it? I had all those doubts.

So I felt from the beginning that the best way for me to develop a relationship with the kids was for me just to be an adult friend. That meant for example never forbidding the kids anything — except in a crisis — because forbidding things would be using parental authority and I didn't feel I had that, or should have it. We left it to the kids to ask about the relationship between their mother and me, so that we could tell them as much or as little as they wanted or could take at a time. That worked well with Beth. She asked about us and we told her the truth over a period of time as she wanted to know more about our relationship. The really big affirmation came when she was pregnant and she asked us to be co-grannies to her infant. From the time the child was born we have been Granny Laura and Granny Sarah to her. Now our little granddaughter is two years old and clings to whoever's neck or arm or leg is there to cling to. She has decided Granny Sarah colours best with crayons, and I'm the best one to tell her stories, and Derek's the one to play rowdy games with her. So she's got us all wound round her little finger. We all worship that baby. That picture on my desk there shows Granny Laura totally besotted with that child.

When Beth was pregnant the father took off and has never been heard of since. We both talked to her and said we'd support her either way, whether she decided to have an abortion or to have the baby. We said, "It's your choice, kid." And she decided to have the baby. She was clear she wanted the baby. So my way of relating to Beth worked out. She gradually came to trust me and to turn to me for help. During that difficult time deciding about the baby she was open and trusting and talked it all through with me as well as with her mother. That felt very good.

With Derek it's been more difficult. Sarah adopted him when he was nearly a year old, and before that he'd been around foster homes and in care. He is much less articulate than Beth, so you can't sit down and talk things through with him. I've learned you have to be doing something else and just let whatever it is come out casually in the spaces between. At Christmas he and I cooked the Christmas dinner together and we enjoyed doing that. We got on. With Derek you have to baste the turkey and let drop a few remarks while you're doing it. He lets drop a few remarks back and you are learning about his concerns. At home he seems to be accepting me. But while he's accepting me personally he has trouble with the idea of lesbians. He's at college now and his friends at college say homophobic things about "lezzies." He gets confused because he wants to be in with his friends at college, and laugh at the same things, even though at home he sees we are not like that. But I think a lot of his present problems are to do with the insecurity of being one of "Thatcher's children." It doesn't matter whether you've been to college or not, or how evolved you are as a person — there are no jobs and you can't find directions in life. That hasn't to do with Sarah and me, but sometimes everything gets mixed up into one big problem when you're growing up and there seems nowhere to go with your life.

The good thing is that although both Beth and Derek have left home now to get on with their own lives, they both keep coming back to stay with us. And Beth comes home with the grandchild we all adore, the grandchild who treats Sarah and me equally as her grannies. I never expected to have a grandchild because I never had any children of my own, so that little child is a never-ending source of joy, as well as learning, to me.

Chapter 5
Parenting

Tradition and change

When people today hark back nostalgically to traditional family values they often focus on an imagined family in some golden past, where the woman stayed at home being a full-time wife and mother and the man was the breadwinner and father who exercised discipline, however distant, in the home. Everybody, it is assumed, felt secure because they knew their role boundaries, and found fulfilment in sticking to the clear gender identity that society and the churches prescribed for men and women. At the beginning of our century many indeed were content, for it was what they were brought up to expect, and alternatives were few and far between. Marriage and children were a woman's way of acquiring both status and occupation. Working-class women who had to go out to work to help the family finances envied their better-off middle-class sisters who could luxuriate in full-time domesticity. Elizabeth Roberts in recording the oral history of women's lives in the Lancashire textile towns in the first half of our century found that:

> Working-class married women displayed an ambivalence towards their wage-earning work. Those who worked were proud of their skill, their efforts, and their contributions to the family budget. But they rarely had any ambition to go on earning wages all their lives, and regarded it as a matter of social progress and of status to be able to give up their wage-earning work. Their emancipation lay, in their estimation, in the move away from work and into the home. It is impossible to find ... any signs of a trend (clearly observable in more recent decades) of women staying at home to raise their children, and then returning to work in early middle age ...

Part-time work was preferable to full-time work, and wage-earning work in the home was preferable to outside work because it meant less disruption to home routines. (Elizabeth Roberts, *A Woman's Place,* 1984)

But however much the Angel in the Home ideal was adopted by middle-class women, and aspired to by working-class women, some women managed to hand over their domestic role to their husbands and went out to make their mark on the outside world. Verena, a woman now in her eighties, recalls how her formidable grandmother rejected the Coventry Patmore vision of woman as pure angel whose soul (and sole) aspirations were to be self-sacrificial wife and mother:

My grandmother simply insisted on a life of her own. She went around lecturing on Shakespeare and Tennyson and so on, "for her own self-aggrandizement" according to family history. She didn't need to earn money, as they were comfortably off. She just refused to be the good angel in the house. She was clever, by all accounts. She had a mind and she was determined to use it. So my grandfather did the cookery and bathed the three little children, and organized the household and the servants. The way people talk about role models today is rather naïve, I'm sure. Because you could not have found a more original model of female emancipation than my grandmother. But her three children were not at all won over to her ideas. It was quite the contrary. To them she was a missing mother, and they resented that. They did not suffer in any obvious way, because my grandfather was such an excellent — "househusband" I think is the word I am looking for. My mother had been taught how to make pastry and do special cookery by Grandfather, not Grandmother. She taught me to cook very well, but she did not pass these skills on to her sons. She brought us up in strictly conventional masculine and feminine ways. She was so shocked and horrified, you see, by my grandmother's rejection of domesticity and her failure to mother them properly, that she tried to "out-angel" even Coventry Patmore's Angel in the House.

Another grandmother at the beginning of the century made a fortune running a chain of pubs in South Wales, but this time with the approval of her family:

> My grandmother was brought up entirely by her father and her brothers because her mother died giving birth to her. They cooked and sewed and knitted for her until her father married again and there was a stepmother to take charge of the house. My grandmother was delighted with her stepmother, because at last she had a female friend to talk to in the house. In the course of time she married a ship's captain and got so bored alone in the house when he was at sea that she acquired a pub, and eventually a chain of pubs. So *she* made a successful business out of her domestic woman's skills, and was able to bring her kids up at the same time.

Now at the end of our century, dynamic mothers and grandmothers are on the increase. Full-time angelhood in the home is not enough for most women. Mothers go out to work not only to bring in income but to find self-expression beyond domesticity. They are often the sole family breadwinners, as the number of single mothers increases because of marriage breakdown — or rejection of marriage as a restricting convention which trapped our foremothers but is not going to trap the younger generation.

Men who in earlier generations were so often remembered by their children as absent fathers because they came home at night too late for bedtime storytelling, are gradually learning to do more active parenting. The word househusband is slowly creeping into everyday use, not only among "thirty something" professional couples who believe in shared parenting, but in some of the last bastions of heavy masculinity. Sheer economics is beginning to create househusbands in unexpected places like the South Wales valleys. There the old coal mines have in ten years been greened over and become sites for electronics factories employing women rather than men. Even though macho mates may make men feel shifty about staying home and looking after the kids, more are having to swallow their male pride and take on parenting as a full-time job, while the wife brings home the bacon. Some fathers are even finding that they enjoy getting to know their own kids and seeing they get a proper start in life.

The latest Social Trends shows a growing number of women putting off having children till they are in their thirties and have made a life of their own beyond the gender roles that pressured their foremothers' lives from birth to death. Among women born since 1962, 37% have not given birth by the age of thirty, compared with 19% at mid-century. A growing minority of women, moreover, are deciding not to have children because their lives are full enough without parenting. These shifts in life expectations mean that there is an ever-widening gulf between the memories and images older people have of their childhood homes, and the way the younger generations are reshaping parenting. Is the habit of caring which we learn from good parenting being squeezed out by the time famine young parents now experience?

What women have learned from their mothers

Avril's whole way of life radiates a sense of caring, even though she is now (in her forties) debilitated by chronic exhaustion because she is an ME sufferer:

> I was brought up in a kind of medieval Scottish Catholicism. I brought from home the Catholic idea of caring for other people in a practical way. We were brought up to believe that home was much more than just a physical space where you ate and slept and did pretty much what you wanted. Home as a way of living one's life and caring in a practical sense was more important. I experienced a real culture shock when I left my childhood home and went into other people's houses in the southeast of England. Their way of life seemed very alien to me, because they had such a secular approach to home and family. I suppose that influenced me into going to help in a therapeutic community in London. There I married the person who founded the community. Home was then whatever free

space was available in whatever project we were engaged in. The community and the people in it, both helpers and those who needed help, became home, rather than any physical space. The ethos of the community was voluntary poverty, with which I agreed, so even when I had a child we had very few possessions and travelled from one project to another all the time. Emotionally I saw them all as containing and being my family. At times that gave me tremendous support, but at other times it was very difficult because it was no privacy, no private space of my own. It was my childhood home all over again!

In this latest home I have, in my second marriage (my first husband died), and as I get older, I have new urges to, not decorate, but *adorn* the home. That worries me because it's a contradiction to my ideas about possessing very little. The other thing I feel is the need for a space of my own, my individual private space where I can work and think and keep the trivia, the bits of wood and pebbles of no meaning to anybody but me, that I have acquired along the way. There's not a space of this kind yet within our present house, wonderful though it is. It is a proper Jungian house. It embodies Jung's idea of the house as a representation of one's psyche, or one's life, or what have you ... It has a cellar with cobbles of river pebbles, and above the two living floors are attics (like Jung's tower) containing unpacked remnants of the past. Before I make my private space (maybe in the outhouses), I'm making the big kitchen more hospitable, because that's where you welcome people and make them comfortable, where you sit down to eat and to share your feelings, and that's the beginning of real caring.

Chrissie, now a career woman in her late thirties, has brought from her childhood home an abiding need for the company of women. This currently takes the form of well-developed female networks in her life. Her form of parenting is not literal parenting of children, but parenting of external projects in the world:

I don't think I've found again that sense of the generosity of women that I had at home till I was eleven when I was packed off to boarding school and became very unhappy. As well as my mother there was the housekeeper Maud, whose ideas of home were sitting together as a family on Sunday afternoons watching the telly and eating chocolate. Maud's way of caring for you was to be generous to you, especially with food. Then there was Edith, who was taken on to look after me when I was born because my mother nearly died. She was generous by always explaining things to you to make you not afraid. Her famous phrase was, "You see those stinging nettles? You want me to brush them aside for you, but they'll come back and sting you. But if you grasp them hard they won't sting you." So every time I was ducking any issue she'd remind me of that, and now I'm famous in my work for "grasping the nettle." Edith gave me the courage to try out new things for real. She gave me real syringes to inject my teddy bears with, and a real camera when I was seven. My mother took from my grandmother a generosity of spirit, but whereas my grandmother ran her own business, my mother had only her home and us children to exercise it. Her creed is that you give to your children, never take from them. Now she is very old and fragile I have a huge problem trying to persuade her to take caring from me, because it breaks that life-long pattern of a mother's unstinted devotion that gave meaning to her life. I see the problems of that one-sided self-sacrificial giving. In my own networks the generosity of spirit mustn't be one-sided. There has to be mutual giving and receiving, whether you're talking about your home relationship, or your work connections, or wider issues in the world. That generosity of spirit I learned as a child is only limited by the mutual capacity to give and receive that I meet in my various networks. But that can be quite a big "only," because more women now want to take and see giving (even when it's mutual) as the old trap of self-sacrifice.

Sister Teresa, who has lived all her adult life in religious communities, sees the good mothering she got in her Irish childhood as a source of security and stability which has stayed with her throughout her life:

> I had great stability in the sense of certainty that my mother was always there. She took her share of the farm work too, so she was a working mother, though her work was home-based. Since I've lived in religious communities I'm very aware of what I learned from home. I'm aware of the need in any community for each to be encouraged to develop her gifts and encourage others to develop their gifts, the way my mother brought up us eight children to do at home. I learned too to deal with the dark in myself, and to accept it in other people. You need to be able to deal with the envy and the jealousies among the people you live with and care about, whether it's a family home or a community. Playing with my brothers taught me that early in life. There was a strong sense of the male and female cultures in opposition, and it was accepted that girls would not be as good as boys at the games that mattered — the boys' games. You were never as good as your brothers because you were playing their games. That can get difficult if you're sensitive and compare yourself to others to your disadvantage. You have to face the envy in yourself and move on to discover what gifts you can give to the world. At boarding school I had very caring sisters teaching me, and they showed me that I had a gift for academic work. They brought that out in me, whereas at home different things were important. There was always the singing and the dancing together when the older ones came home from boarding school or college. Neighbours came in as well, so doing your own entertaining was part of the homebuilding, with my parents and us eight children and the neighbours all taking part.
>
> The strictness of the Irish culture meant that you had to keep up the family ethos of respectability in what you did and in the language you used. I hear now young people on the streets swearing every time they open their mouths. You didn't do that in my home. It wasn't only surface rules about not

swearing. You were taught the values of personal courtesy in your dealings with other people. It was part of your consciousness of the presence of God in everyday life. Sometimes of course that could be oppressive — putting the fear of God into you, with God as the Big Policeman. But more often it was "Thanks be to God," which was often said, and deeply meant, by my mother. When something awful happened you were helped to accept it because it was part of something larger. When a sister of mine was dying my father brought me home from school and said to me in great tragedy of feeling, "It is God's will." You learned to carry pain and loss and separation without despairing, because you were taught an awareness of the presence of God. You learned to care for hurt people and people in various ways dispossessed. The great problem in the world today is the dispossessed, those made homeless by poverty and war and lack of public and private caring. The Christian concept of hope is about giving back home to all those dispossessed people. Re-making home is about re-making hope for the dispossessed, and you can't begin to do that having a personal sense of the values that underpin home.

Many of the older women contrasted the "natural" way that girls used to learn how to mind babies, with the anxiety and insecurity of many new mothers today:

We were a family of four children, living in Thaxted, and my youngest sister was ten years younger than me, so I was allowed to mind the baby — change her nappies (the terry-towelling ones you washed and hung out every day), dress and undress her, wash and feed her, and take her out in the pram. I was as proud as anything being allowed to push the pram by myself and do everything for the baby. In those days you learned to look after babies from an early age. I'm sorry for today's mothers because most of them don't know the first thing about looking after a baby till they have one of their own, and the shock is terrible. They have to learn it all of a sudden, when they're done in after giving birth too. In the days of the bigger families you picked it up from your family as part of growing. It's different today too because children don't do things around the house like they used to. They seem to live separate lives as if the house was only there for their convenience, and making it a home is nothing to do with them. They don't learn to make and mend things like we used to. My mother was endlessly sewing or knitting or mending clothes when we were children. People were thrifty and didn't throw anything away until it was falling to pieces. Most of the sewing Mother did was darning or patching or stitching up burst seams to make clothes last a bit longer. I never remember her sitting with idle hands. And I wasn't allowed to have idle hands either. Once I'd done my schoolwork I was making an apple tart or angel cakes, or knitting a jumper, or embroidering a tray cloth with a crinoline lady in a big bonnet. Women were always sewing or knitting or crocheting or embroidering. Then for a long time girls didn't want to learn any of their mothers or grandmothers' skills. They just threw it all away because they wanted to be "liberated." Now I'm glad to see a few young women being proud of their sewing or knitting again. Even wanting to learn how to make apple crumble or gooseberry fool. It's like they're beginning to want back their women's heritage, whatever else they do ...

University lecturer Caroline is one of those who admits to needing her mother's domestic values, as well as the "liberated" values she has acquired in her professional career:

I get important things from my mother — certain com- forting aspects of domesticity that I learned in my child- hood consciously or unconsciously. I still get great comfort coming back home on a weekend after the big weekly shopping, lighting the fire and making good food. I remember as a child those Saturday afternoons in winter, sitting in front of a blazing fire with library books, and everybody eating toasted crumpets. If my mother were still alive she would at least give me her approval for my Saturday afternoon domesticities, even if she wouldn't know what to make of the rest of my life. I was brought up in a lower middle-class suburb and I became a university lecturer. I live in a really beautiful big house in a national park. In our modern lives we move from one class to another through education, and we move freely according to our work or relationships or just our individual choices of places that appeal — often changing partners along the way. All that is so alien to my mother's rootedness in what might now seem a narrow life. But I'm glad I retain some of her domestic values — like her ability to create an everyday atmosphere of warmth and comfort, and to offer informal hospitality (no dinner parties!) out of very little but a generous spirit and an instinct for reading people's emotional needs.

How do parents today give children a sense of home?

The foundation of home is good daily routines and consistent structures which give a child security and stability in everyday life. That does not mean being stuck at home, because the routines can be taken with you wherever you go. One mother said:

We travel in the security of our own family routine. My husband and I and the two boys are comfortable with strange places because we all know at the end of the day we'll do the family routines that mean home, whether we're in a hotel room somewhere or in my mother's house in San Francisco. They feel comfortable and I feel comfortable whenever we do our home routine of eating together in the evening, story reading, and putting the children to bed. If those patterns are missing it isn't only the children who notice. It's the parent as well. I recently had a week doing my own thing at a literature festival, and I felt very, very alone and inadequate. I missed the parenting routines which are now as embedded in my everyday life as they are in my children's. But I said to myself, "You

are a mother, but you are someone else as well." I was there to
do creative writing and that was the only security I had. I
could sit there with my paper and pen and write. Doing that
made me feel at ease and at home in a different way from the
family routines, but I realized it was equally important to me,
once I started doing it.

Modern parents search for ways of combining parenting with
developing other parts of themselves, whereas earlier generations of
mothers often found themselves left high and dry when they children
left home, and suffered the empty nest syndrome. They knew how to
be a mother, but they did not know what else they could be. It was
tempting therefore to cling on to their children beyond the age of
dependence, to send in a post-dated emotional bill for the parenting
they had done. But good parenting is about giving children independence as well as security and stability. Modern mothers consider it
fortunate that children need to learn independence as much as mothers
need to interweave their parenting with a life of their own:

Bringing up children and being part of their development is a
creative process in itself — until they get to the point where
they don't need your input any more. My youngest is a six-
year-old but he is getting over that dependence now too. I've
instilled in them a sense of independence because they need it
and because I wanted independence myself. I've encouraged
them to entertain themselves because I had a limited amount of
interest in entertaining them. It's working, because the children
don't need me in the same way as when they were little. The
ten-year-old closes the door of his room and reads, writes,
draws, records things on tape. The eight-year-old constructs
things happily for hours and hours if you give him a cardboard
box and Sellotape. The six-year-old uses Lego all the time,
making things and talking to himself. So they're learning
independence and I'm free again. A lot of women at this time
of renewed freedom from the kids go back to work, I'm going
back to creative writing. The energy is coming back into my
imagination ...

I want my kids to develop their imaginations as well. That's
part of becoming independent. We don't have any video games
or computer games for them (except on special exceptional
occasions) because we wanted them to learn to use their
imagination and to entertain themselves with their own
materials, before they get to the ready-made accessibility of
technology. If you sit them down in front of a screen at a
tender age they get only predigested fast fodder for the
imagination to work on. If you come to computers too soon it
supplants the natural imagination.

Good parenting means talking to children from their earliest days. It
does not matter that they cannot talk back. Talking to them from the
start helps to produce a responsive human being for life. But in the
1990s there seems to be a widening gap between underprivileged
babies who are passively parented, and overprivileged babies who are
surrounded by mountains of brightly coloured toys from the Early
Learning Centre, and continually stimulated by articulate parents or
nannies. Active parenting is heavy work, and very different from
earlier generations of mothering fashions, when the baby was put out
in her pram by the front door while the mother got on with the
housework or ran the local shop. A first-time mother experiencing the
shock of full-time active parenting told me:

The baby gets an awful lot of attention, and you and your
partner no longer go out anywhere on your own. You tend to
go out separately with your own friends, or you do everything
as a threesome with the child. So you need to be able to put up
with that. Before we had the baby the two of us always used to
go out once a week to dinner and the cinema. But since the
baby was born we've only been out, the two of us, four times
in seven months. But we accept that. While they're awake
you've always got to be aware of them and give them
attention. They come first and you can't leave them to get on
with your own things. That's what is so exhausting about
looking after the baby. But that's also how you get positive
feedback from him and are amazed at how he is developing

new things he can do all the time, from week to week, from month to month.

Parenting has always included passing on ways of behaving, and values, from one generation to the next, consciously or unconsciously. You need to start as you mean to go on, with the ordinary everyday domestic routines:

> Cooking and eating together is important. If children don't know how to behave in pubs and restaurants it's because they don't learn to eat socially at home. Even babies need to see table manners from the start. Everybody needs to sit down and share one meal a day together. Food isn't just a petrol filling re-fuelling operation. Even now if Tom at seven months wants to join in our dinner in the evening, he can, because that's how he finds out what eating together is about, and learns to share things with us, as we try to do with him.

As children get older it gets harder to pass on values, because of the need to rebel against parental control as a gesture of independence. There is also the dilemma that some self-confessed "wishy-washy liberal" parents find themselves caught in. On the one hand they fervently hope their teenagers are absorbing decent values from them, but at the same time they are anxious to avoid imposing their dominant values on their children. Claire, the mother of a teenager and a professional woman imbued with left-wing liberal values, says:

> I'm Charlie's handicapped hamster sometimes. Sometimes he treats me like a mate and sometimes like a nuisance. We do talk about things when there's a crisis. Recently he went on an overnight sixth form thing and came back grumpy and not talking to us. He said he'd like to go off and live by himself, but he wasn't serious, he just wanted to be nasty to us at that moment because somebody had been nasty to him on the school thing. Recently we decided he should have more freedom by having an allowance that he could use on his own without us interfering or deciding for him. We thought he

needed a way of feeling more independent. But there's always a danger of mixing up independence with a sort of uncaring neutrality. The problem is when you create a neutral environment for your children you don't give them enough to react against, or you may even give the impression you don't care, when you're trying to let them make up their own minds instead of going on about values. Recently Charlie and his friends were sitting on the stairs talking about whether their parents cared how they did in their school exams. I couldn't help overhearing and I heard Charlie say, "Oh, mine don't care at all." I realized that trying to be neutral and not impose your values is dicey, because it may look like indifference. If you don't impose your value system on your children you're not enriching them. They may want to change a lot of it for themselves, but they need to be given a value system to work on.

My own parents were well-heeled and family conscious in the sense of passing on values and resources and ways of behaving. Yet although they believed in all that rather upper middle-class stuff they never imposed it on me. That left me with a lack of richness, a sort of arid liberalism. I was doing the same thing with Charlie, I realize now. So I try to discuss things with him. But we don't always, or if we do it disintegrates because Charlie says I'm out of touch with him — "You don't know what kids of my age think." Or his Dad says something ridiculous and inapposite, and I go off in a hump. End of another attempt to pass on liberal values. That's home!

One of the fashionable tenets of modern parenting is that everybody shares in the emotional and practical work of making home. Democratic sharing and cooperation is one of the values parents want to pass on to their children. But there seem to be a few hiccups in putting these ideals into practice, even in the most value-conscious families. Children appear to do less in the home than ever before in domestic history. They are no longer sent at the age of ten to factories or fields or up chimneys, nor do they do much work in the home either, although a majority of mothers now go out to work. Why is this? An increasing number of women complain that men do not do enough in the house, but it is women who still mainly parent their sons, so what are mothers doing to change the situation? Clearly some women, like their mothers and grandmothers, want to retain domestic control in spite of the dual burden of outside work and housework. But others are determined to bring their sons up to be domestically literate and fit to do real sharing with their future partners:

> I think men have a blind spot about various domestic duties because of the way they've been brought up. So even when they try to share the cooking or the parenting they are not very domestically literate about the whole thing. Women have eyes for the point of no return when the squalor is unacceptable, and they will start cleaning up. Men are just not aware of that point of no return. They do domesticity in a crude mechanical way which my women friends and I are very critical of, because we think we've got domestic ways of knowing which are missing in men — so far. But I'm going to make sure that our son is brought up from an early age to clean and cook and make home comfortable. He'll be taught the basic domestic skills that everybody needs to know if they're going to be able to look after themselves and others.

This is a fair enough resolve, but putting it into practice is not straightforward, because of the gap between what parents say and what they do. Children are adept at spotting the hypocrisies, and as long as adult males are not seen to be housekeepers in the same way as mothers, little boys will jeer and refuse a domestic role. Men who might want to share more of the housework and the parenting are likewise put off in traditional communities where male and female roles are rigidly separate. A young American couple who moved to a traditional rural community in Britain because of her work, would like to have a child, but they are undecided because he would be doing the parenting while she carried on working, and that would make him distinctly odd in this particular community:

I would not feel at ease here looking after a kid because it's always the women who look after the kids in this village. If I were taking the childcare responsibilities they'd look at it as very odd and I would feel even less at home than I do now as an urban American in rural Britain. The women and the men here do very different things and relate very differently to home. The men go to the pub and drink fairly heavily. The culture of male drinking puts me off. The women meet up and talk about home and kids so much that my partner once came back in tears when she was invited along to join them, because with her career concerns she felt so excluded. The women's group meets once a month in somebody's house for drinks and all they talk about is their kids and their husband and nothing else. It's that side of women being seen as exclusively the childcare parents that men doing parenting would never have access to. It's women together — old-fashioned female solidarity — and a man senses a kind of excluding even worse than a woman does whose interests are not exclusively parenting but who has her own career.

Choosing not to have children

Anita (34) is a high-powered professional with a life too full and interesting to leave space for parenting:

The life I live in my professional career simply doesn't leave me time or space for children. That annoys me when I stop to think about it, because I can see that although women like me can have very successful careers in what were previously male preserves, we have to put up with work structures that were designed around men's life patterns and so don't fit women's life patterns. So if I took time off to have a baby, or wanted to work part-time for a few years, I'd fall off the career ladder with a heavy thump. I wouldn't be treated seriously as senior management material any more. I've fought quite hard to be taken seriously as a woman manager as it is, so that would

undo years of steady work and aspirations. If I had a child
they'd assume I had only half a mind on the job, that I
couldn't be called upon in a crisis, or work long hours as I
have to do from time to time. And they might be right to make
those assumptions. Because I've seen it happen to a friend of
mine who used to be as ambitious as me before she had her
baby. Now she says she wants a better balance in her life
between career and parenting. Perfect in theory, of course, but
since the world of work is so geared to men's lives and not
women's lives, a balanced life is suicide as far as your career
is concerned. If I chose to combine work and parenting it
might well be the case that — for a few years anyway — my
energy and my attention would be divided, and that would be
the end of my glorious career. It's all very unfair that the cards
are stacked against us career women having "a balanced life,"
but I don't know how you change it, because women in
powerful positions are still in a minority, and you tread
carefully in case you lose what progress you've made just
getting so far up the ladder. Anyway there's something else I
have to confess. I would be very nervous at the prospect of
spending a lot of time at home alone looking after a baby,
when I'm so used to the cut and thrust of sharp adult company.
I'd miss too many things in my present life, which I enjoy
tremendously. And it would be tough on the baby, because I
wouldn't know how to be with it. I don't believe in a miracu-
lous maternal instinct that bubbles up all of a sudden when you
have a baby. I've seen too many of my women friends
struggling with mothering (although they are stacked with
worldly talents) to believe in that. And it is still women who
end up doing the mothering 99 per cent of the time. So I and
not my partner would be the full-time parent if we did have a
baby. He'd expect that. But I doubt I'd be prepared to give that
much in a relationship which has so far been very fifty-fifty. It
would change things between us too radically. It would change
me too radically, as well, from being the person I know I am,
to being a dreaded *wife and mother,* which I wouldn't at all
know how to do. Even if it turned out I could turn my hand to

that role, I would still have worries, because it's such a very "loaded" role I might not be able to shake off past oppressions and make it over for myself the way I can do at work.

Madeleine (42) is a woman farmer. She used to run the farm with her husband but they are now divorced and she bought out his share of the farm because the farming life was more important to her than to him. She occasionally thinks about the absence of children in her life, but her conclusions are these:

I enjoy my own independent life running this hill farm. The photos I carry around in my bag are not of my children. They are pictures of my family of barn owls. I was doing up the ruined cottage for my father to come and live in when he retired, and when the builder was stripping off the tin roof over the old thatch he found a nest with four beautiful big eggs still warm in it. The barn owl parents had fled when the builders disturbed them. I phoned all around to find out what to do. They told me there was a fine of £3000 for destroying a nest (not that I wanted to anyway), and they put me in touch with the local owl expert. Kev carried the eggs off in his special in-cubator and four fine birds were hatched. When the time came Kev brought me back the three that had survived. They were in a cosy warm box which we installed under the apex of my barn roof. He put a grill over it till they got accustomed to their new home, and instructed me in the skills of pushing day old chicks through the grill twice a day, without making my alien presence felt. They have flourished. Here's the picture of them I carry in my bag. That's one of the sharpest images of parenting for me.

I sometimes think it would be nice to have a child because it does keep you in touch with completely different generations. I tend to live very much in my own age group. But I meet my friends' daughters and I find them very impressive. Girls grow-ing up now are much more liberated than I was at their age. They have their own interests and ambitions and aren't just waiting for things to happen to them as in the old sentimental days. But you don't have to have a daughter of your own to appreciate how young women have changed since I was growing up. You can enjoy and be impressed by your friends' daughters.

Some feminist women are critical of the way mothering is limited to biological birthing and the nurturing of children. The world needs public mothering as well as private mothering, they argue, if we are to stop ecological pollution and find a quality of life based on something more lasting than consumerism and unsustainable growth. Chrissie (37) explains:

> Being at home in the world is about carrying nurture beyond the parenting of children. It is about doing public mothering as well as private mothering. To the great annoyance of my mother I have not married and had children. In her youth that was a woman's only way of doing mothering, and she can't understand my attitude. I don't feel I have to be a mother to fulfil my potential in the world. I can do nurturing in what are for me more significant ways, out there in the world, in my teaching and in my networks of friends and colleagues. Working as I do in the field of theology, I believe in sacramentalizing every part of everyday life. That means working at nurturing in everything you do, and not seeing nurturing as only to do with bringing up children. You try to discern the outer and visible signs of inner grace in other people, and hope you are giving forth the outer and visible signs of your own inner grace. As well as holding that key belief I've also discovered that I need to do my nurturing out there in the public world because I'm an introvert and I need outside stimulus. Otherwise I'm tempted to stay inside my shell and say "sod the rest of you," and that isn't doing much for my inner grace. So I'm into parenting the world in my own modest ways — staying mobile, taking my nurturing out there and spreading it as widely as possible, not staying hunched up in my own little box with my 1.8 children, teaching them to say "sod it" to the rest of the people who share our planet.

Chapter 6
A day in the life of a househusband

To father a child traditionally means the act of procreation, a brief ecstasy which may or may not lead to a man parenting the child. To mother a child means a continuing practical dedication to the rearing of the child. But gender roles are becoming more fluid and more fathers are doing mothering. What is it like for these fathers who do mothering? How do their partners and friends and erstwhile colleagues react when these househusbands blur the boundaries between fathering and mothering? How do female mothers accept this male invasion of their ancient territory? In this chapter two couples talk about their experiences of househusbanding. Grace and David are thirty-something North London professionals, starting out as parents. Judy and Jim are rural dwellers and experienced parents whose children are now nine and seven.

A day in the life of a househusband

Grace and David's story

Grace is a marketing analyst with a city firm. David was working in educational and arts administration before he became a full-time househusband, but a central aspiration lies in developing his print-making skills, which consume whatever spare time he can find. Having lived together for seven years they mutually decided to have a baby. Their son was born a year ago and was cared for by both of them equally for the first four months. Then Grace went back to work and David turned househusband. He says:

The present arrangement is a step on the road but there's another step to make. What we planned was that eventually I would get a part-time job, and we would have some child-minding support. Then I'll be better able to do more print-making and other work which contributes to my development as an artist. We talked about this before he was born, but we didn't know how much I would be free to do my own things while looking after him — while he would be asleep or playing on his own. I have taken him with me to art galleries and exhibitions, which are part of my development. We went to the RA summer exhibition and that worked very well. But looking after him doesn't leave a lot of time for concentrating on other things.

A typical day works out like this. Grace wakes up before Tom and makes up his bottles for the day while getting ready to go to work. She goes to work at 8.30 when he's in the middle of his breakfast. When I've given him his breakfast we'll normally go down the street (with him on my shoulder) to buy the paper. We'll get back and I'll have my breakfast (which he has some of), while scanning *The Guardian* to see about part-time jobs. This morning period of the day is a very good one. He enjoys the walk down to the newsagents on the corner — the flowers, bushes, cats and people. Everything he sees he takes in and enjoys. He's seeing it all with fresh eyes. After that I'll put him in his cot and nine days out of ten he'll go to sleep from about 10.15 till about 12.15. I'll either be working on something to do with art, or on finding a job. I've been working on a football painting in oils which is a commission from a friend, a wedding present for her partner who's into football. Tom's lunch can happen anytime between 11.30 and 12.30, so at some point I'll boil up the kettle and get his lunch ready. That means purée and baby rice now as well as his bottle. We'll often listen to the radio over lunch — Brain of Britain or a John Le Carré serial, that kind of thing. After his lunch we go out to the shops and I have my lunch when we get back. I feel it's important to go out then because it gives me a break and gives him more things to look at, whether we're in the car or on foot. He has his afternoon bottle at 3.30, an hour after we get back from shopping. Sometimes I flag then and feel sleepy. Maybe it's because there's not a lot of structure between 4 and 5.30. I have to summon up enough energy to start playing with him. Once you start it's really enjoyable because you get such feedback from him. Times when he goes to sleep I can rush around doing my own things, but when he's awake and demanding attention I can flag. I drink a bottle of Lucozade to keep me going, and we play together or listen to his nursery rhyme tape. That lasts half an hour and it's a positive thing, a set thing he likes, and there are actions to some of the rhymes.

It's important to structure the day and have some set patterns. It's nice to go out somewhere special for an afternoon, but you need the basic patterns, even if they're invisible to other people. You find yourself doing things like going out shopping for the dinner because it's necessary, but it's dual purpose because it's part of a vital pattern you need to give your day. As he gets older I think we'll build in a big outing once a week to vary the daily pattern.

Tom normally goes to sleep about 5.30 for an hour, and during that time I'll make his tea. He has real food such as mashed potato, cabbage and grated cheese, so it takes longer, but if I have any time over I use every spare half hour, because I'm working on this painting. Sometimes Grace gets home before he wakes up about 6.30. We'll then decide which of us is going to give him his tea, and which of us is going to make our dinner. Slightly more often than not Grace gives him his tea and I do our dinner, because she is really pleased to spend time with him immediately on coming home from work.

From then on it's much easier and less tiring looking after Tom, because when we're both doing it we can give him quality attention. He has his bath about 8.30, and we both do that together. Grace gives him his bedtime bottle and I normally put him to bed and read him his bedtime story and see him to sleep.

The washing-up comes at the end of the day when his bottles have to be done as well as our dishes, so it's half an hour's work. I think we're good at recognizing which of us is tired, and the other does it.

It's important for Grace to have a bit of time on her own to read or whatever, so she goes to bed often later than I do, though she used to go earlier. But if I'm really into a painting I might paint late at night, because I too need that time on my own.

Early conditioning makes me sometimes feel that what I'm doing doesn't have the credit or the value that it should have, though rationally I've worked my way through that to recognizing the value of bringing up a child on a day-to-day basis. I'm becoming conscious that my attitudes have changed significantly in the last year. I've had a number of interviews for part-time jobs, but not been offered one yet. Potential employers are very concerned about these changes I've made in my life. I think you have to separate out the fact that I'm doing childcare, and the fact that I've left a career job because of my interest in doing art. It's the individuality of the choice I've made in my working life that bothers them. There's a certain stigma attached to you if you've left a professional job and not got another. I feel that quite keenly when I've gone to an interview and not got the job. Once or twice I have regretted my decision to give up my job, because of that stigma. But in general I am convinced I am right. I want a better balance in my life. Before I gave up my job my mother's death too made me evaluate what I was doing at work and what that meant to me. I came to realize I wanted more independence, and I wanted to take my printmaking skills seriously as something in me I wanted to develop. I want to do art and to make art from my own spiritual point of view, and because it is a very positive thing to give to people's lives. The other big thing that counteracts the stigma of having given up my job is looking after Tom in this first year of his life. I've made space in my life for my art and for Tom, and that feels right, though I suffer twinges of self doubt when potential employers reject me. You are supposed to convince the employers that you've been yearning all your life to give them your whole time and energy. But once you begin to discover what is really important to your life, it's harder to give them the answers they are expecting.

Once you give up full-time working (I'd been working ten years since I left college) you discover as well that there's this whole day time world in the area where you live. It's been going on all the time you've been commuting to your job five miles away. There are so many people about, and often they're with young children. So there's a source of solidarity there. But being a man looking after a young child does often make me feel self-conscious. Older people often assume I'm looking after the baby just for the day. I am very much an exception still as a man doing full-time childcare. There's only one other man in the street like me. He's a naturalist and manages to run children's wildlife classes in the park during the summer. He also fits in the occasional wildlife research project or study in the local park. I've talked to him about doing parenting and he's been very open talking about things — their first child died a cot death. But we're the only two "househusbands" in the street. So it can be lonely compared with other kinds of work.

Through the NCT (National Childbirth Trust), which Grace and I joined before Tom was born, I also know a number of young women with babies of about Tom's age. They are very nice and sympathetic to what I am doing, but again there's only one other man in our area of the NCT doing the same thing. So I do feel embarrassed or self-conscious sometimes, even though I tell myself I'm stupid to feel like that because I believe in what I'm doing. It's little things like when I'm wheeling Tom past the little nursery place in the park on the way to Muswell Hill, and there's often groups of mothers there with their babies in pushchairs the same as me, only I feel I'm separated from them ... early conditioning again, probably. On the other hand people in the area respond very well to Tom when I'm out with him, so that's positive. I get to know a number of people in the local area through him. That reinforces our feeling that we're bringing him up in the right way, because he's not only healthy, he's happy and contented and responds to people. Among my friends (former colleagues or people I

know through being involved in art) I've experienced a bit of
solidarity and support over what I'm doing. We know a lot of
people who are having first or second babies over the last year,
and there seem to be more things uniting us than making us
different in our experiences in bringing up a child. There's an
element of sympathy and understanding from women friends.
But people in the services sector accept what I'm doing more
easily than people in the commercial sector, who find it really
strange that I want to order my life in this way ...

We'll work the present situation for two years and then
review it, because we might want another child. At some point
Grace might want to work part-time rather than full-time, and I
might want to go full-time for a while. But whatever patterns
of work and home emerge I think it's important to give to Tom
more than just childcare. It's important to demonstrate to him
by the way we live our own lives that you do have an element
of freedom of choice in your life, both in the way you spend
your time, and in the way you go about changing a pattern of
life if it is not satisfying.

Here is Grace's response to David as househusband:

I think David does really good mothering. He is the physical
person who looks after the baby every day. I don't think it's
true what the baby books say about baby loving the mother
best. I don't think there's a difference between the mother and
father as far as the baby is concerned, once you get beyond the
first four months, while I was breast-feeding him. I sometimes
feel a little bit jealous because Tom might turn to David first
rather than to me. Then I think, well, no big deal, that's the
way we've decided is best for us now. And sometimes when
I've had a whole day with him on my own I even think I
couldn't do this full-time, I'd rather go to work. Because after
you have a baby your whole life is concentrated in the home,
whereas before you had a lot of choice. It's just the three of
you, a little family unit, and part of that is nice, but part of it
is claustrophobic. Apart from us needing the money from my

salary, I wanted a change from just being in the house by the
time he was four months old. I got back to work and am using
other parts of myself besides being a wife and mother. I need
to have my own separate identity apart from mothering,
however marvellous that is. And it *is* marvellous. I knew my
life would change completely when we planned to have a baby,
but I had no idea it would be so marvellous to have a baby.
You get so much positive feedback from him all the time. He's
developing from one week to the next, and surprising you with
the new things he can do.

How you are going to share the childcare with your partner
should be a big part of the discussion when you are deciding to
have a baby or not. It's about sheer economics but it's also
about how each of you feels about doing parenting. Both of
you need to be involved in making real down to earth choices,
and not allowed to get away with just making assumptions
about the woman doing the mothering and the father doing the
fathering (whatever that means).

Ten years in the life of a househusband

Judy and Jim's story

Judy and Jim have ten years' experience of this pattern of parenting,
and are sensitive to all the ups and down for each parent. Their two
children Janet (9) and Jamie (7) go to the local primary school in the
village where they live, and are happy and confident about themselves
and the way their family works. Clearly the parenting they have had
has so far been a great success. At this stage the family are reassess-
ing their lives once more. Jim, having been a househusband for nearly
ten years, is beginning a part-time job doing information technology
for a distance learning project in a nearby college. Judy is negotiating
with her employers to go part-time, because her very demanding job
in scientific research and advisory work is giving her too little time to
do things with her partner and growing children. The whole life

balance is skewed. They talked to me (and to each other) about how they have shared their parenting:

JUDY: When we moved into this house over ten years ago I was getting into my thirties and we thought if we were going to have children we had better start. We talked about it and decided we both wanted to bring up the children, share the parenting equally between us.

JIM: Yes, it was very planned, very deliberate. I'd had a full-time job selling computers when Judy was pregnant with Jane, and then I took a part-time job programming while Judy was breast-feeding Jane during the first six months. So we were both sharing every bit of looking after her. We took it in turns in the early days to get a good night's sleep, because it's exhausting work looking after a small baby, and you need to bring energy to it.

JUDY: I went back to work (part-time at first) when Jane was about seven or eight months, so we were both doing two and a half days a week looking after her while the other went out to work. From the moment she was born Jim was there, and when I got home from work in the evenings he was there. We really shared every bit of it. We'd always shared the cooking, washing, cleaning — all the household chores. Jim is fairly domesticated and I'm looking for balance in my life between domestic things and outside work, so it's always seemed natural for us to share all the housekeeping side. Sharing in the parenting followed on from that.

JIM: It's to do with career ambitions too. What seems to be different between me and other fathers is that I wasn't tied to a job. I didn't have any great career ambitions for the future. A lot of fathers just don't have space in their lives to look after their children. They haven't got the energy you need either, because they're so tied to their jobs. I don't think I've ever had the urge to get myself set up in some career or profession. I

feel like I'm lucky to be able to do this for the kids. I feel
sorry for old friends in high powered jobs because it's pathetic
how little time fathers spend with their kids when they're in
"successful" careers. When I'm with friends like that I don't
go on much about what I'm doing, because I feel so sorry for
them. If I did feel able to be honest with them I'd ask them,
"What the hell do you think you are doing with your life?"
They are just missing out on so much of their kids' lives.

JUDY: There's awful financial pressure on people, though. We
were lucky that way because when Jane was born we'd got this
house together and it wasn't desperate for Jim to have a career.
We had enough financial security for one of us not to have a
career, and I had a career.

JIM: Yes, Judy does like working. She likes having a career
job, so she's the one who's been working more or less full-time.

JUDY: Some men would have a problem over the woman being
the breadwinner. Have you ever felt guilty about living on my
money?

JIM: Never, because bringing up the kids is a really important
job, even if you don't get credit in our society for bringing up
kids well — though you get blamed if you bring up kids badly.

JUDY: Anyway we decided we wanted another baby and when
Jane was three Jamie was born. I had another seven or eight
months at home breast-feeding him, and then went back to
work part-time as before. But soon they offered me a plum job
on condition I went full-time. That was a very difficult
decision to make. I was very drawn to the job because I knew
it was going to be interesting and the money was going to be
good. I was starting to think seriously about my career,
because one day the children wouldn't be here and I always
need something demanding and interesting to do. I needed to
climb the career ladder, so I decided to take the job. It did turn

out to be really demanding, and after that it was role reversal with Jim and me alright. I was really dominated by the job, as a lot of fathers are by their careers. I took it on when Jamie was a year old and Jane was four, and for the next five years I was absorbed by it. It was a new job and it built up. I enjoyed the demands it made on me, but sometimes I felt a bit guilty about how much of my energy went into it. I always felt the kids were fine, because Jim was so good with them. It was I who was losing out, not having more time with them. But on balance I usually felt it was worth it because it was fulfilling and bringing in a lot of money.

JIM: I was happy looking after both children when Judy went full-time. We were really enjoying Jamie because it's always easier with a second baby. You're more relaxed about it because you have more experience. But you don't have many social contacts when you're at home with young children. You have to get used to being isolated, even here living in a small village. But I'd been without social contacts before. I can be a bit of a recluse. I made one reciprocal arrangement with another parent in the village. I looked after her child while she went out cleaning one morning a week, and she looked after mine while I did one morning a week in the school giving computer lessons.

The whole thing about being with the kids full-time was very liberating in a way. Little old ladies speak to you when you have a baby with you. When you're carrying a baby or a toddler it's quite hard to suffer social isolation for long. You go out for walks and meet all the people who are around during the day, the ones who don't go out to work. They're the people who are invisible to career professionals, but they are there, and they take an interest in you and your kids. I took the children to the mothers and toddlers group in the village, and I never felt excluded by the women, though I was the only man. It was never, "He's a bloke and he doesn't know what he's doing." I think I was credible because I was doing the same things for the kids as they were, so I got their respect. Perhaps it is partly to do with being in a small village where you know everybody. I was even asked to do baby sitting in the village.

But three and a half years into Judy's full-time job it was getting ridiculous, wasn't it, Judy? You were taking up whatever they threw at you, and having to bring more and more work home to sort it out. That was the result of your attitude to work as well as a product of the job itself?

JUDY: Yes, I admit I was getting so exhausted I had nothing to give Jim and the kids. I was even working Sunday afternoons sometimes and wanting Jim to take the kids to the swimming baths so I could get on with it. I was seeing less and less of them. So it was decision time again. After those five years of really demanding full-time work I've now managed to go part-time again. The civil service have been very good about flexibility in my career. Without that flexibility from employers we could never have shared the parenting the way we have. That's really important, or sharing parenting is just impossible. Anyway, going part-time again meant that Jim would need to get a part-time job as well, rather than relying on risky bits of self employment to bring in extra money.

JIM: I was lucky. I have computer skills, and last summer a friend told me she was putting in for a distance learning project in the college, but she didn't want to go full-time. She wanted a job share, so I put in or the other half of the job share, and got it.

JUDY: After Jim got his part-time job it took me nearly a year to arrange to go part-time. That was a strain, though by then both the children were at school. At the moment I'm only four weeks into my new life of working part-time instead of full-time. It's nice to be at home without feeling exhausted. It's nice doing ordinary things like seeing the children off to school, on the two days a week I'm at home. But at work I feel as if I'm not doing enough. I'm not feeling so valuable at work and I'm not so much in the swing of things.

There *are* disadvantages going part-time. I'm sure you're seen differently. You sense you're no longer seen as such a valuable member of staff. I can understand that because in my job anything can crop up during the two and a half days I'm not there to deal with it. Someone else now has to take it on because I'm not full-time. There is no one at work who would see me as not committed, because I'm known for my commitment over the years. But I found it very hard to go to my boss and ask to go part-time, because I felt I was giving the impression of less commitment.

JIM: It's become a huge joke in the media when government ministers step down "to spend more time with their families," as if nobody in their right minds could really want to spend more time with their family, so they must be hiding something disreputable! There's the hypocrisy of pretending to give "family values" top priority. That's what you're up against when you are trying to do good parenting. Anyway now we're both working part-time we're reaching a better balance for both of us. Judy's no longer working her guts out, and it has been good for me to get back into work. It does help my self-esteem. At first I didn't feel I'd be taken seriously in a workplace when I'd been a house husband for years and years. I can understand why they have to put on access courses for mothers returning to work after years of bringing up the children. Little kids take up all your time and divide your attention from whatever else you're trying to do while you're with them. It's very demanding but very different work from my part-time job which needs single-minded concentration and communicating with grown-ups. I feel it helps my employ-ability and that's good for my future as the kids get older. Already they begin to have lives of their own and don't need you in the same way. It can be annoying when you rush home from work to be there for them, and you find they've made their own arrangements and are playing in a friend's house.

JUDY: They need you in different ways as they get older.

Children change all the time. It's hard to tell how much difference it makes to them having me at home more since I've gone part-time. I suppose I'm better tempered. When I was combining full-time work and mothering, there was the Getting Home Exhausted syndrome. I wanted to come home from work all warm and energetic to make up for lost mothering time, but I was so tired I might find myself yelling at them instead. There were times when all I wanted to do was to come home from work and go to sleep. But Jim would be waiting on the doorstep for the car to get off to his evening class, because all he wanted to do was to get out of the house where he'd been working all day, and it was my turn to take over the parenting no matter how tired I was.

JIM: When you're a househusband you have to build in breaks for yourself. That evening class was an important break for me. When you're at home with the kids you've got to know how to give yourself a break as well. Sometimes I'd put my feet up on the sofa and have a cup of tea before getting down to reading stories to them. You try to combine a lot of things (at home or on outings) so that both you and the kids get something out of it. That takes a lot of imagination sometimes, trying to do things that are educational and instructive as well as the things they want to do — like throwing mud around or whatever.

JUDY: A lot of the everyday work of bringing up children and doing the cleaning and cooking and washing is pretty boring. A lot of men wouldn't have the endless patience you need, wouldn't want to do it. Jim is very patient and caring, and he has some of the female qualities you need with children. He is very physical and cuddly with the children.

The problem with bringing up children is that you don't get acknowledgement and praise for it, the way you get rewarded for other work. I go to work for the motivation and the social aspects. Those are very necessary to me. I do need outside recognition, someone to tell me I'm doing a good job. You don't get that when you're a full-time mother at home.

JIM: Me being the househusband has worked for us because we have different attitudes to work. My jobs have been more like hobbies or interests than careers. I taught myself building by rebuilding this house. I taught myself computing by doing programmes. I'm not interested in the dominant work philosophy of achievement and recognition, which men especially are supposed to have. I don't need outside recognition. I don't want to be "organization man." It's the technical side of my work that fascinates me. I suppose I'm into men's mindless collecting of data external to themselves — the fascination that makes sports quizzes and other information trivia so popular. I think I know when I'm doing a good job, whether it is building work or computers. So I don't need the acknowledgement of that from any organization people.

JUDY: The role models we give the children are important, too. They see that mothers can have careers and fathers do parenting, as well as mothers parenting and fathers having careers, which are still the dominant images in society. Now they see us both doing parenting *and* having outside jobs. It's important as well to share the parenting, because, let's face it, children can drive you crazy, and when they accept you as equal parents you can just walk out and get relief when things get beyond you. Jim's support of me and mine of him makes parenting much easier than if I were a mother at home all the time, bearing the brunt on my own.

JIM: We are really glad that we've been able to arrange things this way, but you have to start with a real strong will to share parenting, because you're not getting support from our society. The career ladder pressures are heavier on men than on women, and that makes it harder for fathers to share parenting even when they want to. It would have been harder to make this recent shift to both of us working part-time if Judy had been the man. She would have felt perhaps she couldn't have gone part-time from her demanding full-time job, because men hardly ever see other men doing that, and so it seems unacceptable or impossible.

JUDY: Maybe, yes. I think it's more acceptable for women to say they want a balanced life between work and home. It's not alright yet for men to say they want a balanced life. And that puts huge pressures on women as well as men. Women, including career women like me, are supposed to carry on doing the full-time mothering, and suppress all the other parts of ourselves. And men are supposed to do the full-time career thing and suppress their parenting side. We've tried to get a better balance for both of us, and show our children how you can balance the different parts of your lives. But we're still a rarity ...

The way ahead: supporting shared parenting

An increasing number of fathers in the younger generation are being more active parents, or would like to be, but are frustrated by financial pressures, inflexible work structures and the male ethic of the one-track achievement culture. Many obstacles need to be faced and overcome before women and men can more fully share in bringing up their children. First is the career orientation which puts pressure on professional people to work full-time and not take career breaks, especially career breaks "just" for doing parenting. A few employers are sympathetic to women or men who ask if they can move from full-time to part-time working for the sake of caring for their children. The majority in our market driven work ethic regard such requests as a sign of lack of commitment, a loss of achievement motivation. If people want to work part-time it is too often assumed they have lost interest in promotion prospects and professional development. It is time for more employers to see job shares and flexibility between full and part-time work as advantages rather than disadvantages. These are, after all, ways of keeping expensively trained staff in the organization, and motivating them for future successes, even if the employers lack any communitarian impulse towards good parenting of the future generation of employees.

Then there is the problem of how women are to make psychological space for men to do parenting and the domestic work that is so much a part of everyday parenting. We have seen that many women, including career women, however much they approve in principle of sharing, have emotional problems admitting men to "their" domestic domain, or "their" playgroup space, or even "their" womanspace at the school gate. Consciously or unconsciously women fear losing control of these last female arenas. They may not want to live the same domestic lives as their mothers or grandmothers. They may have rationally decided to combine motherhood and a career. But the traditional fears of male incursions into a women's world still gnaw the dark corners of the psyche, and undermine the best laid plans for sharing parenting with a partner. Men can only learn to share in creating home when women are more hospitable in welcoming men into "women's things"; when women cease to criticize male ways of doing domesticity and childcare because they are different from their own. The world of home cries out for biodiversity as much as the world of nature. We must become more hospitable to the newly emerging species of househusbands, female breadwinners, mothers with careers.

Househusbands suffer too the loneliness of being in a minority with few role models to guide them. They need continuing recognition of the value of their work, from their partners, their friends (and erstwhile colleagues), and their communities. A central problem for househusbands seems to be the blurring of a secure masculine identity that your culture knows and values, while trying to shape a new masculine identity based on parenting and homemaking, which your culture does not value as "real work" or "men's work." The househusband who retains the strongest sense of identity is the man who "never felt that going to work was anything to do with my maleness. So now at home I'm the same person I was before. I get as much satisfaction out of doing this as from my previous job." Househusbands need to be welcomed by other mothers, by teachers and employers, church and social policy pundits, and by every one of us who wants our children brought up to be emotionally intelligent — open to diversity, flexible in our roles, self-motivating, and creative in relating.

Chapter 7
Bringing up kids on your own

Single mothers and their values

Single mothers have to overcome practical and emotional problems on a number of levels. They have to build up enough confidence in the value of what they are doing to counter the negative images of single mothers reflected back at them from their immediate neighbours and from religious and political establishments. They have to face a period of loneliness and low self esteem while at the same time struggling to give their children extra emotional support to make up for the absence (intermittent or permanent) of the children's father. If they are sharing the parenting with their ex-partners they have to help their children adjust to having two homes which often have conflicting styles of parenting. This is especially difficult when their ex-partners live with another woman and the children are being mothered, distantly or intimately, by her at the weekends. There are nearly always money problems facing single mothers, so they have difficult decisions to make about whether to find a paid job and spend less time with children who need a lot of reassuring mothering, or to concentrate on full-time mothering and experience social isolation on a small income. It is not surprising that, faced with these everyday stresses, single mothers are prone to bouts of depression and guilt. How they work through these depends on their own inner resources as well as the degree of support they can draw on from family, friends and community. Here are the stories of three women — a Buddhist, a pagan and a Christian — who are bringing up children on their own. They talk about their everyday experiences, the problems and the satisfactions, and explain how they are sustained by their personal value systems.

Maggie's story

Maggie (38) is divorced and has three children, now ten, twelve and
fifteen. She is bringing them up in a council house on the edge of a
rural village, and money is tight, especially now the kids are becoming
teenagers and needing more things bought:

> I'm not very well integrated in the village because I'm the only
> single parent around and this is a small community. When I
> was with the kids' dad we lived up on the hill for ten years,
> and all the kids were born here. But now I'm a single parent
> and we've been in this council house for the last five years.
> When we came first I used to feel that being a single mother
> threatened people in formal families. The women would feel
> threatened by a woman making a go on her own, and by an
> available woman who might try to run off with their husbands.
> I don't feel that so much now on the estate, but I still get the
> feeling I'm treated differently than if I had a man in the house.
> My kids get shouted at a lot, and I think that wouldn't happen
> if there was a father around. When I've complained about it
> I've had the door slammed in my face and I think if I had a
> husband they wouldn't dare. At the school gate I feel a bit out
> of it because our life style is so different as a single parent
> family. The kids feel that too in the village school, but just
> now there's one other family where the parents have split up,
> so those kids are like mine now at school.
>   How do we cope with all that? Well, the best thing is the
> kids talk to me about their feelings, and I encourage that and
> give them a lot of time. The positive things about being on
> your own with the kids are that you have a lot of freedom and
> independence. It's a perpetual challenge, but you don't have to
> fight another grown-up about how you are bringing up the
> kids. You can be much closer to your children and there's
> more scope for doing things your own way. If you're a woman
> on your own with kids the dynamics of it is so different
> without the male influence. In the usual family set-up male
> values are often the dominant ones, as in society at large, but

in this house female values are more dominant. My son (12) is better than his friends at getting on with girls because he has his two sisters and me at home, and we talk a lot together. He told me his male friends are quite uneasy talking to girls, though the pressure is on them already at the age of twelve to get romantically involved. So he feels lucky that he's good at getting along with females. Mind you, he also has to assert his maleness quite strongly (through bikes, guns, etc.) as a reaction against the female values of home.

The way I see female values coming out in this house is to do with the way we talk more about emotional and spiritual things. We're more relaxed, informal about things that matter in our life, but where an issue comes up we talk about it and look at it from an emotional viewpoint. If the teacher's been angry with one of them, or there's been bullying, say, we try to talk about why the teacher or whoever's done the bullying has been like that. We try to understand their feelings and our feelings, and deal with it.

With your neighbours on a council estate there's a good side and a bad side, and you have to keep trying to find the positive things. The bad things are a simmering antagonism that comes from being too close to each other's lives. The walls are paper thin, so the woman next door can hear my daughter practising her violin, and we can hear her shouting at her kids. Everybody knows what you're doing and draw their own conclusions. If you have three men on their own visiting you for half an hour each they assume the worst! But there are positive things too about the council estate. There's always an adult around when the kids come home from school, and there's always someone to feed the animals when we're away. So some of the people still have a sense of neighbourliness. When I didn't have a car the old man at number three used to give us a lift to town. There have been times when the woman next door and I were neighbourly and supported each other more than we do now when we're a bit antagonistic. Maybe it's because she's on the up and up, and sees us as a scruffy hippy family she wouldn't want to be associated with ... Any help we

get from neighbours we try to return. My son cuts the grass for
some of them, and now I have an old car I sometimes give
them lifts. The chimney sweep comes once a year and we
arrange that together with the neighbours. So you work out
positive neighbourly things to counteract the negative things. I
don't go any more to any of the local functions in the village,
or even to school things. The old close communities in rural
villages like this have their negative side, when you're on the
receiving end of locals' disapproval — or think you are —
you're never quite sure because they talk behind your back and
never come out into the open. When my marriage broke up
and I moved into the council estate with the kids nobody
would speak to me down at the school gate. They knew who I
was and that my marriage had broken up, and I could feel a
puritanical critical spirit around me. It's five years since then,
and I feel more comfortable because new people have moved
in from Birmingham, London, all over the place. That's a relief
because you don't have to be that close to the local puritans.
So I have very mixed feelings about close community as a
single mother. You want a bit of old-fashioned neighbourliness
to get and give support, because you're on your own. But you
don't want the pressures to conform because when you're a
single mother you can't conform, you're already different from
the rest of the mothers. Sometimes I think it's easier to have
friends a hundred miles away, even if you only see them a
couple of times a year, because you can *really* talk to them. I
can't talk really openly like that with any of the locals, because
there's this set of unwritten rules of behaviour that everybody's
supposed to be keeping to. They gossip away about anybody
who doesn't keep to them, and that includes single mothers. So
there's no real exchange of meaning when you talk. It's just
trying to prop up values that hardly anybody lives up to any
more. They want to believe that nothing's changed, but it has,
so the way they go on in their gossip is all pretend, and
conceal their own shortcomings, while picking on anybody
who's different — a single mother like me.

What about housekeeping? Well, you're trying to do

emotional housekeeping as well as physical housekeeping. But shopping, cooking, cleaning when you have kids are so demanding that there's not often enough time to see to the finer side of home life. A home is like an organism with things going out as well as coming in. It changes all the time as I and the children change. They are 15, 12 and 10 now, and are always outgrowing their clothes, their toys, their interests, so you have to do more than just accommodate. You're moving on to new places with them all the time, inside and outside.

Living on this council estate isn't our choice. This house isn't a house we choose to live in. We were washed up here. We were allocated this house by the council. That's what happens to you when you're a single mother. So the house has limits as a home. I'm always behind with painting and decorating and so on, because there's always so much to do — like cutting the grass, seeing to the car, doing the shopping and cooking. There's only one of you to do all that and support the kids as well, so I'm always behind with how I'd like the house to be. The kids help a bit. They helped with the decorating. Last year we did one of the kitchen walls sky blue with white summer clouds floating across it. We did that together, which makes it a bit raggedy, but they had a part in it, that was the thing. I've joined the local self-help LETS *(Local Exchange Trading Systems)* scheme. I'm the treasurer. You pay an annual sub to join it, and there's a points system for exchanging the members' skills and services. You can build up credit by doing jobs for other members, and when you need a job done you use your credit by getting them to do a job for you. Through the scheme I've been doing a bit of massage and aroma- therapy. I put down my wants as "painting and decorating," but I've changed that, because I found I didn't want anybody else coming in and saying, "Let's have this colour or that for the walls in here." It's a very private space, my home. It's very important to me to keep it private, to do it up my own way, to know what even the marks on the wall mean — those there were made by the kids measuring their height. Anyway I've found a certain amount of womanly independence in doing up my own house. I laid a bathroom floor myself — bought the tiles, laid them and sealed them. I've found a certain pride in doing that sort of thing. But as well as getting better at DIY I've come to value women's old domestic skills the more I see of the instant magic you're supposed to get from instant food and instant everything else in the home. We haven't got the money to go out and fill the house with all the instant things that are supposed to make your instant home. But even if we had, we wouldn't, because the things in your home should mean something to you. They should have associations. The sofa you're sitting on belonged to an old lady who lived on the estate and was like a mother to me when we were having a bad time at first. The kids loved her, and we all missed her when she was taken off to a home. Her daughter came to clear the house, and gave us a few things, including a sack of coal with that poker in it. She'd tended her fire with that all her life, so I see that as a kind of ritual domestic object. You keep things of value and meaning like that, and that builds up a sense of home that you never get by going out and spending a fortune on your colour-coordinated offers — even if you had a fortune! The old lady also taught me crocheting. I found a bone crochet hook that had been chucked out by the new people who must have found it in the house. I used it to make that crochet square for the back of the sofa. When you're on your own bringing up kids you need to value home, and value the women in the past who handed on all the skills.

My spiritual life has to be rooted in my everyday domestic life, or it doesn't work. Buddhism is the tradition I belong to. When I first became conscious of a spiritual side of myself and wanted to develop it, I found a big conflict between the spiritual side and the everyday life at home. I thought I had to choose between developing my spiritual side and having an everyday domestic life. A number of other Buddhists around here go off on retreats regularly, but that kind of individual pursuit of spiritual development is not possible with the kids. Now my spiritual life is much more rooted in my everyday domestic life and what I do with the children. I've been taking them to the Amaravati summer camp for the last eight years, and they love it. So I adapt my spirituality to my domestic rhythms. Rather than concentrate on sitting meditation practice, which you need to have private space and time to do, I develop awareness in ways that fit my domestic life. I can develop awareness while I'm doing simple domestic tasks. Awareness means you take care, you attend to what you're doing and that makes it something different, gives it meaning — even if it's only the washing up. Watching the water, sensing the water, handling the dishes, turns it into a thing in itself rather than just a chore you have to hurry through because you're bored. Practising awareness like that on ordinary everyday things makes the circumstances I'm in much easier, because every time (nearly) I do mundane domestic things my awareness practice gives them meaning. It clarifies ordinary things, having a spiritual practice as part of your daily routine. I want the children to know I follow a spiritual practice, so that it involves them rather than excludes them. When we go on the Amaravati summer camp it gives them as well as me a lot of support, and when we're at home my spiritual practice is seen by them as part of the everyday home routine and not outside that.

As a single mother I value the support my spiritual practice gives me, because there's a lot of heartache bringing up kids on your own, and never enough support. The whole issue of home is very sensitive for me and the kids because they go to their father's every weekend, and they get a different kind of parenting there. They would see this house as home, but he likes them to call his house home, so they are divided between very different homes. Their father's live-in girlfriend is very formal, concentrates on things like their table manners, correct speech, etc., and sees us as very sloppy. So when they come home on Sunday night we always have a debriefing session and work through any awful things that have happened over there. One of the burning issues for me has been letting my children go to another woman with a different way of mothering. You have to be so big-hearted about it. It's different from a traditional extended family, this new kind of extended family that comes from modern breakdowns in relationships. You're just thrown together with this person who shares your mothering, someone who isn't related to you by blood or through having known each other over the years. It's nearly as bad as the way we're thrown together with random people on this council estate. We have nothing in common, and no choice about it. We just have to take it. So we work through the children's experiences with the other mother when they get back on Sunday evenings, and try to make it alright for them and me.

When the children are with their father at weekends I tend to go to my boyfriend's, though it depends because our relationship is very flexible. That relationship helps me no end because he has brought up three kids (grown-up now) and can give me a lot of support. But sometimes I feel caught in the middle of a delicate web of relationships, because both his children and mine spend time with their mum or dad as well as with us. When I'm having to do with his children I feel very sensitive because I know they're his previous partner's children and I don't want to threaten her in the way I sometimes feel threatened by my ex-husband's new partner. There was one weekend when she cut off all my children's hair herself. I felt that was a terrible invasion of my area of mothering. The basic problem is having to share my mothering with a woman I wouldn't have anything in common with at all. The other big question has been how you combine your working life and your home life when you're a single mother. Earlier on when I first became a single mother, I was very low. We were poor and our life was very confined. So I did a correspondence course on aromatherapy and finally got qualified. The idea was it was something I could do from home, and fit in with looking after the kids. I did practise for a couple of years, and put a lot of energy into it. But I found I was giving out emotionally in my job outside the home as well as giving out at home as the centre of our one parent family. I got to a dangerous point where I was nearly burnt out emotionally. I had to drop the aromatherapy and put all my energies into home. Until the youngest finishes primary school in a year's time I see my base as here at home. My own working life in aromatherapy won't start again till the children are through school. So at present I go out cleaning other people's houses, plus caretaking the village hall (cleaning and clearing up after functions), and cleaning the village toilets. People look at me and say I'm wasted on this work. But they don't see the value of what I'm doing at home. That work at home bringing up kids is so invisible to the world outside. But as I see it, it's the most important work I can do as a single mother.

Gwen's story

Gwen (26) is bringing up two children (ages 7 and 5) on social security. Their father has not kept up contact with the children, so they haven't seen him since they were very little, and are forgetting him — "he doesn't even bother to send them Christmas or birthday presents any more." Gwen's current partner doesn't live with them. He has his own place nearby, and that she feels is better. He is "like a dad" with the children when he is with them, but she and the kids also have their own home space without him. Making good home space and doing creative domestic things are still, she insists, the most valuable work a woman can do, because you are in charge of your children's growth — body and soul. She was brought up going to the local Methodist chapel and Sunday School, but now she is a practising pagan, close to the earth and the cycle of the seasons, and concerned for the whole life of our planet. She has made her own little altar to the good forces of nature, and keeps it bright with fresh flowers, shells and stones and other objects that have positive associations for her.

"It's about good relating to people and to the earth," she says. "spirituality is nothing if you're not weaving it in with your everyday life, healing things and not hurting or destroying things."

When you step inside Gwen's small terraced cottage you are immediately aware of the warm nurturing comfort she creates. There is a glowing coal fire burning in the living room, and all around are handcrafted things lovingly made. There is a patchwork quilt covering the old sofa, and a brightly coloured rag rug in front of the fire. The walls are decorated with Celtic hangings symbolizing the spiral of life

energy and the intertwining of all things — animals, plants and
people; earth, fire, air and water. Gwen explains her way of making
home as a single mother, and what it means to her and her children:

> It makes me very angry when they categorize single parents as
> if they're all one kind — the bad kind — and causing all the
> problems for the next generation. My children get as much
> love as a so-called normal couple give kids. I think they get
> more love and stability than most kids. They're well-fed, well-
> clothed, but above all they have care and love to come home
> to every day when they get off the school bus. They enjoy
> coming home, being at home. It's ridiculous to generalize
> about single mothers. I am on income support and I'm not
> well-off but I manage. I feel that society undervalues the
> woman in the home, and glamorizes women working outside in
> a career. I think things need to be made more glamorous for
> the home-centred woman, and she should be given appreciation
> for bringing children up well, for that's really important work
> where you have to use all your never-ending skills. For mone-
> tary purposes I'd be better off if I went to work, but I think
> it's more important to keep a home together for the children.
> I'm giving back more to the community by looking after them
> well than I'm getting credit for. You're not given credit for
> good mothering, and keeping a comfortable and loving home
> together for the children. I'm not saying women should be tied
> to the kitchen sink, but that they should have the time to make
> home a good place emotionally, a place where children feel
> safe within their own four walls, and have someone there who
> really listens to them when they come home.
>
> I have very little money for me and the two kids to live on,
> but it's the way you spend your money that counts more than
> how much or how little you have. My main priorities are the
> food and the coal and the electric. With Christmas and birthday
> presents I make things myself as much as I can, and people
> appreciate them more than bought things. It's a scrimp to get
> the children shoes, etc., and sometimes I feel it would be nice
> to go out for a meal and have a little luxury. But I am able to

make something out of nothing and make the most of what I can afford. The children and I collect fruit from the hedgerows for jam, and last year I made blackberry wine. I make patchwork quilts from scraps of material people save for me. When I'm doing my patchwork I even keep the tiny pieces I cut off to stuff cushions, and the longer pieces to make a rag rug, like that one on the hearth. I find home more comfortable and comforting because I've made so many of the things in it myself. It would cost a fortune to buy children's bedding and curtains, but I have a sewing machine and made them myself. It's personalized as well when you do it yourself. It makes your home different and your own. This year I'm feeling in a creative mood (that comes and goes) so I'm doing a quilt for a door hanging to keep out the draught that comes in from the kitchen. I'm knitting a black jumper, too, for my partner for Christmas.

The way I feel about home is connected with my women's spirituality. As a pagan I see the home as the place which centres you in your life, where people sit quietly, or talk and laugh together, according to the inner and outer seasons that influence us. I believe there's a right time for doing different things, and there are natural rhythms you should follow. I am very aware of the patterning of what I do and how I feel at different phases of the moon and at different seasons of the year. We try to go with those natural rhythms in our home life and in the projects we do. There's a time to be quiet and a time to be active, and the children pick up on that, they seem to slot into that as if they could sense it as well. They accept my whole life style and part of that is an awareness of rhythms and phases to live by. We have times when we are very active, out walking, picking fruit or making the garden. Other times it feels right to sit here by the fire with story telling and quiet inside things. Staying in touch with nature is something I try to do with the children, so they understand about respecting the earth, however young they are. I'm giving them little plots of their own in the back garden so they can learn to grow things themselves and value that. I'm planning something special for next year's garden. I'm going to do a herb garden to

correspond with the phases of the moon. It'll be a large circle
divided in sections that represent the phases of the moon, and
I'm working out which bit particular herbs will do best in.
That's my spring project, planting my moon herb garden. Then
I hope I'll be able to use the herbs I grow to make healing
things. Growing things with a good intent is important and
gives me pleasure, so I want to teach the children how to do
that — helping them get their little plots going, and have them
help me with my moon garden.

My women's spirituality is centred on nurturing life, and it's
natural for me to develop and keep alive traditional women's
skills, because using those makes home a nurturing place for
your children and your friends and your partner. The trendy
thing now is for a very plain home with shop bought furniture
and curtains to match. To me that's a cold and unkind sort of
space to live in, unnatural to me because I believe home has to
be warm and lived-in and have a purpose — to nurture life.
You keep alive that purpose by attending to it and respecting it
in everything you do every day.

I see home values getting lost over the years because everybody's too busy with their own things to put much energy into
making home and community. I see that as a spiritual loss, because the nurturing purpose of home is not being passed on,
and women are losing the skills. I see home as womanspace,
and I don't agree with men looking after children more and
women going out to work the same as men. I'm a feminist
because I'm pro-woman, but I value women for the skills
they've had handed down over the years, rather than for
neglecting home skills and doing men's jobs better than the
men. Our biological patterns mean we're meant to have
children and nurture them, so why try to ignore that? Men can
do the outer work of home, the maintenance of the structure,
whereas women maintain the emotional structure, do the inner
work. A man shouldn't invade woman's space, and the home is
more woman's space than man's space.

My women friends would bash me over the head for saying
these things. Now that my younger child's started school I find

a lot of pressure coming at me to go back to work or to go to
college. It comes at me from the media and my own friends.
My women friends put more pressure on me than the family,
because the family's old fashioned, but my women friends
think that you have to get out into the world to find yourself.
If we all did that, it would be the end of home values, so it
should be a matter of choice for women, how they combine
looking after children and going out to work. The way things
are, though, you haven't got much choice because there's no
proper backup for combining work and home unless you're
well off, and most single mothers aren't. There *are* times when
I do feel stuck in the house, but on the whole I do see there's
a purpose in doing this work every day, so I keep going.
Sometimes it gets on top of you and I ask myself, "What is the
purpose?," because our society expects you to be out at work
all day, and going out for meals in the evenings too. What I
need is more like-minded women around me, but the women
around here do go out to work, so there are hardly any left
with lives centred in home and community, which is my ideal
of home, children or no children.

   When I was brought up here twenty years ago all the
women seemed to be together and helped each other out with
the childcare. The home was a more open place in those days,
with people popping in and out for a chat about what was
going on. This was a more lively place then. Now it's lively
just with your own personal friends, but there isn't much
community spirit. People shut themselves in behind closed
doors and are much more private. There's a lot more people
have moved in here from all over the place, and they make
you feel you're imposing yourself if you knock on their door
just to introduce yourself as one of the neighbours. I was
thinking of taking a cake or something to some new people
who'd moved in, but I didn't bother because I realized they
would think mingling with the locals was a nuisance. People
used to tell their neighbours if they were planning to do something (moving heavy stuff or hedge cutting) that would be noisy
or block the one track road. Now they don't bother. They just

get on with whatever they want to do without caring how it affects other people. Calling on your neighbours is seen more as an invasion of privacy now, but it used to be a way of passing on local news and helping people when they needed something. Someone would be able to produce whatever was needed or would know someone who could. If someone had a baby, or there was a wedding, everyone would celebrate. But they don't want to know any more. It's all kept private for the family and their selected friends. It's really sad this breakdown of community, and it makes the place even more isolating when you're bringing up kids on your own. I make up for that by making a very secure home for my kids, with their granddad living next door. Having my friends call is important to me, especially as the neighbours don't behave like neighbours any more. I meet every week or so with one or two women friends to keep our women's spirituality going. Kay from up the road comes once a week with eggs, and is going to give me a few chickens because I want to start keeping my own hens.

So I have a sense of belonging here even though the old community spirit is gone. I have friends who are new connections, and I have old connections with this house and this place, because this is where I learned the purpose of home from my mother and her sisters. I still feel my mother's influence around the house and I want part of her to live on in what I do, in how I work out the purpose of home. That, and my women's spirituality, are the things that keep me going when I hear people going on about single mothers as if they're all one, and blaming us for causing problems for the next generation.

Kathy's story

Kathy (37) is a divorced single mother with two boys (9 and 6). She was training for Christian ministry when her marriage broke up four years ago and the ministry remains a central purpose in her life. So as well as coping with emotional isolation she has had the stigma of feeling cut off from her church. The failure of her marriage and family life seemed to her to be a personal failure and also to undermine her public role of ministering to other people. She went through a crisis of conscience which she could only survive by delving deep into her Christianity and finding new roads to faith which answer to our modern dilemmas, including divorce and single motherhood:

> At the beginning, when we first split up, I felt very sinful, an abject failure in the most public of ways. I found it extremely difficult because at that time I was lay-preaching regularly. I felt desperately insecure in my preaching role because I felt somebody in the congregation could stand up at any time and say, "What right have you to stand up there preaching to us?" I was feeling that my marriage breakdown was unforgivable in religious terms, so I cut myself off from the people in my church. Although I'd been in that church for years and years, the people were unsure how to reach me, because I was distancing myself from them. My two boys were cut off as well from the junior church because of their disturbed feelings over mummy and daddy breaking up. Each responded in his own way, with Leo (the older one) becoming antisocial and having angry outbursts, and Ian wanting attention the whole time.
>
> After all those negative feelings and that initial time of cutting myself off even from the people who wanted to help, I eventually realized that there was a positive side to my marriage breaking down. It had made me more approachable and more human to some people in the congregation. It came out when I sent out my Christmas cards that year with only one name on them and not two. That was the beginning of warmth and acceptance of what had happened, for me person- ally and for the church members. So the feeling of deep shame that was cutting me off from other people only lasted a few months, before the rediscovery-of-myself stage began. I began to feel I didn't need to go around with a chip on my shoulder about failure. I reclaimed my maiden name as a sign to the world that I was taking back my own identity. I went through

a bit of an angry feminist stage too. I bought myself a pair of
Doc Martens as if to proclaim: "I feel as if life has put the
boot in, so I'm wearing my Doc Martens." I didn't realize it at
the time, but I scared stiff most of the men I came in contact
with in the church. I was pretty angry with the male sex, and
felt sure that with my marriage breakdown I had lost some of
the identity and self-esteem I'd had from my education and
early career and early contacts with feminism. Bringing up the
boys on my own has been a big change for them and for me.
There had never been enough intimacy in my relationship with
my husband, and I realized he wasn't capable of more. For him
what he gave me was what he was capable of, but it wasn't
enough for me. My feelings were repressed for years and years
during the marriage, and by the time I got to telling him significant things the relationship was coming to an end because I
could stand it no longer, but he hadn't even noticed ...

So I'm glad that since I've been on my own with the boys
we've been able to talk more about how people relate to each
other. The first feelings of social isolation after the breakup
have been succeeded by learning new ways of relating, for
both me and the boys. It began when Leo the older boy wanted
to understand what happened between Daddy and me. I haven't
consciously pushed that kind of talk with him because I am
afraid as a single parent of offloading my own emotional
anxiety and frustration on to the boys. There's always the risk
of unburdening yourself by putting it on to them, so I try not
to do that, even when I'm feeling negative about their father.
But Leo is very aware now of how people relate to each other,
and sometimes he wants to talk to me about it, to try and
understand what's going on between people. So we've talked
about the disagreements between the people he cares about.
When the breakup happened I said to him: "Mummy and
Daddy love you still, but not each other." It took time for him
to accept that, because there has to be a healing process.
There's no instant remedy for broken relationships. They have
to get through the hurt. You know when they're no longer
hurting because they stop acting the way they did at first —

not wanting to know, not accepting what's happened, wanting everything to be the same as before, when it can't be. The first sign that the hurt was beginning to heal was when Leo started wanting to know how you could go on being friends without loving each other. He was able to start working on other ways his dad and I could relate, and that was part of the healing. So on the positive side has been that Leo (at nine) is trying to understand relationships. Sometimes he comes home and says, "Mummy, I want to talk to you." It may be something that's happened at school, or some darkness in himself — angry feelings — he wants to talk about. He's bright and articulate but not strong physically so he suffers a bit of low level bullying at school. We've talked about what makes somebody into a bully, what behaviour encourages the bully and what behaviour deters him.

I had developed a pattern of never voicing my own needs for space, in my marriage or in my pastoral work in the church. I saw myself as someone who worked hard at other people's needs, and shouldn't think about my own. If you suppress or deny your own needs for so long, it's very difficult to break the pattern even when you're out of the marriage. You just feel bursting with anger sometimes, and occasionally the angers breaks out. I have a friend whom I lost touch with during my marriage (because my husband didn't want friends of mine in the house except on his own terms) and the talks I've had with her have helped me work out how to reclaim some personal space for myself. At first when I didn't have to fit in with anybody else's plans, it felt really odd. Then it dawned on me how very marvellous it was to be able to do something without having to give it up as soon as you hear, "Mummy, I want my tea." It was marvellous to think about things I wanted to do, what I wanted to spend spare time on, when on my own. When you're bringing up children on your own, you need to give thought to your own need for personal space as well, or you can get ground down.

In my work as a minister I've evolved, I hope, as a result of my experiences of becoming a divorced woman and single mother. After I worked through the first negative feelings of failure and guilt, I was able to use my personal experiences in my work. I found myself preaching sermons coming from the counselling I'd begun to go to. I wasn't doing therapy on my congregation, but speaking to them out of a sense of being swamped with the pain of all the people around me, who (like me) were in broken relationships. What I was on about was how we learn to speak the truth in love, how we can be honest and caring even when relationships break down. What I'm trying to do now in my pastoral work is to use my own experiences of being a single mother (the pain and the guilt as well the new positive relationship with the boys). That way I am trying to keep my home space and my career space interconnected. If my home and my career reflect back to each other, I can see life whole and, hopefully, help others towards seeing life whole. Looking back over the sermons I gave after the breakup, I can see my feelings came out in my sermons, though I wasn't conscious of that at the time. I was doing quite a bit of preaching when we split up. When I was going through the shame phase I was preaching on Moses and the promise of redemption. I was saying God is active in history, liberating the Israelites and us, and it is no good saying (as Moses and I did at first), "God, I am not fit." Because we always have new tasks before us and new places with new friends and new work to do. I was strongly identifying with the burning bush in that sermon. I was trying not to be a shrivelled stump of a person consumed by the flames. I was trying to be a fire of positive energy for renewal — burned but not consumed. I remember liberation theology was an ongoing theme in my sermons at that time. A few months after the Moses and the burning bush sermon I had moved on to the theme of Joshua and the promised land — the struggle to get to where we're supposed to be, but haven't reached. They and I definitely hadn't arrived in any promised land. We were struggling along on the journey we had to make. Liberation theology kept coming into it because the beginning of liberation and healing is seeing ourselves very clearly, our good and our bad sides,

and realizing we are accepted in God's eyes even if the
world's eye does not reflect us back in the same way. Liberation involves getting over the attitude of "Let them think what
they want — I don't care," and finding a way for forgiveness
to come through, instead of clinging to a defiant assertiveness.
I remember another sermon I gave on "Unbinding Lazarus,"
which grew out of my personal experiences. I used the text for
exploring how we experience living death in our own lives,
and how we can unbind ourselves and each other from various
forms of living death — the loneliness of ageing, or crippling
and binding relationships. With my "Unbinding Lazarus"
sermon I had reached the point where I could theologize out of
my own pain as a divorcee and a single mother. I said that
God uses our earlier deaths to inform and enrich our future
lives. The grey clothes keep on binding us in living deaths
again and again in our lives, but our ministry is to keep freeing
each other from the living death of a broken relationship or a
lonely ageing or whatever it is that binds us.

Giving those sermons on liberation and unbinding had an
effect on what the boys and I were going through at home as
well. I was literally having to practise what I was preaching,
and face up to a personal liberation which had to be intricately
negotiated. There was Daddy's space and Mummy's space,
where the boys went at agreed times. I've had to develop a lot
more skills at negotiating emotional boundaries with the boys
and their father. My husband and I can sometimes sit down
now in each other's territory and have a cup of coffee, and
talk. I even ended up counselling my ex-husband about his
relationship with the girlfriend. It has all reflected back into my
pastoral work. It's the burning bush again. When you've been
through the fires yourself and learned not to be consumed, you
can sometimes speak the truth in love and listen to others'
truths in love.

Chapter 8
Living on your own

Loneliness or creative solitude?

At the end of our century the number of "single person households" is rising steadily. A growing minority of those who live alone choose to do so for positive reasons. They want independence and creative personal space where they can freely express themselves. But many who live alone still have no choice in the matter. They are powerless to alter the circumstances that have left them feeling stranded, beached on a shore of loneliness and isolation.

Whether it comes from breakdown of marriage or the dispersal of family, retirement or old age, living alone, when it is not chosen but enforced by circumstances, is for many a long hurt of loneliness and absence rather than a glorious opportunity for self-expression and independence. For career women with good personal networks like Christine (30), who works as a psychiatric nurse in an industrial city, it is easier for women now than at any time in history to lead a fruitful life of one's own. She does not want to get married, but has chosen to build a creative life for herself, with her own house and work and friends for emotional and spiritual support. Living on her own is a positive choice, a creative process.

But for Margaret (49), who is an "unskilled worker" and lives in rural poverty in Northern Ireland, living alone means aching loneliness and an absence of self growth which leaves her insecure and full of regrets for a missing life — the life she would have liked to live instead of the solitary one she has. Having your own space around you is for some a seedbed for personal growth. For others it is that perennial feminine problem of emptiness waiting to be filled.

Living on your own as a positive choice

Christine's story

A few years ago I joined the Quakers, and I was moved by the
Quaker idea expressed in *New Advices and Queries* that you
should try and make your home a place of loving friendship
and enjoyment where all who live or visit may find peace and
refreshment. That confirmed something I'd written in my
journal when I first moved into a house of my own five years
ago: "Time and space in my own home to be quiet and
reflective, and space to joyfully receive visitors. I pray now
that this home of mine will be welcoming to those who visit it,
a place where they can be at peace." Before I moved into my
own house I was sharing with someone in College and I felt
that the balance was all wrong. I couldn't make that house into
my own space, because there was no room or time for renewal
in myself, sharing with Lizzie — along with the TV and the
radio and the tapes and the everyday clatter of activity. I had
no space for the quietness and calm I need. My work in
psychiatric nursing can be stressful, and if we can't renew
ourselves we can't help the people who come to us. As well as
that, one of the things important to me is balancing the inner
and the outer. What I'm talking about is well put by a Quaker
writer (Damaris Parker-Rhodes) when she says: "Unless the
outer is balanced by the inner, the activity part becomes a rat-
race, and what should be part of a cycle of outgoing and
renewal turns into something frenetic and meaningless."

Since I moved into this house and have been living on my
own I have the feeling that the house is my sacred space. It is
the focus for my day-to-day renewal — a chance to come back
from work and the outside world to a place of refreshment.
That matters given the work I do, where you are talking and
giving out to others all the time. But home isn't just for my
personal refreshment and renewal, because I like to offer it as
a place of renewal for other women as well. We have monthly

women's support meetings here. The idea came up at work, because most of the women work in the health services or the statutory services, and we felt the need to meet outside work to nurture each other. We do meditation or healing or whatever any of us has to offer — massage or aromatherapy. I know it's a luxury to have a house to myself, so I try to make it a space I can offer to other women, a space for paying attention to nurturing ourselves so we can return to work renewed for more giving out to others.

There is a downside to living on your own, and I've experienced that at times as well as the positive side. I have sometimes felt that when you live on your own you have to put a lot of energy into justifying — or excusing — being on your own. At first I did a lot of that justifying. Now I don't bother. People tend to assume you're not living on your own out of choice, whereas I think that at different times of your life different kinds of living are right for you, and at the present time living on my own feels right to me. Although it feels right to me some people seem to think, "Why is she on her own? There must be something wrong with her." The attitude is you're like a house that's been on the market too long. There must be something wrong with it, or it would be sold. For me choosing to live alone is a positive thing, but a lot of people don't see it like that. They tend to assume it's a temporary deprived state, and that one day you'll "settle down" properly.

Another part of the downside is that when you live on your own you can feel more vulnerable in illness or accident. When I broke my leg I went through a bad time. I couldn't manage on my own and I had to go back to my parents' house, which was difficult. Then when I had to go back to the hospital to have the pin taken out, it brought up a lot of strong feeling about what my home meant to me. I was off work and alone in the house for three weeks, and one of the upstairs ceilings had literally fallen in (it's an old terrace house), so there was outer as well as inner destruction. I wrote in my journal that "In the silence and stillness of the house I have been faced with myself, my hopes and fears, and I have felt a certain lack of courage." I felt then what Virginia Woolf talks about in *A Room of One's Own* — that life "is arduous, difficult, a perpetual struggle. It calls for gigantic courage and strength. More than anything, perhaps, creatures of illusion as we are, it calls for confidence in oneself. Without confidence we are as babes in the cradle." I experienced that failure of self-confidence and courage during those three weeks I was alone in the house, not going out to work, and trying to pick up the responsibility of getting the house and myself back into running order. I can't do building repairs myself, so I had to do the budgeting and get the repairs done while trying to get back to normal health myself.

One of the issues of living on your own is you have to rely so much on your own resources, inner and outer, and there are times when the courage isn't there. For me part of the problem is living in a society which has difficulty taking women seriously on our own merits. You have to put up with work-men saying things like, "Is your husband there? Can I talk to him about what needs doing?" Or, "I'll call back round and talk to your partner when he's there." One double-glazing chap said, "You must be very frightened here being on your own."

The social message that comes across (and you notice it more when you're housebound), is that you shouldn't as a young woman be on your own running a house. You should be living in a family unit, being somebody's daughter or some-body's wife. That kind of thing is still very strong here in what used to be a heavy industry area, even though the heavy industry has gone.

But the anger and frustration from that doesn't last long. I soon get over it because most of the time I feel so right and centred in my own home, and my confidence comes back. I think we all have patterns of life which are right for us, though different at different times. If you find the right pattern for yourself it liberates you to go off and direct your energies outside the home where they're needed, where you can do something useful. It's important to me that home and outside things, the inner and the outer, connect together. Making a home of my own is about claiming my own space and living by my own light. It's not cutting myself off; it's about being better able to connect with the outside because I'm developing good inner resources.

My dogs are important to me and mean I don't really live "on my own," anyway. They are other bodies, other living presences in the house. Part of it is the joy of looking after them. Part of it is the importance of touch. Being tactile is good and I'm getting more tactile at work and at home. Also the dogs instil a daily routine which is soothing. I take them out both morning and evening, before and after work. My need at those times of the day is to have company without having to talk, because I spend all day talking to people in need. I get that company in a non-talking way from the doggies. But you can talk to them as well — I heard on the *Today* programme this morning that sixty per cent of people in Britain say it's more therapeutic to talk to their animals than their spouses ...

When living alone is the last thing you want

Margaret's story

Margaret (49) regards living alone as a mournful deprivation rather than a self-chosen pattern of life. Coming up to fifty she finds that in conservative Northern Ireland women of her age are treated as nearly invisible socially when they have no husband to give them position or status. Her rural community has changed significantly during her lifetime. Her neighbours are so busy and so occupied with their private concerns that they have no time to be old-fashioned neighbours any more. Margaret has no car (she has never learned to drive, but she couldn't afford a car anyway), and has to rely on an infrequent bus service into Belfast, which is about fifteen miles away. It might all have been different if she had a career, but since leaving school she has only had basic office training and has never got beyond low pay and temporary positions in the world of work. She has been on and off the dole for years, and is at present on sickness benefit after having a major operation "down there — women's troubles."

I've lived on my own since 1979 when my mother died. We're a farming family, and she had bought this cottage because it was time for her to move out of the family farm and let my brother take over. But before she was able to do the work on the cottage (it was a wreck of an old place) her health went. She got more and more confused till she didn't know who she was any more. She went so bad she had to go into hospital — and never came out till her death. So the house came to me, the unmarried daughter. There was no bathroom, no flush toilet even, and only a cold water tap. So it took a lot of time and effort for me to get the place comfortable. When you can't do the work yourself it's a great trouble. You have to make enquiries to find people who are reliable and won't overcharge, because if you're a woman on your own there's plenty of cowboys to take advantage.

When I was first living here on my own and trying to get the house into shape, I was out working in offices in Belfast, so I had plenty of company during the day. But the loneliness hit me every night coming home to an empty uncomfortable house, and being stuck there till I went to work again the next morning. Living here in the country without a car you can get to Belfast and back to your job on the bus, but you have no social life in the evenings. I had only the very occasional visitor to keep me company. A bachelor farmer I had known for years used to come down and have his supper and spend an hour or two with me. He might have thought there was a romantic attachment (or that I'd make him a good housekeeper, maybe, with my apple cakes and my sponges). But I never fancied him, though I was glad enough of a bit of chat in the lonely evenings. A neighbour woman down the road was company too — we were both on our own and were good company for each other. She sometimes took me for a run in the car, up until she died. I had a nice labrador I got from the farm — Bramble — and he was great company. In the

evenings I would get home from the office and light a nice fire
for comfort and warmth, and take Bramble for a walk. He was
a very wise old animal. He got a dose of flu when he was
twelve and died, and I never got another dog because by then I
was changing from office work to Irish Aunts, and the work
I've been doing for them takes me away from home for a week
or two at a time. I'm a companion to old people, relieving their
regular carers for a week or so at a time. The women I look
after are in their eighties or nineties, living in their own homes
but they can't get about any more or do their own
housekeeping. They're great readers and they watch TV — I
watch whatever they fancy, of course. I'm quite a sociable
person when I get the chance, so the job suits me down to the
ground. But the job's irregular, and when I'm between jobs I
sometimes wonder what happened to all the aunts and cousins
in my own big connection, and how it came about that I'm left
sitting here on my own without any company but the old ladies
I get paid for being with ...

I still feel family attachment and support are the great thing,
especially when you are on your own. That's the way we were
brought up here in the country — to give support to anybody
who needed it in the family or neighbourhood. In the early
days on my own my brother and his wife, who now run the
old family farm, used to have me out on a Sunday and brought
me back. But now a lot of the married couples in the farming
community don't seem to hit it off so well with each other.
They want different things. They aren't looking for the same
things out of the farm any more. My sister-in-law wants the
house immaculate, so you're nearly scared to step on her brand
new carpets after you've been out around the farm. She shops
endlessly and terrorizes my brother (and myself) with her
domestic standards. So the atmosphere isn't very welcoming if
I go to visit them. It was better when the children were little
because they took up attention. Now the children are growing
up and off doing their own things. That throws William and
Florence together more and if I'm there I'm very aware they
get on each other's nerves. He's happier outside with the

animals than having to clean up and sit in her house-proud
sitting-room without a word to say to her. She gets her own
back on him by taking the car into town and bringing home
another load of shopping. So I don't get much feeling of
support in that direction, even though they're family. The
younger generation is better. My niece and I sometimes have
evenings out together. She's got her own house and a good
job, and she hasn't married either. Indeed I think she doesn't
want to marry. She's the new breed of woman you hear about
— independent of the men and making her own life. She and I
have good evenings out together. We went to the Lyric in
Belfast to see *Wuthering Heights* and the famous Peter Corry,
and we've been to hear the Rev McRea — the famous gospel
singer — at some Orange Halls in the Mournes. She's great
company, but she has her own life to live and I only see her
three or four times a year. The thing is you don't have a
regular social life living on your own. What I do miss is the
old country habit of neighbours calling in just for a cup of tea
and a chat. But people these days are so busy with their own
social lives and their families and their work, that they can't be
bothered with neighbours. Since the old lady in the next house
dies I can't drop in there in the same way any more. There's a
widower of seventy and his son moved in there. People joke,
"You should be installed there yourself," and that puts me off
being friendly with them beyond casual conversation. And you
don't get to know a person till you get beyond the weather and
the bus service and so on. So the loneliness goes on ... It's
worse in the winter when the evenings are so long and you
have to find enough things to do till it's finally bedtime. I
might be fixing curtains or knitting or doing embroidery. Once
I knit jumpers but they're just as nice, or nicer, bought, so I
thought "what's the use of bothering?" I only knit dishcloths
now. But there's always some bit of sewing you can do to add
to the cosiness of the house, if it's only a cushion cover to
embroider. That Victorian walnut piano (and some of the other
furniture) was my mother's. I've had it tuned recently, and I
sometimes play it myself. My favourite tunes are *Danny Boy*

and *The Last Rose of Summer,* but I like all those old tunes,
and hymns too of course — tunes I learnt back in Sunday
School days, like *What a friend we have in Jesus.* One of the
neighbours has a daughter who's a fully fledged pianist and
plays at socials. She has come over once or twice and can
really make that piano sing. The whole house fills with music
and it's lovely. Most of the houses around me in this part of
the country still have the piano. They send the children to
music lessons privately. Some of the families still gather round
the piano and sing together. That's still common enough here
in Northern Ireland, though they all have the latest CD and
cassette equipment as well. When you live on your own the
piano is company. I know a great hymn player who lives on
her own at the end of a long lane, and has the piano for
company. She does Mission Hall work and can play all my
favourites, like *The Sweet Bye and Bye.* When she's been here
I've taped her playing on my piano. Taping is a great thing
with me. I tape music and conversations when people are in,
and then I play them to myself when I have nobody in.

I've been at home recovering from a recent operation, and it
makes you feel better sooner if you've got someone to speak to
when you come home from hospital. The psychology of feeling
better is all about getting out of the rut of being ill, and getting
your initiative going again. Where there's a helping hand, a
person full of go to look in on you, you're better far quicker.
When the minister calls in, or a travelling preacher from the
Mission Hall, they pray and that soothes me. You need a
person like that to listen to you and to talk spiritually without
it sounding artificial and far from your everyday concerns.
There was a lovely preacher came the other day. A good
preacher talks very simply and naturally but leaves you with a
bit of inspiration. But the trouble with the travelling preachers
is they travel out of your life as quick as they travel in,
because they're moving around the countryside all the time.
This one was living in a caravan and going round the Mission
Halls and the Orange Halls, helping people with praying, and
taking a great interest in youth work. A nice Bible seller came

round one day too. I told him I'd had my own Bible since Sunday school days, so he couldn't sell me one. I should have brought him in and given him tea but I was in a bad mood that day and not feeling sociable. The trouble is you long for company but then when you get a caller you're so used to being on your own you're not in the mood for chat, or it's not the kind of company you want. He said, "I'm taking my Bibles all round Ireland and I'll be back here in four years' time. So goodbye for now, but next time I come you'll ask me in for a day." And I probably will, because living on your own is not easy if you haven't any choice, and there's no sociability. The house feels quite different when people have come in and there's been a bit of talk. It helps you feel in touch with the rest of humanity, and you get a better night's sleep for that.

It's all in a lifetime for me. There are advantages and disadvantages. There's nobody telling you what to do and not do, but there are times when you would rather have guidance than freedom. Holidays are difficult on your own, too. I feel funny going off on my own and wouldn't enjoy myself, so if I have a holiday at all I try to stay with relations. Most of the time I rely on an annual cycle of visitors, old chums to take me out for a run to the Mournes once or twice a year.

You get scared on your own sometimes. You hear noises in the roof and don't know whether it's someone trying to break in through the old skylight, or the wind dragging branches across the corrugated iron roof on the old sheds. One Sunday evening I did come home to find drawer contents all over the floor, and shelves emptied, and stuff dragged out of the wardrobe. Everything in the house was sifted through. They were looking for money because they didn't take the telly. They only found three or four pounds, but it was a bit scary for a while after that. My brother came and nailed up the windows and did things to make the place safer, but it was nasty the feeling that someone had been in trampling all over your house and handling all your personal stuff. You're afraid they'll come back, too. You more than ever want company after that.

What keeps me going is taking things a day at a time, and having a few people who remember me and call in whenever they can. People tell you their problems or admit the same problems as you have living on your own. They tell you it gets better in time. Hope springs eternal. I'm still hoping to meet Mr Right, because I'm the eternal optimist still, at 49! I remember a bit of verse that goes, "Two men looked out through their prison bars. One saw mud and the other stars." Well, I'm the stargazer! I'm a Christian and some Christians find great support in prayer and in accepting their lives as God's will for them. I wish I had the faith to be like that. I envy people like my cousin the preacher and his wife, because they have a spiritual reality underlying everything they do and say. It makes things fall into place and seem part of God's plan. I'd like to become like that because at the end of the day those are the things that matter most. But I can't just put my trust in God and not feel lonely any more. I've tried, but I go on feeling there's something missing in my life and God isn't filling it.

But I wouldn't want to end on a note of despair because I carry on somehow. I have a strong sense of the countryside around here where I've always lived. I love to go for walks in it, and I love certain times of the year — May and June when the nights are long and bright, and the autumn when you go along the lanes and the hedgerows are full of haws, and blackberries galore, and sloeberries (though they're too bitter to do anything with). Living in the country is important to me, and being in touch with the seasons passing. I like to go and stand at the door on a nice moonlit night, before I go to bed, and just watch the starlit sky. Or on a sunny spring day with the clouds rushing by and the first buds coming on the trees ... though these days you're just as likely to see balloons floating by advertising things. Growing things is important to me too. I've planted hydrangeas and flowering cherries and lilac around the place and they've all done immensely well. I grew a beech tree from a four inch slip with a wee root on it, and that's nearly reaching the sky now. Gardening is very relaxing, but as

well as that I like to see the plants come up every year, and
put in new ones to fill the gaps. Every year I'm waiting to see
the bulbs coming up first in the spring, then the wild cherry
and the Laxton's Superb in blossom, and after that the summer
wild flowers, and the rose of Sharon and the forest flame
giving you colour when the days are shortening in autumn ...
Sometimes I feel God's with me whenever I'm out there in the
garden, even though He's not there in the loneliness of the
empty house. But if I could get my faith right He would be
there for me the whole time, and then I wouldn't be lonely any
more. The travelling preacher told me God is lonely for me the
way I am lonely for Him, and I would not feel lonely any
more as soon as I put God out of His loneliness. I'm struggling
with that, but I still feel I'm a loser.

Living alone after marriage breakdown

Suzanne's story

Suzanne (48) has been through a double mid-life crisis involving
alcoholism and marriage breakdown. She has moved back to the city
she grew up in, and is in the process of modernizing her parents' old
terrace house, as a permanent home for herself and an occasional
family home for her student children to come back to whenever they
feel the need. She has taken a backroom job in the media for financial
security and an element of sociability which is very important now she
is living alone after twenty years of marriage and mothering. After a
mid-life divorce a woman can suddenly suffer from having too much
personal space instead of the too little she has as a mother. It can be
a challenge rebuilding self-identity and finding ways of filling this
extra space (it sometimes feels like nothing but emptiness) that is
suddenly yours, as Suzanne explains:

Only in the last few months have I realized that I can grow out
of being a mother and the way that shapes one's whole sense
of home. There will always be space for them here, of course,

but as they're out in the world doing their own things now I
want to develop my sense of being on my own, developing my
own person. The difficulty is I haven't been on my own for so
many years and it's bewildering at first exploring that
experience. It's a kind of positive loneliness I'm aiming at, a
sense of having choices not available to you when you have
partner and children to consider. It doesn't come easily; you
have to grow into it. Because most domestic set ups restrict
one's power of choice, from the colours you want for the walls
and the carpet to the major things in life. When you emerge
from a divorce you have a kind of freedom, but you're scarred.
I am doubly scarred because I'm getting over the drink
problem as well as the divorce. And living on my own is not
something I've organized for myself in mid-life. It's just how
things are, because nobody makes a positive choice to be
divorced. I want to enhance my divorced state and turn it into
something positive, rather than fear it or run away from it. But
every now and then I *am* afraid. I wake up at 3 a.m. and
wonder if all I've done in this house is build a living tomb for
myself. After a divorce you want to build yourself a new safe
place, but you also need to make a fresh start in the world. It
isn't enough to be at home in your own house. Being at home
in the outside world is important. I have always spent a lot of
energy on people, on friends, but some of that is falling away,
leaving me more alone — I don't see that as loneliness (as I
once would) if I can use it creatively. I'm trying to branch out
in different ways and use this new personal space differently.
It's quite difficult because after years and years of having my
mind set in family associations and influences I'm moving to a
stage of being still and appreciating the quietness around me.
But the people element is still the centre of home for me,
rather than the set of good china or the Habitat sofa. So I want
the house to be a thread of security and stability for my
children and my friends. But I want it to be restful rather than
dynamic. I want it to be emotionally uncluttered, because there
has been enough of heightened emotions and raised passions in
the years of the breakup.

I am finding it very hard to let someone else (even a lover) invade the tender new identity I get from my home space. I feel this home is an extension of my new identity as a woman beginning again on her own in mid-life. I would have problems sharing it with someone. But that's not likely to happen because what I and a number of my women friends feel now about relationships is that you no longer look to share your home with anyone. At this stage in life you keep your own space and your home becomes an extension of the individual rather than an extension of the family.

That doesn't mean you don't have partners. It means that each partner keeps their own space and you visit each other more or less as your lives are interwoven. You have shared space with your partner, but you also have your own space to express yourself in.

Madeleine's story

Madeleine (43) is just over five feet, slender in build, and has a delicate almost transparent skin. She is a woman farming on her own. She has 150 ewes on a moorland farm. For Madeleine, divorce has meant the tough blessing of heavy outdoor work and individual responsibility — a combination she relishes most of the time:

The thing I like about living on my own is that I don't have to work things out with anyone else. I can do what suits me without referring to someone else's needs and tastes and preferences all the time. I loved my husband, but I remember feeling the freest person in the world when I left him to the plane taking him to a conference in the United States. That was the summer before we split up eight years ago. I would find it very difficult living with anyone else now because living on my own still gives me that great sense of being free. I can't understand the attitude of people who say, "I can't bear to be on my own." I like visitors, but I also like it when they go away. Christmas Eve is bad because you're supposed to be with people and enjoying yourself, and I'm not. Christmas Day is alright because my husband and his new partner have become like family to me and come here for Christmas dinner every year.

The problem was we didn't have a good enough sexual relationship to keep our marriage going. He was half power on that side of things. I had an affair with someone for five years and when my husband found out he just said he didn't mind. That was rather awful — his not minding rather than his finding out, I mean. That was the last straw. In many ways he is a dear and I like it that he and his partner have become family to me. But I couldn't have stood our marriage going on and on into middle age, with all its wants and absences and frustrations — on my side at least. So the divorce was a relief for me, and we settled it all very amicably — even the finances. We didn't fight over the farm because I wanted it and he didn't. He never took to farming like I did. We had started off in professional careers in the south-east, and chucked all that in to buy our hill farm. We weren't the axe-grinding type of purist smallholders determined to be self-sufficient on the land. We were just fed up with the predictable round of professional life, and wanted more freedom and time to ourselves. My husband is very good at growing things and maybe we should have gone into market gardening rather than falling for this place which is a thousand feet up and basically only good for raising sheep. As it turned out I found myself doing everything — finding the farm, researching what you actually do on a sheep farm, keeping him happy by providing him with the few things he could do ... So in a funny way it was a relief when the marriage ended and I found myself running the farm on my own. I can make my own plans and get on with what needs to be done, without having to worry as well about what he can do.

The financial side is hard because I had to get an outside job three days a week to keep going, and I have to pay for any building work that needs doing, because I can't do that. But though I can't do building I know exactly what I want done. That's my problem — the JCB digger company in my locality won't work for me any more because when I was doing up the ruined cottage on the farm I wanted things done my way, and as a woman in the country I'm not supposed to know how things are done, much less tell men how to do them. That just made me all the more determined not to be one of those women on their own who are badly treated when they want work done to the house because they don't count — they're not supposed to know about building work. So the radius is widening as more builders hear about me and decide they're not going to work for this woman who dares to tell them what to do!

As a woman on my own I have this fear of being anonymous and faceless, so I go on making sure it will never happen — by knowing what I want and making sure anybody who works for me gives me what I'm paying for. I have to not mind being odd woman out in the farming world as well. It's not that the men positively mistreat you. You're just invisible as a woman. In a busy mart you're surrounded by farmers jostling with each other like the animals to see what's going on in the ring. They don't exactly pee on your feet like the beasts, but they often stand on your feet as they jostle about. I try to sell my lambs straight to the slaughter house, but I still have to take my old ewes to the mart to sell. Last week I was standing in the mart from ten till after one, feeling more and more invisible as the men jostled about ignoring me. The mart is part of the social life of the men. They can hang about all day with their male cronies, but it was very inconvenient for me and a waste of my time. The cloak of invisibility descends upon you every time at the marts, because as a woman you can't be a crony.

The solitudes of widows

Doreen's story

He had cancer and I nursed him for two years, so I was exhausted as well as bereaved when he died. I had a job and that was good because although it added to my exhaustion it got me out of the house. You've got to learn to make a new life for yourself on your own, and the first thing is you've got to get out and meet people. But when you do that there's the awful coming back to an empty house afterwards. It's better if you have animals. I had a big red setter and a cat, so that wasn't so bad. There was still some life around the house to greet you when you arrived home by yourself.

I still sometimes, several years on, experience stabs of loneliness like the ones I had at first. I also sometimes dream of him and wake up so happy and content. There's the sense of missing him still because there isn't anybody else to talk to about everything. To learn to live by yourself means you often have to keep your secrets to yourself (even if you've got some good friends — and I send out a hundred Christmas cards every year). Since he died there's no one I can completely trust to say anything I like to, whatever my mood. He would understand and respect my feelings and instinctively know when not to pass something I said on to anybody else.

It still gives me a pang when I see husbands and wives out in a car together, just because they are a twosome and I'm only a onesome now. I feel a pang of self pity. But I don't encourage it. What keeps me going is having people around me to keep the adrenalin up. You need stimulus to keep you going at any age, but at first when my husband died I used to talk to the dog because I hadn't the energy it takes to get out and meet people. Someone who gets me talking is what I need, or I'm in danger of getting pretty low still, living on my own. My husband used to push me into doing things which I could do and enjoyed doing, but was too lazy to get into on my own.

We were both teachers and when I was at home bringing up
my son I thought I was happy enough. But he pushed me to
get back into teaching when Ian started school. I was getting to
be a cabbage when Ian didn't need me so much, but when
you're turning into a cabbage you're the last person to know it,
so I needed my husband to give me that push back into a
career. Now I'm a widow I miss the stimulus he gave me to
keep going and do the things I know I'm capable of but can't
begin without "the push." I have to get that stimulus elsewhere,
and that's the hardest thing, because nobody is as close as he
was, just noticing me and seeing whether I'm up or down ...

When you're a widow at first you see the black side of
everything. I said to myself, "My son doesn't need me any
more." Although he had brought life back to the house I
thought in my gloomier moments, "It's his life, and not my
life. They're his friends and not my friends." What saved me
in that first year was an old friend thinking about me and
ringing me up. He had sensed me being down and seemed to
be able to ring up at my worst times when I most needed to
know that somebody was thinking about me, that I wasn't
completely alone. At first you just feel invisible, that you've
disappeared from the world and there's not one single person
out there thinking about you or caring what state you're in.
That's the terrible thing, that sense of being a non-person.
When you feel like that, you have to force yourself to get out
and start making your new life, or you might as well throw
yourself on his funeral pyre. In that first year I could see how
even *suttee* makes sense. Then I made myself rebuild my life,
bit by bit, friend by friend, a day at a time ...

Elin's story

I have no doubts that there is an afterlife, and when my
husband was dying he said to me, "I will wait for you
forever." We had an extremely happy life together and when
we were not at work we spent all our spare time together. So I
felt I had no freedom to think about marrying again. Because I

loved him so much, when he died I decided this was my
opportunity to love other people. I thought someone
somewhere must need me, so I joined the local Samaritans and
have worked with them ever since.

My husband was ill for fifteen months with cancer and I
knew there was no chance of recovery. My initial reaction to
his death was relief because the pain was at an end, and a
twinge of guilt that you can feel relief. Then there was a big
hole in my life. That's when you have to go out and get
something to do. The problem was my husband was very
outgoing and all our life together I just sat there and said yes
and no. So it took me courage at first even to go out and sit in
a café by myself and order a coffee. Now if my husband came
back he wouldn't recognize me. I'm talking to people and full
of things to do. When you're bereaved you've got to learn to
take the first step yourself, to go out and meet people and do
things. I lost a lot of my own identity when my husband died,
because it came from our identity as a couple. I've now
dropped all the friends we had before (the ones who didn't
drop me first!) because I had to be sure the people who asked
me around were asking me and not my husband's widow. I'm
paranoid about anybody doing anything for me out of pity or
duty — "I suppose we'd better ask her round, poor thing." All
my friends now are my own friends, whereas before I was so
boring and my husband so out-going that all our friends were
his friends. Being a widow has made me self-confident for the
first time in my life. I was married for thirty years and I could
live on my own for another thirty years, so I'm doing my best
to make my own life, though I'm still looking forward to
meeting my husband again in the afterlife.

A meditation on aloneness

We all have times when loneliness or the fear of loneliness is strong in us. But loneliness, for most of the people I talked to, is not to be confused with being alone. Current social styles put huge pressures on us to be consumers of company, remorseless seekers of sociability, so that being on our own is seen as something missing rather than something gained. But in all the great spiritual traditions the merging of our small fearful aloneness with the great alone is a metaphor for wholeness. Christina Feldman in *Woman Awake* (Arkana, 1990) gives us a valuable meditation on aloneness to practise, in which we visualize ourselves standing alone on a high hill, aware of the wind blowing, the high hills around us and the valleys below. We face the aloneness none of us can avoid, and try to experience a sense of connectedness with the never-ending flow of life:

> As you see yourself standing on the hilltop let your awareness deepen, become more subtle. Feel the life around you, beneath you, above you. The movements of the trees and the clouds, the shadows on the hillsides, the endless changes which signal life, rising and passing. Feel the same changes within you, the rising and passing of your own thoughts and feelings. The birth and death of sensations and responses, constantly changing but held within the vastness of your awareness. Just as the vastness of your awareness senses the changes around you. Just as the vastness of the space around you holds your own changes. Open yourself to feeling the transparency of the lines between inner and outer, self and other. Feel the transparency of the lines between aloneness and oneness ...

Chapter 9
Re-making home in retirement

Retiring is an uneasy process. It is something to look forward to, freedom from the straitjacket of work, but the freedom, when it comes, has to be translated into something positive. After the first fine careless rapture fades, there is the business of deciding how to live without the ready made structures of work. Income goes down, the work-based social life dies away, and partners suddenly have a lot more time to spend with each other every day. For many men there is the shock of giving up a lifelong career which has absorbed so much of their energies that they have not managed to build up any networks of meaning outside work. For an increasing number of women, retirement comes too early. They resent giving up a work identity which has only flowered in their middle years after the heavy demands of child-rearing have eased. Retirement raises the terrible question of how to fill the endless hours and months and years that work once swallowed up. The idea of giving up work has great appeal, but it can be a horrible wrench to be torn out of the organizational womb and face the vacancies of a life of endless freedom. Freedom is hard work and makes unusual demands on imaginations deadened by the routine work slog.

Early retirement is increasingly common, and many, given the choice, choose to try out their "freedom" in their fifties while they have the energy to shape a new life. But Caroline (51), a woman now working freelance in the arts world after taking early retirement from an organization job, explains how even chosen change demands emotional intelligence and imagination:

> Starting a new life style is very difficult. Suddenly you have to be a different kind of person after being another kind of person for thirty years of adult life. Certain activities had become habitual to me, like being on committees to drive new projects

forward, or writing exhibition catalogues. There was a clear structure and well-defined tasks with deadlines. But now I'm trying to do my own creative work I have to have a very different kind of single-minded commitment. That's quite a lonely thing later in life, when you've taken for granted all the social and professional contacts that working in an organization gives you. It isn't easy. There are times when your self confidence just collapses totally. And you've chosen this life yourself, so there's nobody to blame. It's you, and only you, who carries the can for your successes and your failures.

Rachel (56), a freelance writer who took early retirement from full-time academic work at fifty, says:

It's been a struggle. People ask me if I have problems getting down to work when I'm my own boss working from home, but I haven't found that. I work harder now than I ever did in the college ambience, because I have to make my own structures, and shape my own goals, and promote my work, on top of actually doing the work itself. Anyway there is more time when you're working at home, because you can't hang about drinking coffee with colleagues or drop into somebody's office for a chat about some issue that's coming up in the department. There's no office politics to enjoy and fritter time away on. You're on your own, and there's a weird kind of loneliness at first, which you have to get used to. It alternately strengthens you or saps your vital energies. Ultimately it's made me far more self-sufficient than I used to be in my institutional job, but it was tough going in the first couple of years. I was on my own. I had no support group to try out my ideas on. Mind you I got a lot more work done. but I think I went through a depression that lasted at least a year. I didn't know it as depression at the time, but looking back I can identify the symptoms — my social instincts going into recession, too many hours spent sleeping, nagging doubts about the value of my writing and my life in general. I had to rebuild my self confidence on the basis of inner belief in what I was doing. Before that I suppose I relied on feedback from colleagues and approval from outside myself. But when you're freelancing you have to believe in what you're doing. You have to have a strong true purpose, which can take all the knocks a writer gets from the outside world and still survive. It sounds grim, I know. Sometimes it feels grim too, when somebody rejects a bit of writing you thought was good, or you have to rewrite a piece to fit in with some publisher's marketing target rather than with your own convictions or writing style. It's always wounding to one's self-esteem to receive crits about work from publishers' readers, because writing is such a lonely activity that you desperately want feedback, but the feedback is always a mixture of positive and negative and the negative bits can get to you emotionally. It ought to be cool and rational having exchanges with an editor who's there, after all, to support you and help you improve your work for publication. But sometimes the creative process leaves you emotionally vulnerable to criticism of any kind, or you just disagree with an editor rationally, or you've got the wrong editor — somebody you're not easy working with. Then when something is finally published you get the reviews, which can be so different from each other that they might not be talking about the same book. Often they seem to be as much about the reviewer's need for self-expression as about the writer's. The nicest thing is when you get appreciative letters from readers, who've taken the trouble to sit down and respond personally to your book. That brings home that what you've written has really gone out into the world and is having some effect.

What with the isolation and the bouts of self doubt brought on by negative criticism, being a writer is never a piece of cake, and from time to time you long to be an organization woman again, slouching along with the team. But I go on writing because I'm in mid life now and what motivates me is having things to say that I think are important and want other people to read — whether they like them or not. In mid-life you have to move away from outer approval and feedback to inner conviction, or you're in danger of losing your soul. In mid-life all the youthful props are gradually knocked away from under you, and you have to replace them with a new source of inner strength. In my case it's my writing that makes me "Me," because that's my base for self-expression. That's what makes me the person I am at this stage in my life, and feeds into my other roles as partner and mother and (recently) grandmother. Occasionally I have inklings of my old age, and I see myself giving up writing and all the achievement things that are so vital to me now. I see myself then in more contemplative mode, but I'll still be creating something as long as I have breath in my body. It's lack of imagination that kills. Probably my last mode of activity will be creating a beautiful garden, somewhere for me and others to enjoy — even if I end up in a wheelchair ...

Creating new structures in retirement

The positive side of retirement is the opportunity to develop parts of yourself that have lain fallow during the time-starved years of work and family duty. For Felicia, a headmistress who had never married, the world was made new two years into her retirement, when her ailing mother died and she was finally free to re-imagine her life:

My mother didn't like people in the house and I had a demanding job, so we never had a social life. That was alright as long as I was working. I didn't make a lot of close friends anyway because as a head teacher you are cut off by your position from being very close to your own staff. When I retired my mother was active mentally but less active physically, so she was very demanding on me. In her mind I was there solely to look after her. I couldn't accept that, but I went along with it outwardly, keeping to her wishes about not having friends in her house. I started an Open University degree to keep my mind ticking over. It also helped me keep my private space in that house which was so much her house, not mine or ours. We managed to get along together, but not comfortably. There was almost always in the house an atmosphere of barely suppressed criticism and carping. Politeness was our undeclared strategy for keeping each other at a safe distance, but it broke down from time to time because we had no relief from each other. Still, we managed on the whole to preserve the niceties.

Then my mother died and I was suddenly free. For the first time in my life I found myself free to do exactly what I wanted. I decided on a long holiday at the seaside, and I spent six weeks in the university town on the coast where I had been a student. I walked and walked and walked. I thoroughly enjoyed myself and decided this was where I wanted to be. I got hold of a house agent and bought a house there. It was the first time I had lived on my own, and I was able to do all the things I had not been able to do in my working years, or in the years of caring for my mother.

I love learning — that is the chief thing that has always sustained me in my everyday life. Teaching and being taught are both important. You need to teach and you need to learn. Reading and learning have been at the heart of my life. You need inspiration to get you started, and that is where good teachers are so important. They give you the curiosity about what people have put into their books. They stir up in you the need to find out about other people's ideas and technologies. But you then have to face up to the discipline of learning. Once you've done that it becomes absolutely fascinating, and there is no end to it, whatever stage of life you have reached. I was a geography student all those years ago in this university town. I had a degree in geography and I'd read geology and botany, which gave me a special interest in exploring the countryside. So when I retired here I would go off regularly and spend a day or two walking a particular bit of countryside with that added interest in the geology and botany. I experienced a delicious sense of freedom on those expeditions. I didn't have to consult anyone about where I was going or what I was going to do. I could go off for a night when I wanted to. I could talk to people I met for as long or as little as I liked, without feeling guilty about straying from the set text, as it were. I had nobody's curriculum to follow but my own. I thoroughly enjoyed myself, as well as learning a great deal about the countryside I had chosen for my retirement.

The other aspect of learning that has always sustained me is the delight of learning with other people in a group. In my new found freedom after my mother's death I was able to go to classes in various wonderful adult education centres. They give you companionship as well as learning. I've always enjoyed working with people for a common purpose, rather than getting to know individuals in a rather random way. So I joined the extra-mural classes here for the same dual purpose of being part of a group while at the same time learning something that interests me and keeps me stimulated. I always want a structure, and so even when I've achieved the freedom of retirement I still need to structure my freedom to get the most from it. But this time it is my own structure, unconstrained by the demands of colleagues or family. That is the true freedom that retirement has brought for me.

Dorothea (69) worked till she was sixty-five, and would have continued if it had been possible, because she only began her career when she was in her forties and her children were growing up. She studied as a mature student and got her teaching qualification. Then she specialized in teaching handicapped children. These achievements meant a lot to her. They brought her a new self-confidence as well as great job satisfaction. So when retirement loomed Dorothea was very worried about losing her working life. Here she is describing how she felt before and after retirement:

Retirement was a real crisis in my life. I had got my qualifications and my career very late in life, and they made a huge difference to the way I saw myself, as well as how other people saw me. The B.Ed. proved I could do it, and the Diploma for teaching handicapped children boosted my morale further. The turning point was when I became the official person with the briefcase, and other people were seeing a different me. I was becoming visible to the outside world in my forties! I learned that if there's something to be said, you say it rather than bottling it up and going off in a sulk. My job gave me great satisfaction — concrete things like succeeding with a reading scheme for handicapped children. So I came to see myself as mainly what I do.

Now that retirement is looming I'm worried because I've learned to judge myself by what I've achieved, and what am I going to find to do that will take the place of work? Without a job what else is there to do? There is the life Clive and I have together — travel, walking, the grandchildren. There's my music, and my sewing. But you can only do so much of that. Homemaking is not going to take up much time, because since I began my career in my forties it's always been a corporate effort. Clive and the children have had to contribute to the cooking and the cleaning, though my influence has continued to be the dominant one in deciding how things should be done. The general ambience matters to me, but I can put up with bits of plaster falling off the wall so long as there are plenty of indoor plants around, and a few nice things. So homemaking is not going to be the answer to retirement. What on earth am I going to do with all the rest of my days?

I went back to see Dorothea two years into retirement, when she and Clive were feeling more positive about finding their own answers to the dreaded question, "Is there life after work?"

DOROTHEA: We've evolved a new pattern for our lives since we retired. We work on our own in the mornings, then we have lunch together and decide what we are doing for the rest of the day. We each have our own work room, with our computers and other paraphernalia. I feel the need still to get up every morning and achieve something in the course of the day (beyond putting a duster around the place, etc.). I bought my BBC Master so I could continue teaching one or two handicapped children on a freelance basis. The first year of retirement I got involved in the local dyslexia group, and as a result of that I got two pupils for a while. That was good because I feel it is an awful waste not to go on using all the expertise I acquired in the eighteen years since I'd returned to work after being a full-time mother. Unfortunately after that first year I haven't been able to get much work. That's not so good, because I still get up early and have this need to achieve something every day. I have one pupil at the moment who comes once a week, but I could do so much more ...

When you retire you no longer have work as an alibi, and you find out about your real interests and priorities in life. In my case that means being there for the children and grand-children, my music activities, and the travel we do together. You have a very different way of using time when you retire. I've found out that you make time for the things you really want to do, and you don't get around to making time for the things you only say you want to do. But you have to control the time or you'll get nothing done. You mustn't watch much TV because it would take time away from the things you really want to do. You can choose for yourself as to how you pattern your days, but you must pattern them to keep chaos at bay and order imposed, That applies to my space as well as my time in retirement, whereas Clive's room is heaped up with papers and materials in a chaotic way which I couldn't stand.

CLIVE: I am comfortable with that because the heaps all represent projects I am working on, or intending to work on. There *is* structure there — though it may not be visible to anyone but me. I agree about the need to structure time in retirement. Structuring the day is very important when you're at home. I do all the meals, though Dorothea helps a bit. We share the shopping now because it's become part of our Monday sociable activity. Every week we go to the lunchtime concert in town, have a sandwich somewhere, and shop afterwards. We have other joint projects during the week, like doing meals on wheels together.

DOROTHEA: But we keep our individual patterns for the week
as well. That's important so that you keep your own activities,
as well as doing joint things with your partner. I've played in
an orchestra since childhood, and music has always been an
important part of my life. Since I've retired I've become secretary of the orchestra. I've learned to use the database because
it makes for smoother running and efficiency. There's the
pressure of three full-scale concerts every year as well as the
constant practice. In the last twelve months I've also had our
own quartet meeting in the house, because in retirement I've
found that music is high up in my priorities. I go off on
orchestral weeks where you just play and play all day everyday
— wonderful. And Clive has his art weeks just as I have my
music weeks. So we manage to maintain a certain independence which is very important when retirement brings you
together so much of the time. Otherwise retirement could be
quite claustrophobic.

Retirement gives you a number of freedoms. There's the
freedom to enjoy family relationships more because you have
more time to give to them. Our grown-up children don't seem
to feel we put so much pressure on them now as when they
were younger. So we probably get on better now we can
appreciate each other as separate people rather than as parents
and children. The relationships in the family keep you in touch
with the latest mores, as well as showing the ways we've
influenced them by our own lives. When their children are
born they decide which of the parents is going to look after the
baby while the other goes out to work. It's not taken for
granted that the man or the woman has fixed roles. We hope
we've influenced them in that by the way Clive and I have
both had careers and shared the homemaking.

Being retired makes you invisible to some people in the
same way I was invisible when I was at home full-time
bringing up the children. You're no longer in the achievement
culture, and for a lot of people now outside achievement is all
that counts. But what really counts in retirement is inner
achievement. That's the hard lesson you have to learn ...

Joining your community's daytime life

People whose lives have been work-centred for thirty or forty years know little or nothing of the mysterious daytime life that goes on in their communities after they have gone out to work. They may not have spoken to the people who live in the same street, or even know the people next door. Working life devours its own children. But it spews them out again on retirement, and then they have to begin again, to learn about the place they have lived in but never known, to talk to the people who have been their non-neighbours rather than real neighbours. Barbara (74) lives in south Dublin, and retired nine years ago after a full-time professional career which had gone on without a break, because she never had a family. She lives in a modern town house which forms part of a square of similar houses, facing each other across a pleasant communal garden with mature trees and shrubs. She has in her retirement become intensely aware of that other daytime world which you never know about when you go out to work. There is still community out there, however splintered and diverse it has become, and she has found it a rich resource for the social and spiritual life she needs now she is workless:

> For the thirty-nine years I was working I wasn't around in the
> community to meet people, and social life, what there was of
> it, arose from people I knew at work. Since I've retired I have
> a new kind of social life, and much of it has grown out of
> various kinds of community where I live. I have met old
> friends and also made new friends who live around here or
> who go to the same things as I do. I now know a far wider
> range of people, and have a quite new feeling of community
> which I never experienced while I was at work. This sense of
> community is very real and comes from being connected with
> the different kinds of people I meet now, and from having time
> to keep the connections going in a day to day rhythm. I
> experience home now as a place where, although I live on my
> own, the people I know support me and I support them.
> There's someone to notice if you're not around, and when you

go away there's someone to keep an eye on the house and keep the key. There are various little parties where I meet people I wouldn't otherwise meet, like well-to-do business men or arts people. That's because the people who live here make friends of their neighbours, and invite them to their little parties, or just ask you in for a G & T with a few friends. That's very important when you live on your own.

There's my church community as well. When I retired the rector asked me to become secretary of a fundraising committee which helps to support an African hospital. That brought me sociable contacts as well as helping the fundraising, though at first I felt strange going to the meetings on my own and not knowing anybody. Meetings at work are different because you've got your formal position and your known role. In retirement it takes more courage and self-confidence to join a group where everybody knows everybody else but you know nobody. But I have strong views on the need for making the hospital in Africa real to people here (as an incentive to fundraising), so I got up the courage to speak my mind and found, of course, that once you've done it the first time, you boost your confidence and become known, and it leads to other things.

When you retire you have to find new ways of keeping your body and your mind fit. Fitness is a big thing when you're getting older, and it no longer comes naturally — if it ever did. So I went with a friend to the League of Health, which is very big here. It started as the League of Health and Beauty fifty years ago when some research revealed the poor physical shape of the ordinary woman and the general ignorance about keeping yourself in good shape, whatever your age. There are classes graded to every degree of fitness, so I go every week to the one that suits me in my mid-seventies. I see how good they are, because no matter how decrepit you may eventually become there's something for you. Some of the women keep their arthritis at bay by sitting on a chair doing hand and arm and neck exercises, even if they can't stand up any more. I've also joined a group of older ladies that goes swimming one

evening a week in one of the local schools' pools. So I'm
taking care of the physical fitness and making more friends at
the same time.

You have to keep the mind fit as well, so since I've retired
I've done a two year diploma in theology. That was one
evening a week, with lectures, projects, etc. I did that because I
was getting more involved in church things but had never
really got beyond very elementary ideas about the theology
underlying it all. The course was very ecumenical and interfaith, so I found out a lot about other religions as well as my
own. And again I made social contacts of yet another kind,
which have led to more party invitations.

Travel has been important in my life, but now I'm able to
let myself enjoy going back to the same places, rather than feel
I have to fly all over the show, which can leave you not
knowing anybody anywhere. I've been going to Donegal for
about thirty years and I keep up with the families of the people
who run the guesthouse and the village shop *cum* post-office. I
know all the local gossip and over the years I've seen their
attitudes to life changing as Ireland is changing. You can see
how the children are well educated and very different from
their parents, but you can also see how Kathleen, who runs the
guesthouse, is the most impressive of them all, though she is
without any formal education. She is so experienced and
intelligent in her emotions, and so perceptive of the things that
matter in the end. I find that very fascinating, that growing
difference between the formally well-educated and the
informally educated in the school of life. I find it sad as well
that so much importance is attached to the formal educated
status, as if that were the only path to success in life. You see,
too, in my Donegal village, the big changes for women in
Ireland that have happened in the last generation. One of
Kathleen's brothers comes to the guesthouse for meals, because
his wife has upped and left him. Once upon a time in Ireland,
in the so-called Good Old Days, women didn't leave their
husbands; they put up with them.

But there's still a place for the old-fashioned woman, too,

and there are some of them left, even in Dublin. When I'm at home here I go out on a Saturday night for a drink and a chat to a local club. The person I usually sit with is the builder's wife, whom I get on well with. She's a very old-fashioned woman, cooking meals for her family at whatever hour of the day or night they come in, and looking after a baby for a working mother. And on top of that she is running a women's organization. At first sight people might think I had nothing in common with her, because she's so different from the people I used to mix with in my professional work. But my sociability is very different now from when I was at work. I choose people for their deeper human qualities, and I'm connected with people from a far wider social range. Before I retired I made my contacts through work. The problem with that is you relate to people a lot more through work roles or professional roles rather than through the wider human qualities you look for in people when you retire. Retirement frees you from the danger of carrying your organizational role playing over into your social life. The problem of spending a large part of your life working for an organization is that work roles give people a sort of alibi for living. You're in danger of role playing through life till you've numbed your capacity for making human contacts with people who aren't in recognized roles or life styles. So retirement is a chance for you to escape all that and meet the rest of creation. Mind you, when I first retired I thought I'd miss all the "in" chat at work about politics and my colleagues' personal lives, and the organization gossip. Everyday contacts and sociability are a big part of work. But I've replaced them with a far wider range of social contacts than I ever imagined was possible. I've learned about the rest of humanity — beyond organization man and woman — and that has been the best retirement gift the world could have given me.

Rejecting the whole notion of retirement

Aiesha the Cook

Retirement is a very modern notion, and there are people who utterly reject the whole idea that at a certain age you lay down your tools and give up your work and adopt a life of enforced leisure till death releases you from the burden of idleness. For Aiesha the cook (70) life and work comfortably coincide, and retirement would be a laughable proposition, were the very idea not so threatening to her very identity:

> All my life I love to cook. All my life I have cooked for my family and my friends. Sometimes I do it for pleasure, sometimes to earn a living — but that is a pleasure too. Why should I stop now when I am seventy, or when I will be seventy-three or seventy-seven? I do not stop being a good cook at a certain age. I think I get better at it even now. I am more relaxed, I am not scared to use my imagination, I am still finding out new things. So this business of retiring has no meaning for me. It is a nonsense. I will go on till I drop. If a day comes and I cannot cook any longer I will sit in my chair and remember all the good food I have made in my life. I will turn the cooking I have done in my life into stories for my grandchildren and great-grandchildren. Always till the end there will be cooking for me — in my dreams, in my soul, if no longer in my kitchen. Cooking is more than my work. It is my life. So it does not end till I end ...

Chapter 10
What does home mean when you're *really* old?

Barbara (74) has in her retirement developed a keen personal and Christian concern about what happens to the really old in our society. She visits many friends and members of her church in old people's homes, and puts into words the fears and anxieties of many women in their seventies and eighties, as they face the prospect of not being able to carry on in their own homes:

> When you're on your own and getting on into your seventies, as I am, you can't help thinking about going into a home some day. However comfortable and well you are at the moment, the prospect of The Home is there looming in the background. I'm very aware of it, not just as my personal destination one day when I can no longer be independent, but because I go and visit people who have already had to give up their home and move into one of these "homes." I find myself planning ahead, as you have to do when you're on your own and have no immediate family — or even sometimes if you *have* got sons and daughters, for they may not want to feel responsible or have their independent life-styles curbed. Anyway, I don't spend money on certain things I might like because I know I'll have to sell the house and have savings as well to give myself five years in a good home when the time comes. Here around Dublin you pay at least £300 a week, so quite simply there's the question of expense, though the Eastern Health Board gives a bit of help.
>
> It makes your heart sink when you go into these "homes" that are often not a bit like real homes. The homes I visit vary enormously, but wherever I go there are shortcomings and

some are a travesty of the very word and meaning of home. There's often nothing to stimulate the residents, so the brighter ones usually descend to the level of the worst off. That's what comes of being expected to eat communally and sit together in a sitting room where there are all grades of deterioration. The residents have all the choices taken out of their everyday lives. From the time they get up in the morning till they go to bed at night they have to follow the set routine. They're not encouraged to be by themselves in their room or to do anything different from anybody else, because it makes it harder to run an institution if you pay attention to individual needs. They often only have two trained staff and the rest are young girls (many of them waiting to go on a nursing course when they reach the minimum age). A lot of the young girls haven't a clue about looking after people or making them comfortable. They haven't a clue either about the indignity of calling old people by their Christian names, whether they want it or not. That's one way to reduce you to second childhood before you're ready for it. So is addressing you in words of one syllable as if at the age of eighty you automatically become simple-minded. I suppose a lot of these young girls have no loving experience of grandmothers and great-aunts in their own families, because the generations are so split up these days. So they have an ignorance of what it is like to be old, and the worst of them can't be bothered to find out even when they are spending their working days with old people. They do not know how to talk to the old as their equals — much less their betters! The accumulated experiences of a lifetime mean nothing to them, because it's the trend to have instant experience and keep moving on to the next bit of excitement.

In case that sounds too gloomy, I know of one or two places that are better than the common run of old people's homes, so they're not all a hopeless prospect. The good ones are more like sheltered housing; they leave you with a bit of independence. You can have your own things in your room and spend as much time there as you wish, only going to the common room when you feel like a bit of company. You can watch what you want on your own TV and have a bit of privacy and personal choice. They have things to go to every week for stimulus to stop inertia setting in. One place I go to has a musical afternoon once a week, either a singsong with someone playing the piano, or recordings of Mozart or whatever for those who want it. The atmosphere in these places is very different from the average run of homes. You can sense in the air that people still have a sense of being themselves, of having a few choices left in their lives. They haven't been reduced to vegetables by the welter of rules and the routines of the day and the way the staff behave to them.

But in the average old people's home there is nothing much to stop inertia setting in. Once inertia takes over you get worse all the time and stop feeling like a proper human being. I'm not saying that everybody in those homes suffers. Of course there are people who if they have enough to eat and a comfortable bed, and a radio to listen to, will settle in without a qualm. There are people in any age group who are happy enough to settle for a passive life, so long as there's an element of material comfort. But I think of one old lady I know who simply couldn't stand that minimal kind of living. She stayed for a week and then went back home till she was bad enough to get into hospital for her final days. She was so unhappy in the home because every circumstance in it made her less of a person at every moment of the day. It wasn't so much a day you lived through as a timetable arranged by somebody else for their own convenience without consulting you, although it was your day they were arranging. In circumstances like that only a minority manage to remain themselves. Others change for the worse because the only way you can assert yourself is by complaining and being cantankerous. I've noticed that one way people cope with old age is by becoming more and more cantankerous, because that's often the only way our society lets old people express themselves. I daresay that's the reason for the mad popularity of that sitcom *One Foot in the Grave.* It's based on endless variations of the cantankerous theme.

At a certain advanced stage of old age people get tired and
want to withdraw from the world around them (and even from
their families). They are preparing naturally to let go of life,
and should be let alone to do their withdrawing process in their
own way. But there's no ambience in the homes to acknowledge and accept this gentle and gradual withdrawal from the
last phase of life. They like them all to be sitting down with
the others, to be "joining in," even if that only means sitting in
a circle with the telly blasting and the heads nodding up and
down endlessly on the ones that are doting. They don't dis-
tinguish between different degrees of old age and the different
needs those bring. They don't recognize the psychological
stages of preparing to leave this world, never mind those of us
who might want to go through a spiritual letting go as well.

Keeping people alive longer whatever the quality of their
lives is another thing our society seems to be proud of. I don't
agree with euthanasia, but I think there's a point beyond which
old people should not be invaded by medical technology
striving to keep them alive when it is their time to go. When
you live in a society that worships achievement and grasping
more and more of everything, dying is harder, for nobody
knows how to let go. But a good death is the final achievement
for us all, and once upon a time in Ireland people knew how to
help you to a good death. The women knew how to hold you
physically in the last hours, for comfort and not for clinging on
to. They knew how to restrain the self-centred emotions of
your nearest and dearest, till they let you go in peace. They
knew when your hour was coming and you wanted quiet and
not talk. But nowadays the staff in the homes aren't trained in
that kind of caring. Running old people's homes is after all a
good business with a guaranteed expansion in the number of
clients. Even homes run by the churches are expected to be run
commercially these days, which doesn't always sit easily in
practice with their caring and compassionate aims. Everywhere
you turn there's business plans and cost-effectiveness
monitoring. It pays, for instance, to have an inhuman timetable
where the last meal of the day is served at 4.30 in the

afternoon, because then they don't have to pay staff overtime by organizing an evening meal at a civilized hour for the residents. And they don't want the old people up at night, as they might be after a late meal, because then they would have to employ extra night staff, and they cost more.

I'm not saying you can't sometimes arrive at a balance between commercial pressure and compassion. Our Lady's Manor near here is run by nuns, and they have to run it on a commercial basis now. But they let one old lady I know take her own bed and a couple of little tables from home in with her, so she can feel secure with familiar things around her. That's important because your personal possessions are a kind of emotional security whatever age you are, but especially so when your other sources of emotional security have diminished in the isolating process of old age. Some old people, I've noticed, become much more conscious of their personal possessions when they have hardly anything left to call their own. That's why getting the wrong nighties back from the laundry is a major source of discontent for some. That can seem trivial to the staff, but to the residents it's a question of feeling secure when there's hardly any security left in their everyday life. Old age disempowers you for a start. Being in a home multiplies all the disempowerments of old age.

Families now in Ireland are torn between losing the family fortune in fees for nursing homes or old people's homes, and the everyday horrors of keeping ageing relatives at home where they upset the life styles of family members, however much they contribute to their moral good. It's a very painful and heartfelt dilemma for many people, because of the long tradition here of the family looking after their own old people. But like a lot of traditions when you scrape off the romantic gloss it's not a simple good that everyone can accept or cope with, the way we live now. It's a big issue. Three quarters of the time spent visiting by the clergy in my parish is used to visit old people in their homes, ferry them to hospital, and give advice and support to young mothers overburdened with

looking after an old person on top of everything else. I can see
how younger people feel about their ageing parents, because
the burden usually falls on the women, and most of them these
days already have a huge amount of work outside and inside
the family. Younger women's lives have changed so much for
the better in the last generation. But old women's lives have
probably changed for the worse. With younger women living
such full lives it's not surprising that the most they feel they
can do for the old is maybe do their washing and visit them
once a week in a home. They don't want them to be in their
own home getting in the way of their already complicated
family arrangements, and invading the limited private space left
to women. There's the problem as well of too little cross-
generational stimulus, so old people become ghettoized. The
young want to be with people of their own age and life style.
They want to be able to ignore the old, at best, or ridicule
them and victimize them, at worst.

So when you face up to all the problems of keeping old
people at home with their families, you can see there's no way
you can put the clock back and bring back the old tradition of
the family taking care of its own old people. You have to fall
back on old people's homes, and try to think of ways of
making them better places to end your days in. There are
positive things to build on. Old people I know in the better
homes feel very comfortable and secure compared with living
on their own. There's always a member of staff to call on, and
they don't have to worry about break-ins and muggings like
you do when you're old and living on your own. There's one
old lady who goes to our church who has her own home and
independence, but she lives in constant fear her housing estate
council flat will be broken into. There are always boys kicking
a football, who catcall and jeer at her as she goes in and out
— for no other reason than that she's old. It's the cross-
generation gap again where ignorant youth have no way of
relating to the old except by making fun of them or imitating
their "funny" arthritic walk. And those are only the milder
youth who don't go as far as muggings and break-ins, like the

rougher sort do on the housing estates, and to a lesser extent in the suburbs as well. You feel physically and emotionally vulnerable when you're old. So a surprising number of old people live in a state of perpetual anxiety and loneliness and insecurity. The physical anxiety is eased by going into any home. But the emotional loneliness and insecurity is only eased in the better homes, where there are elements of privacy and personal choice, and where the staff treat you as an individual human being, instead of shouting at you when you want to be alone: "Come on now, Dolores, why aren't you joining in? It's time for tea and we're all going to have a good laugh watching *One Foot in the Grave* on the telly tonight, aren't we?"

Going for a compromise: sheltered housing

Sheltered housing is a halfway stage between running your own home and going into an old people's home. Here is a way of living a reasonably independent life with privacy and personal choice, while enjoying the security of a resident warden to help in any kind of emergency. Personal possessions in old age are peculiarly important, reflecting back at you the history of your life. In sheltered housing you can keep your own things around you, with all the power of association they have, and, if necessary, be reminded who you are by these Proustian prerequisites. But are the sheltered housing complexes springing up all over the country not just another way of ghettoizing the old, keeping them out of sight and out of mind, while saving the family fortune from melting away in the coffers of some old people's home? What is it that keeps the everyday flame of life alight, when people are in their eighties and their vital energy is burning low?

Felicia's story

I came here to this sheltered housing association flat six years ago when I was eighty. Some of the other people here don't like you to use the word "sheltered," because it implies old age and that gives you a low status in our present culture, which worships youth and sexuality and attractive appearances. They forget we all had those once. They seem to want everything to be *now,* or it's no good. Anyway, I don't mind being an old person, and "sheltered" housing describes just what I want. There are many advantages living in sheltered housing besides the practical conveniences. We're allowed to grow old here, while outside you're under pressure to hide your age and try to behave as if you're younger than you are. But the practical conveniences too are very important when you become physically fragile, as I am now at 86. We have bell-pulls and telephones to ask for help, and there are other people along the corridor in the neighbouring flats. There is a warden when you need help. I feel I have complete security here. I no longer feel nervous and alone as I did in my last cottage. That sense of security is a basic practical comfort, but it is the social life in this sheltered housing block which is important to me. There is a feeling of community here which I did not have before, when I was growing old in the outside world. People where I lived had little time for the old. They were far too busy with their own lives to spare me even a little time, much less to stop and think about what it means to be old and on your own, as we all are in our own good time. Here we have a continuing social life among ourselves, with monthly coffee meetings and fortnightly videos, as well as whatever informal invitations we exchange with each other. We make ourselves feel part of the outside world by sharing our outside companions with each other, even if we don't have any ourselves (as I don't, not being from around here). Although we're not formally structured as a community we have tremendous sympathy with each other, and there's a tremendous amount of helping. Nobody in this house could be forgotten because everybody is in touch. They rally round immediately when there's a problem. Outside it's very different. To be old is often to be invisible, to be forgotten.

I don't go out at all now. I am no longer mobile because of arthritis and osteoporitis. So I live my everyday life within these walls. As I get older and slower and less mobile I still need a structure to my life, though I notice that I gradually fill more of the day with things that have to be done, because basic things take longer and longer. That leaves less time for the things I enjoy, the interesting things.

My day begins between 6.30 and 7.00, because I've always got up at that time and still do. But now it takes me till 9.30 to get dressed and have breakfast, because I've got braces on my legs, and elastic stockings and a corset. And my hands are being affected now by the arthritis, so I'm slow and clumsy. By 10.30 I need a cup of tea, and I have magazines and a talking book to listen to. I belong to a talking book library where the postage is free, but I pay a subscription of £30 a year. I wish more people knew about it because it's an absolute saver. I hardly ever miss a day reading. I'm not blind but I have cataracts growing on both eyes so I can't do much ordinary reading. Before lunch I do letters. Whatever age you are you need to keep in touch. I've always enjoyed writing letters. Now it's chiefly to my sister and to friends. Writing is becoming a difficulty for me now, but I will find a solution one way or another. I *must* keep communicating. I've been thinking I might get an electronic typewriter. At 1.30 I get my lunch and look at the TV — the children's programmes are lovely — and then I've had enough. I go to bed from 3.00 till 4.30, so I don't have afternoons any more! At 4.30 I have tea and friends pop in. I like that very much, but sadly we watch each other getting into further stages of elderliness. When I first came here I thought it was a wonderful place and had no reservations whatever. There were so many new-found friends around me keen to go on and do everything they could. But gradually you watch them getting frail, going off to nursing homes or dying. That's the sad part of being here, living with other old people. It is a constant reminder of your own mortality, which you are only too aware of already, when you're in your eighties.

It's important for me to have young people coming in from outside, because otherwise you are face to face with too much mortality, and I happen to love young people's company.

When you are very old it is too easy to drift back into the past. I think however long you live you should try to anchor yourself in the present — though of course you cannot help seeing the present differently because you have lived so long and seen so many fashions (moral and otherwise) come and go.

The strangest thing about growing old is that you are still the same person inside, but you have changed so much on the outside that more and more people fail to see the you that is still there inside the garment of old age. I have the habit from my working days of keeping myself looking as well as I can, though I am no longer mobile, though I have long ago given up the middle-aged habit of trying to look younger than you are. What matters tremendously is to go on minding that you look as well as you can, whatever age you are. When you're young you think it's only the way the young and beautiful look that counts. When you're old you realize you can look well or ill at any age. A lady here knows she is going to die soon — she has cancer — but she turns herself out with great care every day. It's not any kind of trivial vanity. It's having respect for your unique humanity, to go on making the most of yourself whatever your age and whatever happens to you. But I have to admit there's another less worthy motive for good presentation. It's our dislike of the images of "poor old thing." You fear the stereotypes of the shaky old lady with the shabby clothes and unkempt locks. I'm still the same person I've always been, but other people might not know that if I'm not very careful about my everyday self, because there are prejudices against the old in our society. We're not sages with the wisdom of age now. We're nuisances with the unfortunate tendency of dragging out our redundant lives longer and longer!

What is it that sustains me in my everyday life, now I am in my eighties? The key to life is still the same as it's always been for me. The key to your life whatever age you are is to develop and express whatever potential you have. At my age what sustains me still is carrying on and continuing to do whatever I am capable of doing. We're often missing in this modern world the real chance to talk about what matters to us, and as your friends drop away in old age you have less chance still to talk about what matters to you. But I console myself that even when I am physically incapable I can turn the things that matter to me over in my mind. The mind's eye remains. I do a lot of thinking back over what my life has meant, and that is a positive thing on balance, because, yes, I've tried to do what I was capable of. I've always tried to live to the best of my abilities. I do a lot of thinking as well about what it is like for women who are young now, and it both pleases me and troubles me that women have so much potential to develop these days. They have their families and their careers and their public issues and their relationships and their women friends ... I think they are under great stress compared with my day, when women has less to choose from, and had to be more single-minded. In my day I could only hope to be a good head teacher. Now I would have to be a good head teacher and a good mother, a good lover and a good friend ...

In the same block of retirement flats lives Emily, a practical down-to-earth woman of 84, who keeps herself busy and has no time for the self pity that undermines some old people's life energy. She is a shrewd reader of character, and gets satisfaction from applying her emotional intelligence to this place where she lives surrounded by other old people — "people like me, to outside observers," she comments wryly, "but we are in fact all very different, just as we've always been."

I'm 84 and I've been a widow for over thirty years. So I've had a long time to learn how to live by myself, and that is the main lesson you have to learn when you're old. I do not mean that company is not important. Whatever age you are it's nice to have friends to drop in and liven you up. But the kind of old age we've set up for ourselves in our society these days is basically aloneness. So you have to enjoy your own company and have your own resources, and that's what I try to do every day.

As well as that you've got to get out and meet people, for you get morbid and fearful from being on your own too much. The sad thing is that as I'm getting older my contemporaries are going, but I've found other people to replace the ones who've gone. It takes a special effort to make friends when you're old. You don't meet them naturally as you do when you're young, and going out every day to work or to college or just to enjoy yourself. But you still need to meet people and enjoy yourself when you're old. That's what's nice about having a flat in sheltered housing. The good thing about this place is that you have a choice of socializing. We have enough socializing to keep people together, but not enough to invade your privacy. I enjoy going with the others to the theatre group visits and the pantomime every year. But I don't go to the video showings or to all the coffee mornings because I must have time on my own. I must be self-sufficient. And so long as I have the television and books and videos I'm happy to spend time by myself. I need the time on my own to re-charge.

I'm determined to keep a balance between self-sufficiency in my own flat and going out to meet people. I've seen some of the others here sitting inside their own four walls feeling sorry for themselves because nobody comes to see them any more. I could sit inside these four walls and feel sorry for myself too, but if I did that people might forget I existed. As long as I can get around I'm going to keep going out into the outside world. If you don't do that old age becomes a prison. I've seen that happen here. Oh, we're all very comfortable here. We can't complain on that score. But I've seen the odd one just losing the will to live for lack of human company. Once you lose the stimulus of everyday company, you start to sink. There are days when I feel really low because of the effect my health (diabetes and diverticulitis) has had on my life. But I take the tablets and try to forget it. This is my only life, and I'm determined to live it as well as I can, right up to the end. Here you keep your privacy and your independence and the sociability is never imposed upon you. This place leaves you with choices about how you live your everyday life, and that doesn't happen in the "homes" that so many of us end up in.

When my last dog died I wouldn't have another dog because I haven't the energy to go out now with a dog. So do you see that toy dog there in the armchair? I have that toy dog to cuddle and to keep my hands warm ... anyway there's a neighbour's dog to befriend. There's no nonsense here about not keeping pets, and the great thing about dogs is that they don't judge by appearances. They go on giving you their loyalty and devotion whether you're eight or eighty, well or ill, wrinkled or smooth.

What makes you happy when you're old?

It is easy to overlook the happiness that many people find in the last phase of their lives, because our society more often sees old age as a cluster of problems — financial problems, housing problems, health problems, family problems, social problems ... But for many individuals old age brings its own delights and satisfactions. Their happiness clearly outweighs their difficulties, and life continues to be worth living. This happiness in old age is unique to each individual, and this countrywoman's sources of satisfaction are very much her own. But her connectedness to her cultural roots, her creative interests, and her continuing zest for new experience and new company are perhaps the common bedrock of a satisfying old age.

Elinor Thomas's story

An old chap in Montgomeryshire once said to me, "I never thought I'd be so happy when I was old." I think it's true of me. Keeping the connections is the great thing — keeping up friends and contacts, and making new ones as you go along. Retirement is a great leveller, and that's a good thing too, as I see it. When you're working you're a somebody and when you retire you're a nobody. But the top man retired is in the same boat as the secretary after a while. Retirement is a different world where everybody has to learn new ways of connecting. It gives you time to enjoy people. When I was working I'd get home and prepare a meal, and be at my lowest, especially if I'd been harassed all day at work. Now I'm my own boss, and I have time to enjoy people. My friends can call anytime and I'm not bothered. I'm happy to see them, instead of feeling exhausted and having to recover for the next day's work.

I was brought up on a farm in Montgomeryshire, and after school (at Oswestry) I went back and worked on the farm till my brother got married and brought his wife home. Then I left and began a life of my own. I did a shorthand and typing course and then worked as a secretary in various agricultural bodies like the Welsh Breeds Society, because that was my background. My roots were in farming, and I'm still interested in everything to do with agriculture. I worked hard all my life, but I had to retire early on health grounds because of asthma and bronchitis problems. I didn't mind that, because I could relax a bit and enjoy more things. It was nice not be tired out getting home from work. I had more energy for my tapestry classes and pulled thread classes. I'd been going for years and you get to know the crowd. That saved me from being cut off on retirement like a lot of people are. Keeping in touch is the main thing, and it's up to you. I'm never short of company and good talk now because I've gathered up friends over the years and stayed in touch.

You need a structure to your life when you retire. Every day of the week has its own pattern for me. On Monday a friend comes to me while her husband (who has Alzheimers) goes to the centre. The Civil Service Retirement Association meets every month on Tuesday. Wednesday I go to tapestry classes. Thursday a friend from Cardigan comes to lunch. Friday is my day for doing my chores, and Saturday is the day for my African violets. You need a specialism and African violets are my specialism. It's a reminder of seasonal cycles and I like that. I have the satisfaction as well of propagating things and seeing them grow. I set the leaves in March and it's a very slow process. I have little tiny pots of compost and I cut the leaves and put them in and cover the pot with a plastic bag with slits cut in it ... It's one of my great happinesses when they take and finally come into flower.

Keeping up with my own culture and history is important, because I want to be connected with the roots that started me off in life and helped me to grow into who I am. I've spent a bit of time tracing the family history with the help of cousins who are very into that, and the next thing I must do is put the photos in order. Here's an old photo of the Montgomeryshire farmhouse where I was brought up. I have the census record here listing the people who lived in the farm my mother came from, and here's an old photograph of the farmhouse. Recently a lady came here whom I hadn't seen for fifty years. She'd been going through old photographs of us as girls staying with our grandmothers near Welshpool, and she said to herself, "I'm going to find her." And she did find me, because in a small country there's always a connection you can follow. Those connections make you rich and give you a sense that you belong to a place and a history.

I'm surrounded in the flat, as you can see, by other reminders of my roots and my place of belonging. It's part of my own history and the history of my Welsh-speaking culture, to go through the old photos and have these antiques in the flat. Every one has memories and connections for me. The brass kettle is from the farmhouse at home, but the milking stool I got for £1.50 at a country sale. The corner cupboard I bought, but the fluted Coalport china in it came from the chapel after they'd bought a new set for the opening of the new chapel. I enjoy having all these bits of china on the shelves around the flat because every one has a meaning for me. I can tell you where it came from and when I got it and the associations it has in my memory. That old clock on the wall is from home. If it stops I hear the silence and it's terrible. It's 150 years old and doesn't strike properly any more, and I miss the striking at night if I'm lying awake. But it's still there and it's still going, and it's part of my roots. If you have no roots anywhere you don't belong to the history of your own country, and that is a kind of loneliness. Without roots there's an absence of connections, and it's always connections that give you a sense of belonging. The connections you have from your family and your place are a good beginning. But as you go through life you make your own connections and they're part of you too. When you're old you need to have strong connections, because so many things fall away, like your job and your public status and the generation above you. It's then you're glad you've kept up with the friends and the family and the people from the old places. But connecting is a two way process. You have to make connections with other people too, and be alert to their lack of connections. I pop in every day to the old lady next door because she can't go out any more, but I can. So I feel it's something for her if I pass on a tale or two from town. There's nothing like a bit of storytelling to keep you going!

Chapter 11
At home on the road

The nomadic urge

To outsiders the life of New Age travellers may look like escapism, a flight from personal inadequacies, a failure to live up to the demands of our achievement culture. But the travellers see it differently. For them it is a choice between good and evil. The evil they reject is the greed and corruption and destruction of the planet that "straight" workers and home-dwellers bring about (consciously or out of ignorance). The good they seek is the lost Eden before original sin, the simple life which does not deplete the earth's resources or require humans to exploit other humans. It's about making connections, relating to other human beings in a loving and cooperative way, instead of using them to further your own purposes. Julie explains:

> The ideal way of living for me is the tribal life style, which
> I've known at festivals and green gatherings. In those places
> I'm interacting with the people around me as well as having
> my own space. I've known it in the canal network too. That's
> a good kind of floating community. On the canal boats you sit
> outside and you get to know the others. It's usually very
> supportive. You're connected up with the others and you share
> the cooking and the child minding. Everybody knows
> everybody else's business and you look after each other
> because it's quite a fragile, vulnerable existence. Kids and
> vandals interfere with the boats if they get the chance, so you
> look after each other, bail out each other's boats, keep an eye
> on the moorings. The canal people come from a lot of different
> backgrounds, but they stick together. You belong to the tribe.
> You get support and you give support. You don't get that kind

of support any more if you are stuck in a house on a council estate, like I was when I was married.

Although I have this nomadic streak in me I'm a very home-centred person. Just because you're a traveller doesn't mean you have no sense of home. Only your home isn't a little box shutting you off from the world. You're at home on the road or the canal. Home is anywhere you earth yourself. It's the place where you feel right with yourself and with the other people sharing your space, and they feel right with you.

Rose lives in a bender adorned with her favourite Taoist texts, which she has patiently worked in needlework. She believes being a traveller is about the inner as well as the outer journey through life. It is about working for "the rainbow revolution," which will transform people into peace-loving cooperative beings, whose energies go into nurturing the earth and each other. Being a traveller means turning life into a pilgrimage, finding the soul in things, seeking the Way. Sometimes it is the Taoist way, sometimes it is the native American way, but always it is about being at home in the whole earth, and that means turning your back on the fixed abode that is home for most of us. Not being at home is being at home, just as, according to the Tao, or Way:

> Not knowing that one knows is best.
> Thinking that one knows when one does not is sickness.
> Only when one becomes sick of the sickness can one be free
>   from sickness.
> The sage is never sick because he is sick of the sickness.
> Therefore he is not sick.

Another of her chosen texts is from the native American tradition:

> Teach your children what we have taught our children, that
>   the earth is our mother.
> Whatever befalls the earth befalls the children of the earth.
> If people spit upon the ground they spit upon themselves.
> This we know: the earth does not belong to man; man
>   belongs to the earth.

All things are connected like the blood which unites one
    family. All things are connected.
Whatever befalls the earth befalls the children of the earth.
Man did not weave the web of life; he is only a strand in it.
    Whatever he does to the web, he does to himself.

Rose's story

June 1983 I went on the road. It was summer solstice and I
went to Stonehenge for the first time. The man I was with
went for the week of the solstice. He had his bike and I had
mine. After the week he went back. I stayed on. I still travel
there in the spirit every solstice, but I've never been back in
the flesh because '83 was the last year they left the festival
alone. From '84 the massacre began. Pregnant women were
pulled about and kids were cut with the broken glass flying.
The government wanted to stop those kids, and they want to
stop all of us travellers because they are afraid of the rainbow
revolution we are working for. But Stonehenge '83 was still
OK. I got in with the druids, got talking to them, began to
understand a lot of things I'd only half worked out for myself.
And Sid Rawles was there. He used to call himself the King of
the Hippies. He was marrying and baptizing people on the big
stone, with everybody singing and celebrating.
    Then I met a guy called Curly. He was sitting cross-legged
by his fire and I was walking by. I sat down opposite him and
he looked up and said, "Do you want a peanut butter sandwich?" He had one of those old yellow British Rail trucks, and
I moved in with him. Before that I'd only had a small tent. I
stayed with Curly all that summer, and we went to festivals
around the place. At the festivals I used to see little old
ambulances parked-up, and it was always girls living in them.
I said, "I want one of them," and I stuck to that. When I
went back to Milton Keynes August that year to see a friend,
there was this old ambulance sitting outside her council house.
It belonged to the woman my friend had just swopped council

houses with, and she had just left it there. She had no use for
it any more. It was just what I wanted. That was my van.
Only I still had to get the money for it. I left it outside my
friend's house while I went to do the hops with Curly. We
were three weeks in September doing the Guinness hops, and
then I had £300 in my hand, and that was my money for the
van. I was over the moon, but Curly wasn't. He said, "You'll
not be my woman now, you'll only be my neighbour." And
that was that.

It took me months that winter to get the little old ambulance
roadworthy. Then when I got on the road with it at first I
didn't know whether to travel on my own or stick with the
people I knew. Only once did I live any time with other
travellers. That was in a little place outside Aylesbury. Most of
them were people I'd known for years when we were living in
houses. They were as fed up as me. We were all living in little
boxes and working in other little boxes and not having a life.
When I got the van they came and looked at it and said,
"Where you going, Rose?" I told them about the festivals and
said I was going on the road. It ended up a lot of them bought
trucks, buses, old ambulances, and went off to do the festivals
in '84. They saw me and my black cat Toots happy on the
road, living without ties — free to choose my own life. They
thought they could do the same thing — get out of their Milton
Keynes council flats and make their home on the road. But it
didn't work out for a lot of them. I do what I do because I'm
doing it. I'm a traveller but I haven't anything to prove. A lot
of them had something to prove. There was trouble, trouble,
trouble on that site in Aylesbury because they were all trying
so hard to prove they were free.

Freedom's a load of trouble when there's a group. When
you're on your own you don't have to cope with anybody
else's karma. I try not to have bad nasty thoughts about other
people because that's all part of your karma. Some of these
people didn't know that and they would bitch away. They were
spending the months of the winter together incestuously —
having it off with each other to show they were free, and then

bitching about who was having it off with who. It got to be
like Peyton Place. The coach wasn't talking to the truck, and
the truck wasn't talking to the bus, and one day a very dear
brother took a lot of pills to kill himself. I got him to hospital
and said to his partner Dot to look after him. Then I told them,
"I love you," and I pulled out, blowing them kisses. I can't be
doing with other people's heads. All that storytelling is too
much — I mean the way human beings are so two-faced, nice
to your face and bitching away behind your back. That does
my head in. Now most of those ones who went on the road in
the early eighties are back where they were, in their council
flats in Milton Keynes. Freedom turned out to be too much
trouble. My friend Dot's still travelling, but she was born on
the road. Now she has a narrowboat on the canal. That's a
good way to be because those people look after each other. I
would like to do that, only I haven't the money for a boat.
They cost you, boats like that.

Not every site is like that first site I was on, but after that
winter I decided to travel on my own — me and my cat Toots.
The place we ended up was Lake Vyrnwy in the middle of
Wales. I was so happy there because it was the first time in
my life I'd had my own space. Before that there'd always been
Mam or Gran (they brought me up), or my husband and
daughter, or some bloke putting me under pressure to do things
the way they wanted. My time at work wasn't my time. It was
always their time, never my time. I'd been working in an old
people's home for ten years, and they took advantage of me all
the time. They kept putting me on nights and most weekends.
My man and I weren't even seeing each other, and my young
daughter was going off the rails. I couldn't go on like that. I
had to get out, so I gave in my notice. But a week later I was
straight into the spastics through a friend who told me about
the job. That turned out worse again. My time at home became
their time as well as my time at work, because they were
always asking me to do shopping for them, although there
were carers supposed to do that. It invaded my time even
worse. That was April '83. I got out and it was that summer I

went to Stonehenge and my whole life changed. I wasn't made
for living and working in little boxes. I was a traveller.

That first spring and summer at Lake Vyrnwy was a time I
always remember. I was so happy on my own. I got there early
spring and there weren't any visitors driving around that early
in the year. I parked the van in a lay-by along the lake. There
was a little wood where I got firewood for the stove, and Toots
hunted voles and rabbits. He got his own food and sometimes
brought back a rabbit or a squirrel for me to make into stew. I
had my bicycle to go to the village down the road and get
shopping or phone my mother. It was like heaven spending
time on my own by that beautiful lake — fresh water running
down the rocks, pinewoods next to me, no human being to tell
me what to do again. It lasted till one day some ladies drove
up in their car for a picnic in my lay-by. Spring was getting on
and I knew they were only the first. So I moved on.

After I got to Wales I just wanted to stay on there — and I
have — because it's so beautiful. But the first couple of years
I was travelling I was having to go back to Milton Keynes to
sign on and get my money. Then I was signing on in Brecon
for a while, because I lived one summer in the Brecon
Beacons. Once a fortnight I had to go back to wherever I was
signing on. So long as the van was in a safe place that was
OK, but they make it harder and harder for you now to get
your money when you're a traveller.

I had this idea of travelling the whole length of Wales from
the top down. So I made my way up north to Bangor. But I've
never got further south than the middle, because this is the
place I love, this is my place now. It took me about a year to
get here from Bangor, travelling in the van and stopping wherever it felt right. On the way I helped a couple of farmers with
feeding the cattle and with the lambing. I only met other
travellers when I was festivalling or signing on. I believe if
you're on your own and not a threat to anybody you're alright
travelling. Whenever I'd park I'd go straight to the nearest
farm and ask if it was alright. When they realized I was on my
own I wasn't a threat to them. The wives would sometimes

say, "Are you alright? You're very brave, on your own. Are you not scared?" But I wasn't thinking bad thoughts, so I wasn't scared. You build up your own good karma inside your head.

If someone said to me, "No, you can't stop here. Clear off," I'd be gone the next morning. No hassle. I wouldn't rile them. The only trouble I've ever had with straights is kids throwing stones or drunks banging on the van, nothing serious. Sometimes you'd get busybodies telling you what to do and not to do. That was like being back at work, back home in Milton Keynes. One day early on in my travelling life a woman in a car stopped where I was parked up, in Brickhill Woods in Bucks. She said, "Excuse me, excuse me, what are you doing here?" She was furious though it wasn't even her woods, because it was on the Duke of Bedford's estate. "I'm just staying here for a while," I said. In those early days I tried to stay near a church for sanctuary like. I was doing that then. I said to her I'd seen the vicar and it was alright with him. We got talking then and she realized I had no bad feelings towards her village or the people in houses like her. Instead of being furious with me like she'd wanted to be, she was nearly in tears in the end. Yeah, she was moved to tears, but I didn't take advantage. I don't want to build up any bad karma for myself. There's plenty of bad karma around without travellers adding to it. In a couple of days I was gone from there because if anyone starts to invade my space I go, and she'd invaded my space with her bad karma.

When I was travelling around North Wales I didn't give nasty thoughts out so mostly I didn't get nasty things back. I got some real good things back. There was one farm I stayed for a month because the van broke down, and the lady gave me a big box with a dozen pots of her own home-made jam in it and black binliner bags of clothes. Another place one bank holiday a lady done me a huge roast chicken leg — fresh chicken off the farm — which lasted me and my Toots three days. When you get good in you need to give good out. I was doing tapestry bookmarks and giving them away to people. I was working out texts for them from the Bible and the Tao. I did one that said: "If God is for me who is against me?" and ones from the Tao about knowing and not knowing. I've not been lonely travelling with my cat and doing my tapestry and talking to whoever wanted to talk to me. I've always got a diary exercise book I write in, too. Sometimes it's only shopping lists or things to remember. Other times, if my head's not right, I have to write it out in my diary. There's a lot of prayers in those exercise books because I needed to sort out my head. Some of those prayers and thoughts I'd do out in tapestry. I'd sit and listen to the radio and do my tapestry. I'd talk to the people on the farm if they wanted to talk to me. I was respectful of their space and wanted respect for my space, so if they wanted me away I'd go. You can slip away easy when you're on your own. When you're travelling in a group and one turns nasty — back answering the locals and that — the whole lot has to move on. There's no way you can stay even if it's only one of you bad-mouthing the locals. I never bad-mouth, even with the police. I say to them, "I know it's your job to move me on, but I live like this, I'm not doing anybody any harm by the way I live." They've said to me, "How can you live like this?" And I've tried to explain to them. I say, "I've had nothing all my life, for 38 years. Now I've got this van and this is my home. It's my own space and I can go where I want." They look inside the van and see it all clean and tidy, with the bicycle parked outside. But they still don't know what it's about. They don't get it when I tell them, "You get back what you give out. You begin in your own head." Once they shone a torch around the van and said the local farmers were worried about sheep rustling. "Have you a dead sheep in here?" they said. "I'm a vegetarian," I said, "what would I want with a dead sheep in my home?" They laughed and said, "Alright, dear," and left me alone.

It's got a lot worse now with the new Criminal Justice Act. They can get you for "aggravated trespass." There are fewer and fewer places you can be safe when you're a traveller. The culture now is different from when I started off on the road.

There's less trust now all round. The people in the houses
don't trust even each other, so they aren't going to trust
hippies of any kind. They say all hippies are dirty and lazy.
Well, you can't be lazy when you're travelling, because
travelling is hard work. Every day you've got to make sure
you have food, and wood for the stove, and time to go busking
when you're near a town. So it upsets me like when the people
in houses think it's easy and lazy to be a traveller. That poor
old Romany who parked his caravan here last winter was out
every hour of every day after scrap, to turn it into money for
things for the kids. He wasn't lazy, was he? And she was
bringing up all those kids really well. They are lovely kids, but
they wouldn't be any more if they let them go to school. So
they keep them at home and she teaches them reading and
writing herself. If they were at school they'd soon learn bad
language and nick things out of shops and bash each other like
the rest of the schoolkids do. But they get chased after for not
wanting their kids to go and learn bad things at school.

It's getting totally hostile on the road now. I used to cry
when someone would come up to me and get me to move.
Now you'd be in tears the whole time because you can't find a
place anywhere where nobody's going to come up and get you
to move — even if you think you're in the middle of nowhere.
The thing now is to stay in groups when you're travelling. You
have to stick together in groups because there's so much
harassment from the police and farmers. I don't go for groups.
I want my own space. So I'm glad I've got a good quiet place
tucked away in the woods, with me in my old ambulance and
my man in the trailer, and all my animals around me. Because
I'll never find another place like this, with the stream, and the
little birch trees growing up and hiding us, and the woods
around me. I have six cats (Teddy, Janey, Paddy, Lena, Yellow
Cat and Mog Mog), and two rabbits (Blackberry and Lady
Grey, but they usually get called Munchkins). There are the
two cockerels and fourteen hens, but one cockerel's got to go
because I want to put the little ladies in one run and the
cockerels will kill each other if they're put together. I call this

place "William's Rest." William was the white rat I had when
I first came here. The other white rat with the dark hood was
Miss Piggy. When they had eight babies I put some in the
wood and kept the rest. William would sometimes sleep in my
jersey and come down the inside of my sleeve when I had a
snack for him. My man Davy used to take William out to the
pub with him. Sometimes the white rat would appear out of his
sleeve and some woman would start screaming and Davy
would be asked to leave. One night when Davy was drunk and
sleeping it off at a friend's William got out in the night and ate
the toes out of the friend's socks. They still laugh about that
when you mention William the white rat at the friend's place.
So William was a character and that's why I called this place
after him when he died.

This patch of earth I'm on, and my animals, are all part of
the life I'm making here. I'm still on some kind of journey,
even though I'm not on the road these days. I sometimes get
the wanderlust for a while. I don't want to go anywhere in
particular. It's just an impulse inside you to keep moving on. It
would come into my head suddenly I was going to pack up
and go. There's travelling in my blood, because my mother
told me my great-great-grandfather was a traveller from
Ireland, but the thing that started me travelling was the thirty-
eight years I had of being a robot at the beck and call of other
people. Then I discerned the travelling impulse in my blood
and that freed me from everything that was crushing the life
out of me and turning me into a robot.

Once you discern that travelling impulse in yourself and
become a traveller, you belong to a new family — the whole
family of travellers. That first time I went to the solstice at
Stonehenge I just knew those travellers were my family. and I
still feel they're all my family. If I go out to a bender or an
old bus I know they'll put me up and feed me if I need it. And
if they turn up at my place, like Jock and Robbie did recently
for a couple of weeks, there's food and a bed for them,
because we're all part of this family of travellers — even if we
have rows among ourselves like any family. When I go into

town on Thursdays (hippies sign on then) I pass them in the
street and there's a wink and a nod because you want to
recognize each other as part of the family. There's sometimes a
crowd of those kids busking in the supermarket carpark and
bongoing on their drums. I give them sweets and apples,
because it's so hard for them now on the road, and I'm so
lucky to have my old van parked up in those woods. It's so
hard now for travellers that I don't know what will happen. I
think some of the family will be lucky like me, get an acre and
live in peace on a patch of ground that nobody else wants. But
the rest will turn militant because you aren't free to go on the
road now with this latest Criminal Justice Act. The family of
travellers is being made homeless by a police state, and that's
sad, because that's the death of a whole way of life. But some
of us are turning into road protestors, and that's getting us a bit
of sympathy from the straights. Swampy and the tunnellers are
the new kind of travellers, and suddenly they're top of the
pops with the media. Those eco-warriors travel from one
protest to another. They're out to save the planet from death by
traffic, and nobody can say they're idle or lazy. So the rainbow
revolution always finds new ways of carrying on ...

When you're a traveller you have your own values, and you
try to live them. You respect the earth, 'cause the earth is our
mother. So you make your bender out of bendy young
branches and cover them with polythene, That way you're not
cutting down trees. You gather dead wood and not living wood
for your fire, and you live off the land as much as you can.
Like in late summer you gather magic mushrooms — the
"fairy nipples" were early this year, I started finding them as
far back as August. I dry them and pound them in my pestle
and mortar. I get fairly good honey and I mix them into that.
I've got other "naughty" things — my opium poppies as well
as my magic mushrooms. Somebody I know made themselves
ill with those little yellow poppies you get in Wales, but I
think that's because they took too much. You have to have the
balance in everything. Anyway it's winter solstice and there'll
be plenty of hippies flying today on their magic mushrooms. I

barter my magic mushrooms for other things I need. That's
part of being in the family of travellers. You share what you
have, and you don't waste anything. You give it to somebody
who has a use for it, and they do something for you in return.
You don't need that much money when you can barter. It's
good as well because it gets everybody coming up with
something they can do, something they've got to offer other
people. In the robot world nobody wants to know what you
can do. They just want you to do what they say and not
answer back. They haven't time to listen to you. When you
join the family of travellers it's different. There's give and
take. You share whatever there is.

You can't make a home on the road without a good stove.
You can't give out good energies when you're cold or hungry,
so your stove is the main thing when you're travelling. You
can't live right without a stove. That's the first thing you need
in your van or in your bender, because in this climate a
campfire is useless. You can make a stove out of anything —
an old gas cylinder, oil cans, any metal container. You go
tatting on the skips (or did — you could get nicked these days
even for that), on the lookout for flexipipe or old iron drain-
pipe to make the flue. On the road in the van I never had an
oven so I learned to cook everything in one big pot. I used to
make a boiled cake in a big enamelled pot on the stove. I was
almost living on boiled cake at one time. I made it with mixed
dried fruit and oats, marge and brown sugar, milk powder,
lemon and water. Then for a year or two I was almost living
on bean stew because you mix that all in one big pot as well. I
used to sling in green and brown lentils, aduki and mung
beans, onion and garlic and Oxo cubes, and boil it all up. Not
kidney beans — they're too fleshy. That time I was travelling
on my own with my black cat Toots, before I met Davy, my
diet was nearly perfect. I was eating brown rice with raw
vegetables, chopped boiled egg and the occasional can of tuna.
I never bothered with potatoes because they are too heavy for
what you get — only two or three meals in five pounds of
potatoes, but you get an awful lot of meals out of two pounds

of brown rice. Once though we were parked up near a potato field and if somebody came to visit we'd go out with the torches and pick a few potatoes for the guests. There was fifty-seven varieties of potatoes to offer them, because it turned out the field belonged to the university, and they were growing all kinds for an experiment! You can bury potatoes in the ashcan under the stove and bake them like that. They taste great if they're cooked enough. There was another time I was travelling in Norfolk when the peas were ripening. I had these army pants and jacket with pockets all over them. I used to pedal out on my old-fashioned bike and fill all the pockets with handfuls of the ripe peas just before they sent the big machines in to cut them down for the canning factories. I reckon it's OK to rip off the giant companies in your own small way like that, because they rip off the planet in a really big way. You're not doing bad to people. You're fighting the machine and putting the balance right. My head was really strong when I was travelling on my own and eating well like that. Most travellers are veggies, but you shouldn't make a big thing of it. I used to try and explain to the youngsters I met on the road that if somebody cooks you a meal and there's meat in it, you should eat it and be grateful. If you run over a rabbit on the road you've got the makings of a good stew. A rabbit can go with beans and onions and garlic or whatever you have. You come across hedgepigs in traffic accidents as well. I haven't tried baking them though I know how you do it. You wrap them in mud and when they're baked long enough the spikes come off with the dried mud.

Now I'm with Davy my diet's ruined because he's into supermarket junk food and he's dragged me down with the food he eats. The rubbish I eat now is bogging me down. I'm trying not to make a big thing of it, but I can feel the way I'm eating now is real bad. My good energies are low. I know when I'm giving out good energies. It goes up and down with the kind of food you eat and the way you give out to the people you meet.

Living with Davy has made me a meat eater, but he's taught

me a whole lot as well, and he is my man. Whatever happens I stick by him. I'm an earth mother, see, and he knows that. He knows I'm here for him and he can always come back to me. I learned to skin animals by Davy showing me how to do a mouse first. Then I skinned guinea pigs. We've eaten stewed guinea pigs. They're a dark red meat with a gamey sort of smell. I just skin them and gut them and stew them with potatoes and onions and vegetable cubes.

I got good enough at skinning to skin a sheep we found caught in a fence, dead, and a dog that had been run over on the road, squirrels, rabbits, a calf ... We've used the dogskin and the rest in the bender for rugs and hangings. When you're a traveller you don't waste anything. You find a use for everything and you don't destroy anything. You make your home wherever you find yourself. You respect that place for as long as you're there. Home is what you make for yourself out of whatever there is. You never take more than you need of anything, and you try to give something back for what you have taken. You're one of the family of humans and animals and all living things, and you try to live with them in peace same as you hope they'll live in peace with you. All a traveller is trying to do is just be at home in the only earth there is, and share it with others, and not be one of the little people in the little boxes. Because the little people don't care about anything beyond their nice little box homes ...

Chapter 12
The electronic home

Surfing the Net

Electronic networking is making the global village an everyday reality, for work and play and social relating. Enthusiasts in the new technology may not know the people who live in the house next door, but they regularly communicate with people across the globe who share their interests and provide mutual diversions. The Infobahn, the information superhighway, is rapidly bringing about the third communication revolution. The spread of the printed book was the first, the universal telephone was the second, and the Internet is the third. Who still needs a place-based community when you can link up with an ever-expanding electronic community? Now you can build your own social networks according to personal choice, instead of having to put up with the contingency of neighbours and the clash of life styles where you live and work. But there are snags and snarl-ups on the Infobahn. The electronic superhighway is attracting many more men than women. Is it in danger of providing a new escape route for youngish males with poor social skills, who prefer the virtual world of the Internet to the real world of face-to-face encounter? Is it encouraging the next generation to hone their technical knowledge at the expense of their emotional intelligence? Is the new God Supernerd cruising the airwaves, and interconnectedness only electronic? Here is a female enthusiast's view of the Net:

Christabel's story

Christabel (40) is the information technology specialist in a big university library. She has access to the Internet at home and at work, and is very much at home on the World Wide Web. But she finds the Net a rather macho community, with far more males than females participating (unless the females are using male pseudonyms, because you can be who you like in cyberspace). But, she says, there is a new joke going the rounds among "us lady librarians": "We play with the mouse now instead of standing on a chair and screaming." She says:

> I've just got the first issue of a new Internet mag. I find it really irritating although it's got loads of information about things I'm interested in. It's quite macho and uses heavy sports jargon. "Surfing the Net," the phrase that's got on in the last few years, is typical macho jargon, growing out of the image of bronzed he-men on Bondi beach, hanging about in the water being bored while they wait for the big wave that makes it all worth waiting for. The general style irritates me no end, because it's so Wow! and Gosh! and radio-hammish. There's a *Boys' Own* flavour about it with lots of jargon carried over from boys' comics. Like Terry Pratchett is interviewed in the first of a series of profiles they call "Infonauts." That name "Infonauts" carries for me overtones of man alone surfing on the great information superhighway, going where no man has ever been before — out there conquering cyberspace. Well, all I can say is, *"Don't* beam me up, Scotty Nerd, so long as it stays so macho in cyberspace."

> But leaving aside the macho and nerdish cult elements, I have to say that since I started using the Internet I've found it fantastic. Sending an e-mail is an immediate connection with friends or colleagues anywhere in the world. I can communicate with people wherever they are, in a way that combines the best of writing and phoning. E-mail brings back the written word, but it's more like talking to someone than writing a letter. If everyone had access to the Net it would be revolutionary. It would be like when people learned to pick up a phone and forgot how to write letters. It's developing it's own etiquette. It's typical of the juvenile jargon that you call that "Netiquette." Part of the Netiquette is that you don't "shout," that is you don't use upper-case letters. "Spamming" too is not on. That means sending out the same message to all the people on more than one network list (usually for advertising

purposes), or blocking somebody's mail list with the same message over and over again.

The way I use the Net has a number of strands. One strand is communicating with individuals — friends or colleagues — and building up my networks at home and at work. Another strand is getting on to the Internet and logging on to remote services, getting information out on anything from the trivial to the totally interesting. That's the main thing I do at home. There's for instance a North American database on popular music which I can download on to my PC. I wanted the words for Tracy Chapman songs, and the words for Patsy Cline's *Sweet Dreams*. One Sunday afternoon I was fiddling about on my guitar trying to remember the words of *Sweet Dreams,* and it was fantastic just being able to fool about on the Net and get the words and the chords downloaded on to a disc so I can bring them up on the screen whenever I need reminding. For me personally the Net means the ease of being able to browse around the world and access information on some distant computer. The Net shrinks the world, at work and at home. Or to put that the other way round, it expands your personal boundaries at work and at home. You can go global. It gives me the beginnings of much closer professional links with colleagues all round the world, in North America and Australia as well as in Europe. There's the challenge, too, of getting hold of any info you want on anything, and also downloading software packages on to your own disc and getting them to work as a program. You sometimes get "boo files" which you can get instruction for "debooing" and "unzipping." One thing that fascinates me is that challenge of getting at files and making the software work. The other big thing is the global communities you can get into. You're at home in the big wide world. You can go anywhere, find out anything, even while you're just sitting in your little terrace house in your little city street.

There's something for everyone in the Internet Yellow Pages, and they're expanding exponentially. You don't just get access to work information or official information. It's very much part of your home life too. If you're into cat mania like us, you soon discover that "Basic Cat Care" is a FAQ (frequently asked question) on the Net. So you can see if anyone else has got a cat like ours that cries in delight when you open a second bottle of wine in the evening, because it knows you'll throw down the cork for him to chase. You can dialogue in real time about cats, or about alt.sex if you feel like it. The Yellow Pages have headings like "Romance and the Internet" and "Alt.sex wanted." You don't even know if the people you're in with are m or f, because you can assume a different gender on the Net if you want. You can reveal as much or as little of yourself as you want to, so you have elements of choice and control that you don't always have in the real worlds of work or home.

I'm a lurker. I tend to subscribe but I don't contribute. I'm lurking there on the Net in the shadows reading other people's messages, and only occasionally responding when I am moved to do so. World Wide Web is really user friendly because it uses natural language. I'm a lurker, so I mainly browse around to see what's on offer, without looking for anything in particular or having anything in particular to contribute myself. It's a new kind of social life, so you don't know what will come up. You can come across anything from recipes to the complete text of the Bible which you can search through using whatever search words you choose — if that's what turns you on. I was browsing around one Sunday and got a list of recipes organized according to ingredients. I homed in on my favourite garlic, and got a recipe for "Forty cloves of garlic chicken" which I've tried and found to be good. You can download your favourite stories from classic texts like *Alice in Wonderland* or Dickens' *Bleak House,* because Project Gutenberg stores the texts of writers who are out of copyright. But it ain't ever going to replace the book (like you hear some idiots pontificating), because what you get is just a file of text with none of the qualities of the book. Whereas there's a CD Rom of *Halsbury's Statutes,* which *does* look like the printed volume, so you can use the screen version like a desk top,

literally, browsing and putting in book marks and creating
your own links between volumes, as well as doing fast text
searches for whatever topic you're looking for. I haven't seen
anything as good as that CD Rom on the Internet yet, but it is
very near.

I'm sure commercial interests will get in on the Net and
make loads of money out of it. But at the moment there's still
masses of stuff you can get absolutely free. You can strike up
dialogues on an ever expanding number of subjects with people
everywhere, so it gives you a world wide community to belong
to. I like that, because I don't want to be labelled in quaint
old-fashioned ways, like where I come from, or who my family
are, or the street where I live. I want to be out there, connected
up with the rest of the world, finding things in common with
people everywhere. There's a kind of democracy on the Net
which means everybody can link up with everybody else. You
can e-mail President Clinton or Terry Pratchett (if that turns
you on) as well as your friends in Oakland, Cal. or Gosforth,
Lancs. And Lislink (a Library and Information Science service
I'm in on because of my job), for example, is open to inputs
by Mabel Nerd, new library assistant, as well as to inputs by
Big Man librarians. It's more personal than other ways of
communicating. It's a surprisingly intimate medium, with
people soon picking up the jokey, personal style that's
considered "cool" — or whatever the latest word is for
what's OK. Of course when it's more personal there's a
down side as well as an up side. A rude message came
through recently from some American librarian blasting
British librarians for being the "information poor." That's
not Netiquette. That's a flame. But a lot depends on the way
it is done. When you start sending and receiving messages
you're not sure how to get the style right, but you soon pick
up on keeping it light and making it personal, even if it's
work. I found at work that you move easily from the working
stuff on to the personal — "Next meeting's in London on
such and such a day. Fancy a drink?" I find myself using
e-mail as well when I want to avoid formality and possible

confrontational situations. You can cover yourself at work by
sending your boss a casual e-mail about something new you're
doing, rather than putting it to him more formally and maybe
making it an "issue."

The side that fascinates me is the home access to ever-
expanding information and services. The fibre optic cable is
coming down our street soon, because we're in the
Metropolitan Area Networks scheme. That will change things
because once the cable is passing the door you have the
potential for getting video on demand, graphics, all sorts of
advice and shopping services. I don't think shopping services
will ever be a big thing. Shopping services are bound to be
boring because it's more fun going down the shops. But other
leisure things would be fun for me. I could, for example, visit
all the art collections of the world without leaving my own
house. I could use Mosaic, say, with World Wide Web, to
download the pictures in the Vatican art collection on to my
own PC. And instead of walking to the public library in the
rain on a Saturday afternoon you could access whatever you
wanted in your own home. It's changing the way you get the
information you need as well. Using the Internet is starting in
schools, so when the present kids grow up they'll want to get
their info that way. Already in the US government information
is going on the Net. At the moment in Britain you still have to
go to your local DSS offices to get info, but you could access
all that in your own home with your own ID.

Being enthusiastic about the Net doesn't necessarily mean
you have to turn into a house-bound nerd — the sort who can't
face real people and has greasy pizzas delivered so as not to
miss anything exciting in cyberspace. You wouldn't have to go
out to boring places for information and support systems.
You'd have all that at home. But you could then go out for
different reasons, better reasons. You'd have more time to go
for a walk, say, and enjoy the countryside in whatever way you
want — pubs, paragliding, whatever. You'd have more time to
lurk in your local leisure centre, or in B & Q if you're DIY
fanatics like us.

The only scary thing about it all is that if you rely on electronic networks for all your information there could be an absence of alternative info. You might not get access to non-mainstream ideas outside the control of big business and government interests. Take feminism for instance. Texts written, and interchanges in the feminist movement are not going to have much of a look-in on the Net, because somebody's got to pay a lot of money and give the go ahead to get information on the Net. So the big questions are who's going to control what goes on the Net, and who is going to have access to it. It worries me that there's always going to be vast numbers of people who can't afford to have access, in this country and in the third world countries. You'll get a new range of underprivileged — the electronically underprivileged. The government could make it even harder than it is now for the information poor to find out what they're entitled to, if they closed down the DSS offices and expected people to have electronic access to all that information.

There's another question I sometimes worry about. Is it unsociable to do things electronically? If you're at home on the Net does that mean you're down and out in the traditional meaning of home? Is getting on to the Net so very different from sitting around the communal fire passing on your tribe's songs and stories and store of wisdom? I don't think so. At work and at home I've found you expand your social contacts on the Net. You're still you, only more so, because you have more choices of who to communicate with, and that brings out more sides of you. You always have the choice of lurking or being an active contributor when you feel like it. It's not so very different from the old ceilidhs when there were listeners as well as performers, and (if you were lucky) you might meet the occasional stranger with news from the big wide world beyond your shut-in community. There's a crit you often hear, that electronic networking is cutting people off from each other, distancing us from personal contact at work and at home and in dealings with officials. I don't think it's like that. With officials you might have more control getting your answers from the Net and not having to interface with officials who are not great at social contacts anyway, and these days are often remote behind thick glass for security reasons, which is not exactly welcoming. My social life and leisure is expanding on the Net. I can dialogue with people who have the same interests, and I can download all sorts of stuff I want, from recipes to guitar chords to cat mania. Of course there's a downside, just like there is anywhere you try having a social life. There's the macho mystification, like in the first issue of this new Internet mag, which announces that "This magazine is going to change your life!" when it's really just a bunch of wimps doing something very simple, once you get through the mystification barrier.

When you're dialoguing on the Net you also run the risk of wimpish nerds sending messages like, "I like to keep abreast of affairs" and "God knows we all need a bit of breast" and other boring little nerd jokes. But we've always had to put up with that kind of chat in the local pub, and it's harder to get away from it in the pub than on the Net. On the Net you're more in control of who you talk to and about what. You can make your own community instead of being stuck with the one you find yourself in. Old Style community gave you no choice at all. You put up with your neighbours, and you were under pressure to conform or get out. Electronic networking is the ultimate choice. You choose your community for yourself, and you have the whole world to choose it from.

But if you make your home on the Net how much time and energy does that leave you for home in the real world? Some cyberfreaks eventually lose touch with real-world home and community, and take off into cyberspace for good. At the other end of the spectrum are those who see the Internet as a way of strengthening or recreating old style community, as well as giving people the chance of global networking and expanding their *too* close-knit communities. Residents in the little village of Kington in the Welsh marches, for example, are taking part in an experiment to find out how this rural community of two thousand souls might benefit from telecottaging and hooking into the global village. Utopian surfers believe in merging the best of old-style community with new style networking. They point to the Net's potential for reconnecting people in local communities which have become fragmented and have stopped talking to each other. Their dream is an electronic recycling of "the pre-industrial revolution culture, when most folks didn't live in overcrowded cities, travel on overcrowded roads and infrequent trains, or breathe polluted air. This isn't yearning for a return to the values of a bygone age either, but a practical solution to urgent problems facing the entire world" (Net guru William Poel speaking).

But how likely is this optimistic scenario of cybertopia, where old and new community virtues are merged and clothed in a seamless electronic robe? The Net can only mirror the values of our time. so not surprisingly it reflects back to us all the individual yearnings of our acquisitive age, with our in-groups, our style fiefdoms and our peer group conformities. Lonely cyberhearts seek the perfect mate on Cyberotica, which came online in 1994. Cyberdiners can satisfy their appetites in the London café Cyberia, which provides a line of Pentium PCs for customers to get on the Internet and chat with global villagers rather than speaking to each other over their cappucinos.

We cannot ignore the tidal wave of new services flooding on to the Net, for work and leisure, for information and fun, for chatting and dating, for virtual sex and virtual friends. How then can you belong to the electronic community without losing sight of the real people around you in home and community? It is too late to bury our heads in the sand and pretend the electronic community doesn't exist, because that is to crave virtual unreality. Nor can you disappear into your electronic home and shut out everyone who is not into your Mondo 2000 technocool life-style. Re-making home for the millennium is not just about making real homes hospitable to the Internet. It is about making the Net more hospitable to the whole people we are, with our continuing human yearnings for relating to others in family and community.

Matt, a computer student in his twenties, believes IT can bring life back into the home, make home more hospitable to people's emotional needs well as their "control freak" tendencies:

In most places now you build your own networks. You can
choose your friends and link up with them wherever they are.
My electronic house will have the communications technology
for keeping up my emotional support networks — work and
social life. An important part of my scenario of home is
working from home. When I've finished studying I'd like a job
where I could work from home and be linked up with the
external environment by my range of communications systems
like the e-mail and the Internet. Because working from home is
coming back now, even when you live in the country like I do.
Electronic networking means you're not cut off. You can work
and live in the same place. That's what I'd like to do, because
I would like to spend a lot of time in this electronic home I'm
designing. It will be an environment I really like, with my own
private space, and my work space, and hospitable spaces for
grown up friends and visiting kids. I'll be able to work to my
own timetable. I'll be able to do as much networking as I need
to keep in touch with people at work, and friends, and with all
the amazing stuff on the information superhighway that I might
want to know about. My friends would appreciate my
electronic home, because they're thinkers and I could
communicate with them wherever they are. That's important to
me because I'm not a pub or party going person who likes
mixing casually and chatting to people I happen to meet. Even
with real friends coming to visit I'd still want private space for
myself in the house as well as shared space. Home only
becomes claustrophobic when people have no space of their
own to go, and are pushed together with the other people in
the house. It's being able to choose that's important. In my
house you'll have your own private space to go to when you
need to. Feeling at home is about having control over your
environment. Everybody needs too an environment that you
can change to suit your activities and your moods. Some
people move the furniture around or have different colour
schemes. In the electronic house I could do it by designing a
system which uses optical fibres to reconstruct all the
constellations of the real heavens, say, on the bathroom walls

and ceiling, so that when you put the lights out you're no longer in a room but lying in a bath under the heavens — preferably with a glass of Baileys in your hand ...

My electronic house would be very hospitable to kids, my own or visiting kids. They should not be dumped in a corner or told to be quiet and read a book. So I'd have a secret room for them, an electronic version of the treasure chest we used to hide coloured beads and things in when I was a little kid in London. We used to give kids a map of the house to help them find the treasure. I'd incorporate into the secret room theatre and funfair effects, and fantastic lighting effects, to help kids have fun. Kids need magic, they need to explore. In my electronic house the treasure chest might be in cyberspace, but what's the difference between real and virtual magic?

Chapter 13
Running on empty

Re-making home with the poor and the abused

Elaine is a teacher in a residential home for disturbed children. Their images of home are stunted or distorted by the abuse and neglect and emotional chaos that they associate with the place other people call "home." Elaine lives in a staff house in the grounds, and so she meets the children around the place when her official timetable is over for the day. In these encounters, as well as in her formal work, she often has insights into their emotional illiteracy in the meanings of home.

Elaine's story

I find myself contributing to a kind of homemaking for them. I try to give them something stable whether I'm on duty or off duty. The kids know I'm living there, and I let them know I'm there for them when, say, they meet me walking the dog in the evening. It means something special to these kids if I say to them in school, "I was thinking about you last night," or, "I was thinking up a project for you to do." It's special because in their lives hardly anybody has ever thought about them or cared about them. So when I show them that I've been thinking about them and preparing something for them personally to do, they will often come up and cuddle you, they're so pleased that anybody's thinking about them. For them home has been a disaster. They've had none of the ordinary things of home, like just the everyday contact with people who give you support and security. One of the girls I teach has had thirty five "homes," and thinks nobody remembers her. So I try to hold her in my mind, even when I'm not with her, and I find her memorable, and I let her know I'm doing that, because it gives her some feeling of home.

I took some of the kids swimming one evening and they asked me, "Are you taking us as a teacher?" They said to me, "If you go in the water with us you're more like a friend than a teacher." I went in the water with them, and that too was part of trying to give them a sense of home, although they are in this institution. That's one of the hardest things for them to develop, that sense of what home might be, because they have never had a home that taught them a sense of respect for themselves. They've never learnt respect for their own space or for anybody else's space. Social Services tend to throw money at them and expect that to work, assuming that if you give people decent things around them they'll respect them and look after them. But it doesn't work because the kids have never learned about making home-space good for themselves or for the people they live with. They're given beautiful rooms but they rubbish them. All of them fling stuff up into the air and trash belongings, because they have no feeling for home or what it should be like or why you should bother to respect it. They get new clothes every couple of months. They have a chance to choose their own clothes. But it means nothing to them having their own things and looking after them. They take other kids' clothes and wear whatever they can grab if they take a fancy to it, because they sense that nothing is really theirs.

They act up all the time to grab your attention as well, because otherwise they don't know who they are. Nobody at home ever paid any attention to them except they were acting up, and then they belted them for acting up. For these kids home is associated with chaos. So they try to create that chaos wherever they are, because, I suppose, that's the only kind of home they've ever known. I'm not sure how you would really give them a feeling of home as a good and safe place to be in. As from September we're hoping to start up a foundation workshop where the kids will go through learning by play. It's to re-establish a sense of security and self-development in them, which they've missed out on. We're trying to open up

blocked channels of development, to re-start them with the
things they never had in the homes they've come from. They
need to learn the most basic things you expect from home,
because they've missed out on so much. They have no sense of
security, like knowing the food will be there, that mum or dad
will be there, that there'll be someone at home to take your
side if there's a threat of some kind on the street or at school.
So we're going to try taking them back to the beginning and
see if we can maybe bring back a sense of self, a sense of
security, a sense of home.

The Fourth World movement

Aid in Total Distress (ATD) — the Fourth World movement — began
in 1957 when Father Wresinski, a Polish priest, built up a network of
volunteers to work with the socially excluded and listen to them on
their own level about what life is really like in the worst housing
estates. Now there are Fourth World family centres, nursery schools,
life-skill workshops, arts centres, in eight European countries and
across the world, where the poorest families can meet and do creative
work on their own futures. Karen (30), a volunteer worker, explains
how the Fourth World movement works:

Karen's story

I'm on a three months' training course for volunteers. We
work with the very poor to help them keep their families
together. I've been mainly down at the family centre in Surrey
where families come for short stays. There was a Christmas
stay of ten days this year and I found it really amazing being
with the families. There were ten families, some with children
in care, including a couple who had only been allowed an
hour's access to their children a few days before Christmas.
The more that can be done so that children don't go into care
the better, so the stays with us are a time away from everyday
problems, a chance for families to be creative together rather

than just struggling along trying to cope with the difficulties of daily life. Parents can see their children doing creative work, and children can see their parents making things or fixing things in our workshops. At Christmas we had computer workshops and woodwork workshops. One mother made a set of shelves to take home to display her children's special things on while they are in care. Somebody else made a cassette holder. A twelve year old boy I was working with made an elephant jigsaw. What I was doing was being with them in the workshops, or doing driving or cleaning. Everybody's invited to help keep the place clean, but the families are having a break so the helpers like me do most of the cleaning.

How does the centre affect people? Well, I remember there was somebody at the beginning of the Christmas stay who was very stretched and tense, and by the end she was far more relaxed. But so would I be if I'd been entirely controlled by strangers like she was in her home life. What we're doing here is not trying to change people into different people from who they are, because who are we to change people? It's about valuing people for who they are. The people who come here are in extreme poverty. It's not just financial poverty but a whole lot of poverties to do with poor health and bad housing and children in care ... Some are not able to read or write, and many have problems getting their voices heard by the authorities they come up against in their everyday struggles to keep their home together. Our movement is dealing with a particular kind of poverty — generational poverty — where people are excluded and stay excluded from one generation to the next. Their children do not achieve in school and often get taken into care because they come from families that are themselves excluded from "respectable" society. They have all the difficulties piling up on them. They're out of work, in poor health, dirty — because of not washing enough or not having anywhere to wash properly in their bottom-of-the heap housing. They are not treated the same as the rest of us because they are seen as "not worth anything," so not deserving anything. They are constantly bombarded with indignity and injustice because of being seen as excluded, as unacceptable.

What I've learned as a volunteer here is just being with people as they are, accepting them. I came with a number of questions in my mind about poverty. I was feeling there's a difference between poverty here and poverty in the third world, and that third world poverty must be worse. But I realize now that poverty covers a wide range of things. The poverty we work with here has an injustice side which comes from these people being treated as excluded persons. I realize there's something wrong in a society where there are people who are so excluded, so much not treated like other people, not given the right to have a home and family or be "respectable." These people are so excluded they're invisible as far as most people are concerned. Somebody working here was trying to find out the best way of getting in touch with the poorest families in an area. She said you can't find out by asking, "Who are the poor?" Because these families are not known to people, being excluded. So she asked a different question. She went round teachers and doctors and found the excluded ones by asking, "Where do you fail in this locality?" The teachers would point to certain children, and the doctors would refer to certain patients, and people living in the neighbourhood would talk about problem neighbours. Those are the people who come here.

Our movement is made up of the families themselves, the volunteers like me, and the Friends who do all they can to make links between the excluded and the rest of society. It is about creating community which recognizes that nobody is an isolated individual, nobody is excluded. Everybody is linked up with the rest of society by being included in a group or a community. During my time here I have been changed by the changes I have seen are possible in others. I have done practical manual work like everybody else, because that is part of learning skills and using them in everyday life — painting and decorating or woodwork or mailing magazines or whatever. It is also part of learning to work with other people. The important thing is for people to have a group where they belong and find they can do something that needs doing. Working together with the families is what it's all about. As well as working in the family centre I go out and visit families. Other volunteers move into a locality and run street libraries — reading books or doing computer workshops on the run down housing estates where the excluded are to be found. Whatever you do it is a way for the excluded to become part of groups and get some basic security and ordinary human dignity in their everyday lives.

I find the Fourth World movement amazing because of the consistency between its aims and the way we work. I've never come across an organization before that has so much internal integrity. The groundwork of everything we do is where people are in extreme poverty. People in poverty are the starting point for re-working home. There have to be some places where things work for them, even though things go wrong for them with so many aspects of home — children in care or threatened with going into care, needing basic literacy if they're going to be able to read even officials' letters ... Here we are giving them a place to come where they can see that things can work, and they are involved in the working. It's only short stays because we haven't the funding for the longer stays of six or nine months we used to do.

Although their homes are places where they are often *not* learning to care and be cared for, taking them from their homes into "homes" is not the answer because that deprives them of home and family. The family is the only identity and security even if lots of it is negative in terms of good upbringing. Just taking that negative away does not bring something positive, because, as one girl in care said, "I feel poor when you tell me to speak and then you don't listen to what I say. I feel miserable when I can't say who I am to anybody."

The voices of the excluded

Children's voices

Listen to the voices of children from some of the families that the
Fourth World movement has worked with, for they tell us just what
everyday life is like when you are one of the excluded. School can be
a problem for a start. Derek (7) says:

> I don't like school, the other people in the class are snobs.
> They're always talking about models or electronics, and we're
> not interested in talking about things like that, we want to talk
> about other things. Well, about what was on TV the night
> before and well, nothing really ... In school they don't care
> about what I know. The others don't listen to me. It's because
> of where I live.

And Doreen says:

> I was scruffy going to school. My mother could only afford a
> uniform for my older sister when she went to secondary
> school. None of us others had uniforms. When I was eleven
> and went to the school they wore a gym slip and a blouse and
> cardigan. Well, I didn't have the right things but I had just an
> ordinary skirt and cardigan. They were the right colours but
> not the proper things. Some of the kids use to make fun of me
> because I was so scruffy. I sometimes had a fight with a few
> of them.

But it can be equally humiliating if you get the right clothes through
charity. Another girl remembers not with gratitude but with continuing
shame "the day all the children brought clothes for me. They brought
dresses and pants and socks and I had to try everything on in front of
them."

Excluded children especially suffer as they get older from the
unending boredom of not going anywhere and not doing anything:

It's embarrassing at school to be asked what you've done or where you've been at the weekends, or what you've seen on holiday. You don't know what to say. We never go anywhere. We don't talk about holidays in our family.

We just get bored. We're not allowed to play in the street because of the cars, so we stay indoors and we make so much noise that they're always shouting at us to keep quiet. If we fight too much and they get really fed up, they send us outside again.

But then "on the streets you get bored so you go around breaking things and getting into trouble."

It's not all doom and gloom. Once Nancy's father bought them a big colour TV they couldn't afford, and she knew just why:

You have to understand my father. He said, "Just because I'm on unemployment doesn't mean you won't have a good Christmas." So to make himself feel better he wanted to buy something really big, to forget all about being out of work. You can't be miserable all the time. You have to understand him. For days we didn't eat meat, but that doesn't matter. The important thing is to keep going.

Imagining other ways the world could be helps some excluded children to keep going. They have their dreams of what home could be like one day, when they get out of the poverty trap. But even their dreams may be tinged with scepticism, for they know the score from when they're very young. A young teenager says:

Often I look out of the window and see the houses all around, full of people who have all sorts of problems, like us. The noise from the traffic going past our house goes round and round in my head and the cars never stop, day or night ... On the other side of town there are some really nice houses where it's quiet and peaceful. Those families haven't got people up-stairs who shout at their kids all the time, or next door neigh-bours who fight, or water that you hear running and doors that are banging all night, or televisions and trannies turned up loud so they can't hear the noise the neighbours are making. They're alright and good luck to them, but do they know how lucky they are? Sometimes when I'm at the window I start dreaming ...

Then I say to myself, those nice houses aren't for me ... The way things are, my life will always be like this ... slums, noise, shouting ... I can see myself living the same way, I already shout at my little brother. It's the same thing with my schoolwork: I'd like to pass my exams and work with children. But look at my Dad, he can't get any work ... At 16 I'll get any old job.

Younger children still keep their dreams of home intact:

"It would be a large house where you could invite every-body, people, animals, everybody. Everybody should do that."

"In my house there would be beautiful plates because ours are all broken, and plenty of chairs because we don't have enough."

"My house would be all blue. You know sometimes the houses are all grey, and that's sad."

"If somebody had a baby and no home to go to, I'd take it, so the baby would have a place to live and friends and good food. Because when you're little it's not much fun. You have to be careful with babies."

"I'd like to live in a place that's nice and quiet and has clean walls and lots of room. A place where there's no dogs or pee in the halls and stairs, without people who always complain, like that nut who gets his shotgun when someone messes with his motor bike. And they should have grass for us to play on."

Working with poor families to re-make home

Fourth World volunteers work in partnership with poor families, not in control of them. The aim is for them to move from the powerless-ness of being excluded to feeling that can take more responsibility for their own lives. There has to be a starting point in the ordinary things of everyday life, like children's schooling — but the school has to reach out as well, for one-sided moves are never enough. Sally is a parent who has been through the mill and knows the problems of shifting yourself from inertia to connectedness:

Sally's story

A few years ago my children brought home a school note asking parents to come to a meeting. It was to do with "Home Link." At this particular time I was feeling very much alone due to a marriage breakdown and a lot of problems. The children kept asking me to go to the meeting. At first I kept putting it off, then one day I went. There were a few parents in a room, reading. I felt very nervous but a Sister was not long in making us feel welcome by offering us tea and asking our names. She explained to us about the group she was setting up. It was all to do with getting us involved with our children at school and how it could help our children with school work.

At first when she explained we would read and get involved with our children in the Home Link room, the first thing I thought about was, "I'll never be back," the reason being I was not very good at school work when I was at school. I felt embarrassed anyway.

Time went by and I started going to the meeting once a week. I started to get very much involved with the school. My two girls were very happy that I was involved. I started to feel very confident and worked with my girls and school work. We all got very much involved in the community. We did plays together, reading, and writing. I became a play leader in a crèche. My children and I got more together. Home Link was the best thing that ever happened. I would like to see more of this happening in schools.

But many families have trouble breaking out of the exclusion from community that passes from one generation to the next. Some can make it, but only with the right kind of support. Lynn knows for herself the difficulties of breaking the circle of defeat and failure:

Lynn's story

What I would say is you have got to break the circle sometimes. Children who have been brought up in care and different
institutions, it makes it difficult for them to be parents if they
have not experienced love and security.

To help the child you must help the mother, the parents.
But too often, rather than helping the mother to help the child,
the child is taken into care and separated from its natural
bonds.

I was taken into care at the age of six. My parents too
came from a deprived background and I suffered more in care
than I would have suffered if I had been staying with my
parents. I was physically and mentally abused and I went to
fifty-two different institutions which scarred me for life. I
found that after all the damage they had done, they left me to
cope on my own when I was eighteen. Since leaving care at
eighteen, I had long stay admissions to various different
psychiatric hospitals. I was not classed as mentally ill, but
emotionally ill with personality disorders that stemmed from
my childhood.

There are so many families who are desperate to keep the
family together. These are the families that cry out to be
helped. Why take the short cut that anybody can take by taking
the child into care? They don't find enough ways to help the
parents help the children.

The pain that goes with separation is unbelievable when
people love each other. If you bang someone with a hammer
on the knee, at first it will hurt but after a while you get so
numbed that you don't feel anything.

I struggled very hard to keep my daughter when she was
about a year old. I went to a mother and baby unit. There I
met a wonderful person called Judy. Judy and others try very
hard to keep families together and when I left she continued to
play a great part in both my daughter's and my life.

Telling your family's story

Fourth World volunteers work with individual families to support them in re-making home, as Judy did with Lynn and her baby daughter. Another way they help families out of the cycle of deprivation is to record the family's story in a "family monograph." The family monograph does not change anything on its own, but it helps the family understand what is happening to them and maybe see a way of breaking the downward spiral. It also adds flesh to the bones of poverty statistics and so suggests ways of slowing or halting generational poverty. The families themselves, or with the help of a volunteer, write down their family's story. They go back to their parents and grandparents if possible, and come forward to their present hopes and projects. They talk about the things they have managed to do for their families, and the things they have not managed to do. They say what they do and where they turn for support in everyday problems. They describe their connections with their surrounding community, or their inability to make these connections. They try to explain what is happening to them as a family and how they might find a way forward for themselves. The best way of understanding what the "family monograph" is about is to read these extracts from Gloria and Peter's story (partly written in their own words, and partly in the volunteer's words). During their stays at the Fourth World family centre in Surrey Peter and Gloria have been gradually learning to connect better with each other, with their children and with other people. Going over the story of their family and writing it down has helped them along the road to emotional intelligence in their family and community lives.

Gloria and Peter's story

1978 was a hard year for Peter. His family had thrown him out, he was sleeping rough and had no work. He had tried to commit suicide and was put under strong medication. This was when Gloria entered his life:

Before I first met Gloria I had nothing to look forward to. I was drinking and ruining myself, wasting my life. Then along came Gloria and I've stayed with her ever since. It changed me a lot. She understood what I'd been through. I couldn't talk to my old man, I couldn't talk to my mum. I couldn't talk to anyone but I could talk to Gloria.

Their relationship and then Gloria's pregnancy gave real meaning to their lives but neither her family nor the social services approved of the situation and problems piled up ... Gloria's mother signed her daughter into care and the young mother was placed in a mother and baby home. The Home's records of Gloria are totally negative; they criticized her lack of hygiene and care for the baby, and her violence towards the staff. Gloria says she suffered greatly from being under observation and from the threat that her baby would be taken away from her if she did not conform to requirements. Peter visited Gloria and baby Laura almost every day ... the young couple felt that nobody realized how much they wanted to be a family; nobody wanted to listen to and understand their hopes and ambitions. Peter wanted to marry Gloria as soon as she was old enough. The social worker was against this idea ...

When Peter and Gloria first came to Frimhurst (the family centre), they kept very much to themselves, protecting themselves against any potential criticism. They used to spend entire days locked up in their room. Gloria's inexperience and fear of others made her rely on Peter, and he enjoyed her dependency on him. Gloria's tasks remained undone ... the other families complained of the smell, the dirt ... These criticisms made the young couple even more insecure and withdrawn ...

They had to discover what it is to have a home and to live with neighbours, so many things for which their experience had not prepared them ... but they found themselves accepted as parents and as a family. Because of the support of the other families and the Fourth World volunteers they gradually realized they were not alone and slowly came to make friends.

At Frimhurst we learned to communicate with each other.
There should be more places like Frimhurst, so that young
people like me and Gloria can learn to communicate and know
what the big world is about. You have to learn by your
mistakes. In most cases social services don't give you that
chance. Every time you put your foot wrong they say they will
take the children away. In Frimhurst you can learn.

As Gloria became more confident as a mother Peter was encouraged to join in the work of the household. He learned how to use his
hands and work with tools, as well as the basic arithmetic necessary
for measuring. Having been regarded as educationally maladjusted
with learning difficulties, his achievements now gave him great
satisfaction,

But "They took the kids away from us seven weeks after we left
Frimhurst and after we lost my sister Debbie. What chance was that?
That was no chance at all. They expected me and Gloria to do
everything in seven weeks. It was impossible."

They felt ashamed, helpless and unhappy. There was a great
temptation to blame each other and they were terrified they would
never see their children again. The Social Services had declared that
the family had had its chance and there was no alternative to long
term placement for the children ... But the families they had met at
Frimhurst and through Fourth World expressed solidarity ... The local
mothers supported them through this very tense time (preparing for a
court hearing about their children). They had themselves undergone
similar experiences and could understand better than anyone what
Peter and Gloria were going through. They helped them to keep the
house tidy and to have regular meals to keep their strength up. They
encouraged them to keep up with visiting the children at all costs.
They let Social Services know of their involvement and offered to act
as a safeguard when the children would return home ... The court
ruled that the children should be returned to their parents ...

Peter and Gloria and their children stayed at Frimhurst with six or
seven other families whose experiences of poverty and sever disadvan-
tage were similar to theirs. The weekly parents' meetings enabled
parents to give voice to their worries and difficulties. For Peter and

Gloria, being encouraged to complain, question and make suggestions opened the door to a dialogue with people around them. This was a dialogue that they and many of the other parents at first believed was not only impossible, but would lead to more closed doors, more rejection:

> "We don't have the words to say what we want."
>
> "Every time I open my mouth, I put my foot in it."
>
> "People will know everything there is to know, the minute I speak."
>
> "You don't know what they'll do, that's why I don't tell them anything."
>
> "Whatever you say they'll use it against you. They always do."

Peter and Gloria's experience has given them confidence to establish contacts with people around them. They feel more and more a part of the neighbourhood. In addition they have the will and strength to support other people who face the kind of traumas they have known. Their home has become a place where people can come and talk. It is a point of call for young couple and young families who have no one to support them and nowhere to go.

At Frimhurst the families learn to take the first faltering steps towards re-making home. They learn to tell their own family stories in their own words to listeners who know and care about what is happening to them. When they leave Frimhurst they can go on re-making home, and keep in touch with each other, because there are Fourth World University gatherings for them to go to. Here they can use their new found confidence by talking to the public people who need to hear what they say. "We want the right people to be there, people from the government, MPs, priests who speak up in church, people from education departments who give teachers their jobs."

Breaking the cycle of deprivation and giving people a chance to re-make home for themselves requires emotional intelligence among the families themselves and among the public officials who prescribe for them.

Can you train people to be emotionally literate — to be self-aware, to develop ways of handling negative emotions, to keep energies for positive rather than negative things, to read other people's emotions and respond skilfully? They are trying it at Frimhurst. And once people have learned the basics of emotional skill they can use it every time they are in contact with others — at home in the family, at work, and on every collision course with friends, neighbours and officials.

Chapter 14
Re-making home in community

Ajahn Chah was a Buddhist teacher and founder of many monasteries, but in the early part of his life he had been a wandering ascetic, meditating alone in the hills and forests of Thailand. The problem was that in the brief intervals he spent living with other monks he became angry and intolerant at the petty irritations of community life.

"Well," he realized one day, "it is easy for me to go and be the fierce ascetic off in the forest. What is difficult is to be with other people, to learn how to spend time with others." The monastic communities he formed after this insight were based on his belief that learning to live with other people in spiritual friendship is what holds life together. This applies not just to people living in religious communities but to those outside in the world. There is a word used in Buddhism, *kalyanamitta,* which means the network of spiritual friendship which we all need to practise our whole humanity in our daily encounters. Laws, rules, religious commandments, community guidelines can be imposed on people, but they don't work when the networks of spiritual friendship are threadbare or full of holes. Many people today, whether they have formal religious beliefs or not, are seeking better ways of relating to other people. There is deep unease that so many relationships fail, that so many friendships only last as long as people have a common interest at work or doing sport, that people simply have so little time for other people. Maybe that is why there is a burgeoning interest in living in a community, long or short term, as a way of re-learning how to commune with others, now that the places where we live and work so often fail to be nurturing communities. Living in community is often only one stage in a continuing spiritual quest, but it is a practical and down-to-earth test of how well we practice our values in interaction with other human beings. Emotional intelligence and spiritual intelligence become one in the practical virtues of community. We learn to hear what we ourselves are saying, and what other people are saying — or not saying — to us. We learn to be open with ourselves and others, to acknowledge our grudges and irritations — and then let them go. We learn to sit in the place of listening as a spiritual friend to others, and to respond with active attention to the happiness and pain we sense around us.

Some of the people in this chapter have dedicated their whole lives to God or, in the case of non-theistic Buddhists, to Right Livelihood. They live within the formal rules of their orders, which variously interpret the practice of spiritual friendship in everyday community life. Others experience community only for brief periods of inner refreshment and renewal, when they go, say, to the New Age centre on the Greek island of Skyros for a summer vacation that focuses on spirituality and personal development. Between these two ends of the spectrum we explore a whole range of experiences — Buddhist, Christian and New Age — as we listen to the personal stories of modern seekers.

Relating to the world in an enclosed religious order

Sister Ursula, now a lively and spiritually mature woman in her fifties, joined her enclosed order of nuns when she was a young girl still in her teens. She explains what it is like to live in a traditional community following the medieval Rule of St Benedict, which counsels an unceasing daily round of work and prayer for the world you have left (but by no means abandoned).

Sister Ursula's story

When you withdraw from the world to join a contemplative order, you are not forgetting the world. You have other ways of relating to the world. We try to keep in touch here. That includes taking the *Guardian Weekly* so that we know what is happening in the outside world. We have wide-ranging spiritual networks, which include members of our own order from all round the world visiting us. We have local networks too, for we are connected with the local people here. We need to know what is happening outside so we can direct our prayer energy to where the suffering is. It is our way of channelling positive energies to where they are needed. Also we have bidding prayers at daily mass. When the priest says, "Let us pray for the suffering of the world," we can pray aloud for the people we are holding in our minds who currently need help. That might be anybody from the local people here (who are currently suffering from a factory closure), to the people in Somalia whom a visiting missionary sister has been telling us about this week.

Our daily life in community is built around prayer. We see our prayer as practical, but we are practical in more obvious ways too. We support ourselves by running a successful cottage industry, which we all work at in our turns. Work and prayer, our Rule prescribes, and that's what we do. Our day starts with the prayers called Vigils at 3.30 in the morning, and is shaped from then on by Lauds, Terce, 8 a.m. Mass, Sext, None, Vespers and Compline. In between our pattern of prayers we share out the work, including all the domestic work of cooking, gardening, cleaning and maintenance. A few of the older sisters can no longer work. We give them love and care and security here in the community which has been their home for so long. Life outside is often a terrible place for the old. Here we're not going to leave them out.

At the heart of our lives is the sense of shared community. That is what matter in the end. You don't always experience it in the daily routines. You can lose sight of it and experience all sorts of small irritations, because you're only human in community as anywhere else. But the vision is always there, lurking somewhere, waiting for you to be able to see it again. Sometimes it comes when there's a celebration in the Order and singing the Offices becomes, literally and truly, an amazing grace. Other times God is just there among the pots and pans in the kitchen, as Teresa of Avila reminded her nuns three hundred years ago when they were turning theologically high and mighty on her.

Accepting the dark and the light in other people

Sister Teresa entered her Catholic Order in the 1940s, straight from school. She has witnessed therefore all the changing perspectives on community before and after Vatican II, while at the same time learning from her personal experiences of different convents the skills needed for real spiritual friendship that underlies good community living. She says:

> Good friendships are a central core of life, but in the outside world they seem now to be relegated in favour of less lasting sexual relationships. Perhaps in communities good friendships have more of a chance to grow and to last. They grow through sharing your life stories and through sharing your everyday work with your sisters. It doesn't matter what the work is — gardening, sewing, house chores — so long as you're sharing it in a spirit of mutual friendship and support and good humour.
>
> Wherever I have been in a community I have been faced with different personalities, some more congenial than others, but because of the spiritual content of our training I gradually learned to include rather than exclude people who were not congenial. Spiritual friendship as opposed to worldly friendship tries to be always open and learning from differences, not clever and condemning about "people not like us." Of course it's easy to advocate spiritual friendship. It's much harder to practise it in a particular community. There was a period of intense activity I was involved in, when our community was establishing a school, and all the hard work could tire people and frazzle nerves. We had to develop the skills to deal with that. Most of the time we managed, but not all the time. At home or in community what matters is not so much the problems and differences we come up against, but how we respond to those problems and differences. We were taught to respond by remaining always aware of the immanence of God in each one of us, and the need to respond in our own personal

imitation of Christ. Christ is our model for being a spiritual friend to everyone we encounter, whatever our differences.

With Vatican II came a high emphasis on the importance of community. They set up endless courses and seminars and retreats on building community. But ultimately it comes down to respect and reverence for one another's differences, developing your listening skills, and keeping a constant awareness of God living in each one of us. Those are the foundations of the spiritual friendship at the heart of community. And again they are easier said and taught on seminars, than practised in the day to day difficulties of life in community.

My work has meant that I move around a number of convents, and wherever I am that becomes home. But I go home regularly to my original community, and the people there know the dark side of me as well as the light side, because there's no hiding when you've been with other community members long enough. Openness and trust are part of a sense of being at home, so you need to be able to reveal the dark as well as the light. As in a family the individual needs to learn how to be a good community member. You need to learn how to give support, and how to appreciate and learn from support when it is given to you. You need to learn how to work out some kind of open and friendly way of accepting criticism and accepting authority — or at least work out friendly ways of influencing whoever is making the decisions when you don't agree with them.

You accept the darkness and the light in yourself and in other people. Acceptance of the dark side discourages self-battering and guilt, and enables you to deal with the ever present possibilities of jealousy, envy and all the evils of home whether in a family home or in community. In a big community the problems are diluted, but in a small community everybody is affected by the weakest link. You need congeniality in a community, and that can suffer. You learn from the dark side when you can see its potential for the light. When there is a clash or a conflict developing you can pray together, or engage in contemplative prayer on your own. In contemplative prayer you can face up to your own intolerance of the weak links in the community. You try to accept a weak sister, include her in the grace of God. Then you can include her in everyday community. In a religious community each of you is encouraged to develop your gifts and encourage others to develop theirs, no matter how different from yours. You have a responsibility to yourself and to each of the others. Am I my brother's and sister's keeper? Yes, I am.

Transforming the traditional religious community

The Rowan Tree Centre

The Rowan Tree Centre is tranquilly sited in an old stone house overlooking the Wye valley. The centre offers courses and retreats for people who are open to many different spiritual traditions, though the anchor of faith is Christianity for the New Age. There is a weekly meditation group and regular Desert Day retreats. There is a programme of workshops which includes "Mandalas," "Jung and the search for wholeness," and "Gender issues in cultural and religious traditions."

The rowan tree is a safeguarding tree in Celtic tradition. It is used here as a symbol of the tree of life uniting heaven and earth, a cosmic symbol that occurs in many religious traditions. The sacred tree is the source of life from which comes healing, wholeness and wisdom. It has its roots deep in the life-giving earth and stretches upwards towards the heavens. It puts forth new leaves in the resurrection time of spring, and enriches the earth with its dying leaves in autumn. It matures slowly through its ages, and withstands the buffeting of the elements till in its natural time it falls and returns into the earth from which it came.

Mary is the Director of the Rowan Tree Centre, and explains how the Centre has evolved to meet the changing spiritual needs of people today:

I see what we do here as a new form of monasticism without
the traditional walls or rules. We are growing as a transforming community, like an ashram. We are not just a site
for providing workshops on spirituality. The weekly meditation
group is becoming a sort of community for those who come
regularly. You don't have to have a heavy residential sharing
of every minute of your lives to form a transforming community. That can sometimes even weigh against transformative
experience. And so many people simply haven't the time,
because we all seem to lead such remorselessly busy lives
now. Fewer people are going to church, yet many more
people want some spiritual element in their lives. But we
are only at the start of the new consciousness, and the
transformation hasn't got far enough yet for there to be a
sense of belonging to the new community. If you're a
member of the clergy or living in a traditional Christian
community there's psychological and practical support
available to you. If you're doing similar work on your own
initiative to raise the new consciousness you can experience
terrible loneliness and lack of support. Traditionally minded
people will not want to come to your centre, and time and
distance and lack of money too often get in the way of
meetings with the like-minded. But you are sustained by a
tremendous sense of blessing through the people who come on
the workshops and retreats.

I cannot stand behind the old-fashioned Eucharist any more,
so now on Thursday twice a month we are having a combination of teaching on the mystical contemplative tradition, and a
contemplative Eucharist. We sit on the floor and centre down
into it. The first part is nearly all silence. Then we pass the
bread and wine round to each other — moving away from
patriarchy and sharing among ourselves all on the same level.
We're trying to transform the way we express our Christianity
and our sense of community. There are two foci I am working
with at the minute. One is the recovery of the contemplative,
mystical, cosmic form of Christianity which got pushed out
after the early centuries. It's not just a moral theology but an

inner transformation involving the whole world, yet starting with our ordinary lives.

The second focus is entering the new consciousness. For the centre that means being open to the interfaith dimension, to the feminine dimension, and to the ecology dimension. I'm trying to plan my workshops on an annual cycle that will reflect these concerns. In February there's a workshop on feminist theology and that is the theme for the month. March is dedicated to monastic spirituality and teasing out the inner transformation which can change our outer lives. In June an artist theologian is going to do a mandala weekend, because she has spent twelve years in India and is very steeped in eastern spirituality ...

A number of different influences got us going on setting up this ashram type of community open to people of any tradition who are seeking transformation and personal growth. Our first workshops were shaped by our experience of real hospitality and warmth at a friend's marvellous old house in London. It was a place of such openness and welcome, no matter how many people were sleeping there. It strongly affected my idea of having a home which would be open and transforming for myself and for other people. Then when I was a student of music there was another house like that where the family opened up their home in the summers to musicians and painters. It was a place where you could experience personal growth and be surrounded and supported by other people — all growing in their own way, living out whatever gifts they had.

Another influence was the Taizé Community. In our current brochure I have a quote from Brother Roger of Taizé which explains that influence better than I can in my own words: "The depths of the human being are limitless. They open towards the depths of God. And God is already there waiting for every person deep within them. It is there that creative energy is born."

Our visits to Taizé showed us that it was possible to organize that kind of experience for a large number of people. Then we had a year in India soon after we were married. We

were based in Jyoti Sahi's home which was an ashram. His
background was Hindu-Christian. His wife Jane was an artist,
and she ran a little school in the grounds, while he ran art
retreats to help people grow spiritually, educationally,
theologically.

Along with all these positive influences for setting up the
centre, there was our increasing frustration with the Church.
We had had powerful and empowering spiritual and
community experiences in Taizé and in the Indian ashram.
Back home those experiences were just not there for us in our
parish church. If you can't find it you have to do it yourself.
So we did. That was in 1979. We are still growing, and
helping other people to grow.

A Buddhist women's community

Maitreji (a name adopted when she joined her community) is a young
Londoner living in one of the "right livelihood" communities set up
in Britain since the 1970s by the Friends of the Western Buddhist
Order. She says:

Living in a spiritual community is part of the vision of the
Friends of the Western Buddhist Order because spirituality is
about putting things into practice in everyday living and
working lives. We are trying to create the living and working
conditions most conducive to our growth and development. If
you live with other people who have a common vision of
living together, that's a very good basis for deepening
friendship and furthering communication.

There are six of us, and we both live and work together. We
run a natural health centre in Bethnal Green called Bodywise.
It started in 1984 as an annexe to the London Buddhist Centre,
and now we six women run it as a Buddhist Right Livelihood.
We offer (with some outside help) yoga, massage, shiatsu and
reflexology, herbalism and aromatherapy, acupuncture and
homeopathy. The people who come to us are from Tower
Hamlets and neighbouring boroughs. We started by working

together, and then extended that to living together. In the community we have a yoga teacher, an osteopath, two Alexander technique teachers, a massage practitioner and a finance worker. I do Alexander technique and also do the management of the health practice. When we first set up Bodywise we were all involved with the London Buddhist Centre and came there for meditation. Then two years ago we moved house so that we could all of us live together as well as work together.

In Buddhism we have ethical guidelines in the Five Precepts, so in our community we try to live our lives according to those. The first is not harming living beings, and the positive formulation of that is loving kindness. Second is not taking the not given, and the positive formulation of that is open-handed generosity. Third is not doing sexual misconduct, which is not refraining from sex but living your sexual life ethically, living with stillness, simplicity and contentment. The fourth precept is not lying, but communicating truthfully and honestly. The fifth is not taking intoxicants which cloud the mind, but keeping your mindfulness clear and radiant. It doesn't mean never drinking alcohol (although some Buddhists are teetotal), but that you have always an awareness of what you are doing.

Those are the ethical guidelines, but we're not expecting ourselves to be able to do all that overnight. You work at it, make mistakes, try again. By living in a community together we're trying to put those guidelines into practice in our everyday relations with each other. Ideally we would have a meditation room in our house, but we haven't space, so we tend to meditate in each other's rooms, in twos and threes, every day. Meditation is an important way of being together in community. So is eating together. We each cook once a week and we try to eat together every evening. We make a definite commitment to eat together, and practically it's the best arrangement of resources because each of us ends up only doing the meal once a week. We eat very well — good wholefood cooking — and it's very enjoyable sharing together.

One morning a week we have a business meeting, but it takes a different form every week. One week is a discussion on how the health centre is running. The next week is a study of a Buddhist text by our teacher Sangharashita, to remind ourselves of the aims and goals of what we are trying to do, and not lose the right livelihood perspective in the everyday demands of running a business.

Once a week we spend an evening together, doing something that brings us together more as a community. Sometimes we just talk about how we are — our experiences and thoughts during the past week. Or we might do meditation together, or study, or just do "fun" things like going out to a film or a concert. One person might take us through massage, or get us to draw each other or the room. We've also had life story sessions. One of our rituals is for someone to do that on their birthday — tell her life story. At the moment we've decided to take that further by telling each other our financial biographies, because we're working towards a "common purse." We are talking about what we tend to spend money on, and how it matters to us. Our teacher Sangharashita said recently that people today are prepared to talk more openly about their sex lives than about the ways they earn and spend money. So we are trying to share with each other our attitudes to money. One or two in the community are not sure about going collective in our finances, but the principle of living and working together does seem to lead to collective finances. Because we are trying to create a positive alternative to a nuclear family situation. We're trying to move from being dependent or independent to being interdependent. The way you handle money is a factor in that. At the moment we have a collective kitty for shared expenses. It is just one step further to pool all our money.

In our movement there are a number of alternatives to living in the nuclear family. Some people live together as family groups, with a number of parents and children together. Single parents may live in community with other men and women. Or you have single sex communities like ours. There are reasons

behind the various groupings. Some people prefer to live with
children and others not. Some families with children want to
live in community but have their children with them. The
biggest reason for the single sex communities like ours is to do
with how we express "masculine" and "feminine" qualities in
our lives. The thinking is that when men and women spend a
lot of time together they tend to fall into using more strongly
masculine or feminine qualities (or stereotypes). If we live in
single sex communities we become more fully human by
drawing more deeply on the qualities that are associated with
both masculine and feminine genders.

In our movement we put a lot of emphasis on friendship
relating, to offset the outside emphasis on sexual relating. We
see friendship as a very important part of community life, and
we try to practise friendliness in our everyday lives. The three
jewels in Buddhism are the Buddha, the Dharma (the
teachings), and the Sangha (the community of people practising
the Buddha's teachings). In the Friends of the Western
Buddhist Order we place a lot of emphasis on the Sangha
jewel — friendship relating in our everyday lives.

Living in a community with other people really brings you
up against each other's social conditioning, so of course there
are antagonisms you have to work through. It can take a long
time and years of practice to work through the personal
reactions you have to each other. It comes down to learning to
listen to each other, learning to take in what lies behind the
other's behaviour. That's where telling life stories helps. If you
know where someone is coming from, it can make their
behaviour more understandable. If I'm feeling antagonistic to
someone I work in two ways. First I'll try to be open and
honest about what is happening, rather than trying to ignore it.
Then I'll work through it in my meditation to develop loving
kindness towards that person. We call that practice *Metta
Bhavana,* which means the development of loving kindness.
The practice is in five stages. First you develop positive
feelings towards yourself. Then you bring a friend to mind,
think about what makes them happy and what you appreciate

about them. You wish them well. The third stage is bringing to mind a neutral person and including them in the well-wishing. The next stage is thinking about the person you are feeling antagonistic towards or who feels antagonistic towards you, and including them in the well wishing. The final stage in the loving kindness meditation is bringing together all these people and imagining yourself in a situation of well wishing. You can expand that out to include other people — in the same building, in your locality, in the whole country, in the world ... You include all living beings, as much of life as you can, and you expand it out to include more and more in your loving kindness well wishing.

Sometimes of course you can't get very far in the meditation because you keep thinking, "She said this to me, she said that ..." But even so you find later when you've done the meditation that there's new psychic space for you to be more open when you next meet that person. When both of you do the meditation it makes the openness more expansive.

I have strong feelings about the need to heal personal antagonisms, because in our society we have this sense of wanting to end conflict and wars, but how can we do that when we can't even live under the same roof in harmony with someone like ourselves? So I feel it's very important to start working in the here and now to improve our immediate living situation. That comes of living in community.. You learn to let go of attitudes, particular ways of doing things. If you feel you've been hurt by something that someone says to you, you've got to learn to let go of that hurt, that anger.

There is a good image for living in community: a stone-polishing machine. You put in rough pebbles and grit and mix them together for hours on end, and they come out beautifully polished and brightly coloured stones. In a community there's our individual roughnesses and the grit of rubbing along together, and you have to work at it and go on believing in the polished stones. The grit can be as simple and everyday as coming home at the end of a hard day's work wanting a relaxing bath, but you find there's someone in the bath. Then you decide to make a few phone calls while you're waiting, but there's someone else on the phone ... The big thing you learn is cooperation on a daily basis. It is not valued enough but it is an important spiritual practice, because it is about taking other people into account and remembering you're not the centre of the universe.

Findhorn

Marie (60) lives on her own and runs a word-processing business from home. Divorced for the second time, she has filled emotional and spiritual vacuums with steady commitments. She is active in her church, in Amnesty International, and in her local Ramblers Club. She is a constant seeker, and Findhorn has been a vital stage on her personal spiritual quest:

Findhorn is out along the coast from Inverness, near the town of Forres in the extreme north of Scotland. The original village of Findhorn doesn't like to be confused with the New Age Findhorn Foundation. The Foundation is located in the mansion, Cluny Hill College, and in the Park, an ecologically sound village (with its own wind generator) on what was originally just a caravan site. There are still caravans and chalets there now, some owned and permanently lived in by people associated with the Findhorn community, but who carry on with their own jobs. Often they are self-employed artists and writers because the Foundation inspires creative work.

When I first went I was looking for new openings, and Findhorn opened doors for me. I was newly on my own after splitting up with my partner (in a friendly way). My mother died around that time and left me some money, so I bought a car and drove up to the north of Scotland on my own, just driving around and hostelling. It was the first time in my life I was happy on my own, not worrying about being on my own. The next year I was ready for some kind of retreat place where I could have a chance to develop myself, and I went to

Findhorn. I liked it right away, and every time I've been since
I feel full of good positive energy. I leave my daily worries
behind and just plunge into my group, and take it on trust that
there's a point in what you're doing. At the beginning of each
session you hold hands in a ring and have a few minutes of
silence to get in tune with the others and leave your own world
outside. You pass a lovely stone around the circle and you
only speak when you have the stone in your hand, so that
everybody gets a chance to express themselves. Nobody can
hog the self-expression because you don't just pass the stone to
somebody who wants to talk a lot. You go quiet and open and
attuned as to who should have the stone next. At the end of a
session you attune again for a minute, and prepare yourself for
winding down and going out.

You're in your group in the morning and you work in the
community every afternoon — in the kitchens or gardens, or
on maintenance or building work. You attune to what you feel
you should do. I thought first I should go in the kitchens
because I hate that and was avoiding it and felt a bit
conscience stricken. But in the end I worked in the gardens
and felt I was putting good energy into that.

You tend to stick together with your group during your
experience week. You sit together at meal times as well as
being together for the group activities. We weren't lectured at
or given any pious instruction. We were shown things and
learned by doing them. We were in the dance studio one day
and played games about trusting — like getting into pairs in a
circle, with one curled up like a foetus and the other very
gently and lovingly unrolling you, laying you straight out on
your back. You take it in turns to be curled up and to do the
unrolling. There was another trusting game in twos, where one
kept their eyes closed and the other became the eyes of that
person, guiding them about. You learn to feel that the other is
very precious and you take great care they don't get bumped or
jarred moving about in your care.

Another day we went to a beautiful place by the River
Findhorn, a great rocky gorge called Randolph's Leap, and did

other activities to do with trusting and caring for another person. Again we were in pairs, with one blind and the other leading. When you were leading the blind one you explained to them the beauties of the place by touching them on the ear to get them to listen to the sound of the waterfalls, or you guided them to open their eyes suddenly and really *see* the colour of the trees or the lichens on the rocks. It was a lot of fun, not at all earnest, and it wakened you up afresh to the sensations of seeing and hearing and touching, which can get very stale.

At Findhorn everything guides you towards developing a reverent feeling for ordinary everyday life. Preparing the food and eating is an important part of that, and the food is lovely. It is all wholefood. If you're working in the kitchen you attune so that only good energy goes into the food and it provides emotional nurturing as well as body nurturing. Preparing the food is important for the people preparing it as well as for the consumers. It is a way of caring for the people you are cooking for. I now try to remember that when I'm making food for others, because I don't naturally take to cooking and kitchen work. When I had my son here one weekend after he had split up with his girlfriend, I consciously put good energies into the food I gave him. And it worked. He got relaxed and was able to talk to me about the breakup.

I learned a lot at Findhorn about expressing care for people in other ways than words. Before I went there I didn't believe you can have an effect mentally, but I do now. It's to do with realizing that everybody has a capacity for healing. And that means being able to turn to other people for healing as well as understanding the potential for healing others that we all have. It includes self-healing too, respecting your own needs as well as being healing to other people when they need it.

I learned at Findhorn the Buddhist thing of "doing what you are doing." You put yourself entirely into what you are doing, whether it is preparing food, or chipping concrete off old bricks for recycling, or making a native American medicine wheel for growing herbs ... I met people amazingly wise and mature for their age, young people with great skills who were so straightforward and sweet, with no sense of self-importance.

There are hard things about living in community. One year I spent a fortnight on Erraid, an outlying Findhorn community on an island off Iona, and it turned out to be a bit difficult there at that time. One thing happened after another. Wild minks crossed over at low tide and killed the chickens that provided the eggs. You can't be strictly vegetarian in all circumstances, so it was decided to eat the dead chickens rather than waste them. I volunteered to pluck the feathers out. I sat there for hours, dipping them in hot water and plucking away. It was a horrible job, and then cooking and eating them was not so good for some of the strict vegetarians. The community wasn't all loving and happy either that week on the island, because there were a couple of families whose children were bored stiff away from their urban, plugged-in environment. They had no way of passing the time without their "normal" high tech props and computer games, so they whined and whinged to their parents at meal times and all around the place ...

Skyros

Marguerite is a committed Quaker whose midlife quests have included the New Age centre on the sun soaked Greek island of Skyros which offers "holidays for the mind, the body and the spirit" — wholeness as physical, moral and intellectual goodness:

A friend of ours was physically and psychologically healed at Skyros after going through a terrible time. So Colin and I were intrigued at the idea of staying on a Greek island with interesting people. It offered something quite apart from the usual holidays abroad, a complete break from everyday work and domesticity. There were far more interesting things to do than nude bathing — though that was enormously enjoyable too. It was like a bright sunlight shock being there. It was very clarifying and invigorating for me, and had a lasting good

effect — though you have to come down from the artificial
high you reach while you're there, and that needs very good
debriefing from the community.

I had never been to Greece before. The clarity of the light
and colour there seemed to be echoed in the way I felt
energized in the groupwork we did in the Skyros community.
It began with us selecting people for the group we would work
in. We were asked, "If you were shipwrecked which of the
people around you would you choose to rescue?" You grabbed
someone interesting and went on until we had formed six self-
selecting groups of ten. Each morning we worked with our
group at various kinds of group therapy, like psychodrama or
gestalt. Someone who had something in their life to work
through would volunteer to be the subject of a session. The
rest of us played the roles of those who had been part of that
person's pain. It was very powerful. There was the freedom of
knowing we didn't have to see each other again (unless we
chose to), so we did have great freedom of expression and it
worked. It was the skill of the facilitators to make sure it
became a healing process. My only reservation was that it's
such a strong experience that some people might come away
artificially high, or with problems exposed but unresolved. My
own experience was all positive, but you do need a certain
amount of inner strength to stand up to it, or you could get
churned up. You're given a co-counsellor — someone from
another group — so that you can get support that way if you
need it. Also the people who run Skyros are very experienced
and very open. If a group doesn't gell, the facilitators would
help.

I was surrounded by adults as a child, because my brother
and sister were eight and nine years older, so I was laughed at
and never taken seriously. I carried that on into adult life,
expecting people not to take me seriously. I tried to manage in
a very consensus way, and be always calm and humorous. My
big thing was never to hurt anyone. I'd end up stressed myself,
and have to go off and collapse in tears of frustration and
exhaustion. Skyros gave me the confidence to face up to the

fact that some situations can only be resolved by causing an element of hurt, and that trying not to hurt anyone ever is not going to help in the end. I still back down sometimes in situations where it is necessary to speak the truth even if it hurts. But Skyros has had a lasting effect because now I know when I'm backing down and I can pull myself up and do what I have to do in these difficult management situations.

Absolutely everyone in my Skyros group felt they'd been helped by the end of the "holiday." A number had decisions to make in their lives, and they went back home with the strength to make these decisions. With some it was to end a very negative relationship. With others it was to change the way they were living in relation to their work. They were resolved to stop being totally drained by their work and to take back time and space for the sake of the "whole life." Or they were able to find something good (if possible) about past horrors in their lives. There was a man in our group who had a brutal father and had been mercilessly beaten throughout his childhood. As a result he'd become an alcoholic and had broken relationships when he grew up. In the psychodrama when he'd enacted the horrors, the facilitators said, "Try to think of something good about your father, or of some time when he gave you something you liked." The man did that, and he was able to start trying to forgive his father. In the psychodrama he was kneeling by his father's grave, with all of us sharing his pain, and everybody in floods of tears.

Sharing in other people's pains and sorrows like that gives me a great feeling of oneness, of community. You experience for yourself the fact that we're all struggling along together in our everyday lives, and it helps to be with each other in the pains and the pleasures, instead of being lonely and isolated, as so many people are.

How does Marguerite reconcile the attractions of a New Age community like Skyros with her deep roots in Quaker spirituality? Are there irreconcilable contradictions between the Christian faith and New Age spirituality, as many churchmen would have us believe? Or are both rightly concerned in giving us back better ways of relating to our families, our workmates, our friends and enemies? For some years now Marguerite has been going to Q Room weekends which are for giving and receiving support among Quakers. She finds agreeable parallels as well as differences between her Quaker support groups and the New Age community on Skyros:

> At Skyros you get an enormous cross-section of people. Very few are conventionally religious people. They tend to be seekers or New Age people. Whereas on a Quaker retreat there's a degree of commitment to Christian religion. The Quaker "Q Room" weekends I go on are for getting and giving support. In Q Room we have one-to-one sharing, a spiritual co-counselling. There's also help with learning to facilitate a retreat. You learn the importance of not making everything harmonious and safe all the time. You learn that people also need to be challenged in order to explore where they are spiritually. You bring the one-to-one nurturing ideas and strategies back to your own Quaker meeting (and hopefully the rest of your life). Q Room as I see it is about spiritual self-help. No one gets paid and everyone does their best to be open about their spiritual dimension, and pass on to others new ways of understanding or helping solve problems in everyday relating. Skyros on the other hand is quite an ambitious commercial enterprise as well as being a centre for spiritual and personal development. In material terms on Skyros it's very comfortable but it's kept simple. The Greek word for home is *oekos,* and they emphasize two sides of *oekos.* It is about self-realization, but also about sharing a sense of common purpose — of community. On Skyros, as in any community, taking part in the preparation of food and eating together is important, because that is part of everyday nurture. It does away with a hierarchy of people divided into those who look after and those who get looked after (as in the usual holiday situation). Another thing you learn in a community is the importance of caring for yourself — not as any kind of crude self-indulgence, but as a necessary part of learning to

care for others. You cannot give out to people in a healthy way unless you are in good shape inside yourself. It's good to eat healthy food and enjoy the sunning and take the time to do what you want. It encourages you to acknowledge that everyone needs nurture (especially carers of other people, and we are all carers to a greater or lesser degree). Otherwise when we nurture other people (in our family, say, or at work) we are in danger of becoming either domineering carers or plain nervous wrecks.

Going on occasional retreats in community, as I do (whether it's New Age Skyros or the Quakers), is a way of learning to be balanced about nurturing. Very few people these days want or are able to go into a community as a permanent way of living. As I see it, if you're living and working permanently in a community you would have a rather one-dimensional life. In a permanent community there's nowhere to work through your problems because work and leisure and home are all lived out in the same community of people. Whereas if you go to a community for a break it is a real refreshment. You reconnect with your fundamental energies, and can go back to everyday work and family and friends with the good energy flowing again.

Chapter 15
Emotional intelligence in everyday life

In traditional communities women had ready-made women's networks in the place where they lived. Now most women have to build their own personal networks to fit their work, their interests and the stage they have got to in bringing up children (or in choosing professional life rather than mothering). Elaine, whose professional life as a teacher of disturbed children is a vital part of her self-expression and personal identity, explains that you fit together the different bits of your life like a jigsaw, and it can be quite stressful. You need the equivalent of the old style women's network to keep you going and give you sociability and support. But you build different networks, because you can't put the clock back, and women want more things out of life now than the old home-centred things:

> I was getting really depressed because there were no
> challenging jobs in the part of the country where Gerald and I
> live. I was working at a very humble level in an old people's
> home, and it was really dead end. There was no stimulus, no
> way of using my teacher training or my counselling skills. We
> couldn't move because Gerald has built up his own business
> over the years and all his customers are there. So we went for
> a "commuter marriage." I got a good job in a residential home
> for disturbed kids in the southeast, and now I spend the
> working week there and come home holidays and most
> weekends. I've joined a women's network there for support
> and because you need to build up new social connections when
> you're on your own during the working week.
>   Since I've joined my women's network it's really nice be-
> cause women ring up and say, "Come along to ..." something
> with them. It's really friendly and informal. Whatever we're

doing there's always a good laugh with it. Recently there were two women travellers talking about their trip to Peru, and the joys and perils for females of hitching in Latin America. Another time one of the women invited us to her house to try out dishes, because she'd been to a cookery class and wanted the group to appreciate the results of her efforts. Another needed a bit of ego-boosting after she'd trained herself to do stencil painting on old furniture. So we went to her house and it was lovely to see the work she'd taught herself painstakingly to do so well. It wasn't just an ego boost. It was important to her to have the rest of us come and admire her work, because it reinforced her personal growth.

I need my women's network for real growth in my life, as well as for fun. Those things are more difficult with men because other things get in the way. My women friends don't seem so emotionally needy and demanding as my partner, or perhaps it's that there's a more equal sharing of needs among us. There's a lightness of personality among my women friends that makes me feel very relaxed and at home with them. They ring up, pop round to see me, ask, "Are you coming to something?" You feel connected with the outside world in a different way from how it is at work or in your relationship with your partner. It's fun, it's supporting, and it's a way of working out your values when you're not sure about something.

When I'm at home with Gerald it's difficult for me to make the same kind of women's network as I have when I'm away at work. I'd have to think all the time about how he would get on with my women friends, and they with him. There'd be a whole lot of complicated emotions going on underground, or occasionally breaking out into arguments between us about how much time we're giving to friends and not to the partner.

Networks of women friends are to do with nurturing each other and giving support in everyday life. They are safe havens where you can try out new accomplishments. They are fun because they're risk-free zones where you can laugh with loyal friends about your achievements and humiliations in the work and partnership arenas. Laughter can purge awful incidents of some of their weight of woe. Enjoyment matters, and women's networks are sources of good-natured enjoyment in the company of women.

Professional networking women often have strongly negative responses to traditional women's skills and networks. They are dismissive of the sewing groups, the jam making and the cake decorating competitions that go on in Women's Institutes. But there is another school of thought which remains faithful to traditional women's skills, and is working for more recognition for the tapestry and embroidery, the patchwork and the knitting, the cooking and the preserving that have been (and still are for a minority) a major form of self-expression for women at home. For Gwen, a young mother in her twenties, traditional female skills are a source of solidarity and sociability among women, but she finds fewer and fewer of her women friends are interested, and she regrets their gross neglect of women's culture:

> There's a whole lot of creative skills in sewing and cooking that used to bind women together in their own women's culture, and provide friends — and rivals — and company. That's nearly gone now, except in a few country areas where the women still take a pride in their baking and their sewing, their plants and their flowers. But fewer and fewer can recognize quality, or respect each other's achievements, because so many women have given it up and say, "Thank God for frozen food," or "The wife part is OK, but the housewife part — Yuk, no thanks." So they just throw away a whole women's heritage of really creative things that women learned from each other, and that brought them together socially. You could sit around a table making a patchwork quilt and put the world to rights in an afternoon. If you didn't have the power to really change things, you could at least express your ideas in your sewing. I've seen patchwork quilts with all kinds of messages (open or secret) worked into their designs.

I think it's a spiritual thing as well, making something beautiful and useful with your own hands to adorn your home space. And being there for people in your house is important as well, because there's hardly any community left, and there are fewer and fewer places where people can drop in and find somebody at home to talk to when they're feeling lonely or hurt or badly used by their family or somebody. Most women aren't at home any more as they used to be, and that makes it very lonely and isolating for the mothers with young children who have to be at home during the day, because there's no community support for them while they're doing their parenting. Even in the country villages they're closing down the community schools and shops and post offices where the women can meet and get to know each other. There'll be no proper community left soon, because it's always been home-centred women who have held together communities, and women don't want to be home-centred any more because they don't know what to do with themselves when they're at home. They've lost women's creative skills and the warm natural togetherness that grew out of respect and rivalry for each other's crocheting or jam making or baby soothing magic.

Emotional intelligence is not about judging whether it's better to follow Elaine's superwoman way or Gwen's traditional woman's way. It is about keeping in touch with your true feelings in any situation, at home or at work, channelling your emotional energies positively, and relating creatively to the people around you, whether they are your family or your colleagues. Highly evolved people, whether saints, sages, bodhisattvas or the many wise women who have told their stories here, are not necessarily clever people, or religious people, but they are invariably emotionally intelligent people. How then do the rest of us learn to be more emotionally intelligent, more literate in relating, more at home with other human beings? Not by borrowing second-hand emotions from the media; it is easier to be "emotionally correct" at a distance than with our intimate connections. Not through emotional self-indulgence without discernment; for that is emotional illiteracy. There are many paths, but they follow the same four-pointed way:

— *Practise emotional awareness*
Keep in touch with your real feelings in any situation, so you can handle your emotions better and not give way to heady impulses (anger, malicious gossip, hatred of the Other — do you know your own emotional weaknesses?)

— *Work out your own true purposes in life*
Work at channelling your emotional energies into positive purposes (what *really* matters to you). Go with the Tao, find your creative flow. Don't put energy into negative things.

— *Improve your emotional empathy*
Practise putting yourself in the emotional situation of the people you relate to (or fail to relate to) — family, friends, your work mates, your networks. Try moving your emotional stance little by little closer to theirs, so you can open up your understanding.

— *Be emotionally imaginative in relating to others*
Practise in your everyday encounters a combination of emotional awareness (of yourself and others), channelling your energies into positive purposes, and empathizing with others.

This practice of emotional intelligence in everyday life is about mixing and baking your own life. It resembles in many ways the Zen Cook's practice of breadmaking.

> *The Zen Cook's Tale*
> Food is a necessity for life just as life is a necessity for under-
> standing; you need to eat to live just as you need to have
> tasted the joys, sorrows, love, hatred, gratitude and anger of
> life before you can understand the meaning of all things.
> To an onlooker it might appear that the process of baking
> bread only involves the periods of the cook's action — the
> gathering, preparing and mixing of the ingredients, the

kneading of the dough, the greasing and filling of the bread tins and the putting of the tins in the oven. But the process of baking bread also includes the periods of the cook's inaction when the stove warms the flour, when the yeast rises the dough and when the oven bakes the bread. In fact the process of baking the bread is continuous, so even though you see me sitting in the zendo or sweeping the kitchen floor or collecting water from the stream or washing the pots, I am also baking the bread ...

Just as, when the bread is baking unseen in the oven, filling the kitchen with its warm, welcoming, appetizing smell, the unseen path of my life is continuously unfolding and my awareness is forever growing; the thought-free understanding of the moment which has always been present within me, though often hidden, is also slowly baking within me, fusing and integrating with my everyday existence.

The kitchen, the dining room and the shrine room are now filled with the smell of the bread baking in the oven. Unseen behind the heavy doors of the oven, the bread is ready. Unseen behind the ephemeral, illusory veil of my thinking mind, the nature of the universe is resounding throughout my being, the kitchen, the valley, the skies and everywhere beyond. I open the oven door, to be enveloped by a cloud of bread-sodden steam, to behold the five loaves. Carefully I remove each bread tin from the oven and turn each loaf out of the tin and on to a wire grill to cool off. I always find it a great joy to see the freshly baked loaves lined up together on the wire grill, each perfectly formed in its own way, the domed top, maybe a fold in the crust, the straight sides; each loaf is a splendid testimony to the fact that the age-old process of baking works ... Look, the loaves are ready and Buddha mind is all around and within me, how could I ever have doubted this?

Notes

Page

8   Virginia Woolf, *A Room of One's Own,* shows the shortcomings of the Angel in the Home model. The quote is from her 1931 essay, "Professions for women."

9   Helen Wilkinson and Melanie Howard, *Tomorrow's Women,* Demos, 1997, surveys 3000 women to assess what women want from life.

83   Elizabeth Roberts, *A Woman's Place: an oral history of working-class women, 1890–1940,* Blackwell, 1984, p.137.

156   The full meditation on aloneness is given in Christina Feldman, *Woman Awake,* Arkana, 1990, pp.24–26.

218   The children's voices are from *Children of our Time,* collected by ATD Fourth World in the course of their work with excluded families to rebuild broken homes. More information is available from their British centre at 48 Addington Square, London SE5.

223   Peter and Gloria's story, among other positive narratives about the excluded re-making home, has been written up in *The Wresinski Approach: the Poorest — Partners in Democracy,* available from ATD Fourth World (as above).

253   Examples of practical steps to learning and teaching emotional intelligence are elaborated by Daniel Goleman in *Emotional Intelligence,* Bloomsbury, 1995.

253   *The Zen Cook's Tale* is a classic Zen story. The version given here in abbreviated form is told in full by Tim Blanc (who regularly cooks on Zen retreats) in "Why the cook bakes the bread," *New Ch'an Forum,* 11, Summer 1995, pp.18–24.